PENGUIN BOOKS

THE CITY GAME

A native of Rockville Center, New York, Pete Axthelm graduated from Yale University in 1965. After graduation he became the horse-racing writer and columnist for the New York *Herald-Tribune* and then worked for *Sports Illustrated* as a staff writer. He joined *Newsweek* magazine as a sports editor in 1968 and from 1974 to 1988 was a columnist and contributing editor there, writing a biweekly column on sports and a variety of other subjects. From 1980 to 1991 he worked as a television commentator, covering NFL games and horse races, first for NBC and later for ESPN. His other books include *The Kid, The Modern Confessional Novel,* and *Tennis Observed* (with William F. Talbert). He died in 1991.

Acknowledgments

I WOULD like to thank my patient and incisive editor, Herman Gollob, and an invaluable reporter, Peter Bonventre of Newsweek. For other assistance, I should mention Max McGowan, Jeanne Voltz, Jim Foley, Frank Blauschild, and Jim Wergeles. The idea for this book was available to anyone aware of city sports, but for helping to crystallize and define it, I'm particularly grateful to Al McGuire and Pat Smith.

THE CITY GAME

BASKETBALL FROM THE GARDEN
TO THE PLAYGROUNDS

by PETE AXTHELM

PENGUIN BOOKS

TO MEGAN

PENGUIN BOOKS
Published by the Penguin Group
Viking Penguin, a division of Penguin Books USA Inc.,
375 Hudson Street, New York, New York 10014, U.S.A.
Penguin Books Ltd, 27 Wrights Lane,
London W8 5TZ, England
Penguin Books Australia Ltd, Ringwood,
Victoria, Australia
Penguin Books Canada Ltd, 2801 John Street,
Markham, Ontario, Canada L3R 1B4
Penguin Books (N.Z.) Ltd, 182–190 Wairau Road,
Auckland 10, New Zealand

Penguin Books Ltd, Registered Offices:
Harmondsworth, Middlesex, England

First published in the United States of America by
Harper's Magazine Press 1970
Published in Penguin Books 1982
This edition with a foreword by
Dick Schaap published in Penguin Books 1991

10 9 8 7 6 5 4 3 2 1

Portions of this book previously appeared in
Harper's Magazine in slightly different form.

ISBN 0 14 01.6501 0
CIP data available

Printed in the United States of America

Set in Electra

Contents

Foreword

The cast of The City Game *is impressive:*
Bill Bradley became a United States senator.
Willis Reed became an NBA coach.
Walt Frazier became a broadcaster.
And Dave DeBusschere became commissioner of the American Basketball Association.

But the most compelling character in The City Game *is a young man named Earl Manigault:*

"He was the king . . . a six-foot-two-inch forward who could outleap men eight inches taller. . . . Freewheeling, innovative, he was the image of the classic playground athlete . . . a powerful magnetic figure who carried the dreams and ideals of every kid around him as he spun and twisted and sailed over all obstacles. When he fell, he carried those aspirations down with him. Call him a wasted talent, a pathetic victim, even a tragic hero: he had symbolized all that was sublime and terrible about this city game."

When Pete Axthelm wrote those words, Earl Manigault was "in his midtwenties, a dope addict, in prison."

Almost twenty years later, Earl Manigault returned to the playgrounds of New York, observed by a young reporter for the New York Times.

"Last weekend," the young reporter wrote, "Manigault, the most

gifted New York playground athlete never to make it to the National Basketball Association, came home. Manigault, who now lives on the brink of poverty in Charleston, S.C., returned to the park on 98th Street and Amsterdam Avenue where he was once so popular that in 1977 the local residents played a tournament named after him while he was in the Bronx House of Detention on weapons and drug charges.

"What Manigault found was that nearly 25 years after he ruled the city's playgrounds, his legend remains intact. . . . He is instantly recognized."

The magic of Earl Manigault endures.

So does the magic of The City Game, Pete Axthelm's magnificent study of basketball on the professional level and the playground level, games only miles apart, and worlds apart, the vast differences, the stunning similarities.

Earl Manigault is still alive. Pete Axthelm is dead. The odds against that parlay would have been enormous twenty years ago. Axthelm, who boasted of being a degenerate gambler, would have had trouble resisting them.

Axthelm, like Manigault, was a precocious talent, wise enough, curious enough, skilled enough to write this bittersweet book when he was only twenty-six years old, just a few semesters removed from Yale.

"The book," said Jimmy Breslin, who was Axthelm's hero and his mentor, "was a major move."

Over the next twenty years, Axthelm turned out a handful of books and hundreds of columns and articles and television commentaries, many of them gems. He could make you laugh. He could make you cry. He could make you think. But The City Game, intelligent and insightful, remains his finest work, the best use of his reportorial legs and eyes and ears and his mind and his typing fingers.

The City Game is, in a sense, Axthelm's monument.

It is also, in a sense, his life.

Like Reed and Bradley and Frazier and DeBusschere and Dick Barnett, the world champion New York Knicks of The City Game,

Axthelm was a consummate professional. He knew all the moves of his game, and he could execute them brilliantly. He earned and enjoyed the cheers of the rich and the famous.

But like Manigault and Helicopter Knowings and Kenny Bellinger and Boobie Tucker, stars who never made it past the playgrounds, Axthelm abused his gifts. He loved a bet. He loved a drink. He loved a cigar. He loved a party. He hated sleep. And when his loves and hates dueled with the work he could do so well, the work often lost. He wrote less frequently and less well.

Pete Axthelm died at the age of forty-seven, having achieved so much and having promised so much more.

Patrick Smith was one of the many friends who spoke at the memorial service for Pete Axthelm at the Yale Club in Manhattan. Patrick Smith was a black basketball player from Marquette University and the playgrounds of Harlem. Patrick Smith was Pete Axthelm's native guide to the city game.

"I'll never forget one of the first times we were up at the playgrounds," Patrick Smith recalled, "and afterward we went to the first place we saw, a place on 119th Street and Eighth Avenue. It was a hard bar, a strip joint. It wasn't comfortable, even for me. I said to Pete, 'I think we ought to go someplace else,' and he said, 'I'll take care of this.' And he stood up and waved his arm and called to the bartender, 'Set 'em up!'

"That was Pete. He bought everybody a drink. We went back there three or four times, and they always gave him a big greeting."

Those were beautiful days, when the best basketball team in the whole world performed in Madison Square Garden and some of the best players performed on the playgrounds of Harlem.

And Pete Axthelm was the best writer he could be.

—Dick Schaap
New York City

Introduction

Basketball is the city game.

Its battlegrounds are strips of asphalt between tattered wire fences or crumbling buildings; its rhythms grow from the uneven thump of a ball against hard surfaces.

It demands no open spaces or lush backyards or elaborate equipment.

It doesn't even require specified numbers of players; a one-on-one confrontation in a playground can be as memorable as a full-scale organized game.

Basketball is the game for young athletes without cars or allowances—the game whose drama and action are intensified by its confined spaces and chaotic surroundings.

Every American sport directs itself in a general way toward certain segments of American life. Baseball is basically a leisurely, pastoral experience, offering a tableau of athletes against a lush green background, providing moments of action amid longer periods allowed for contemplation of the spectacle. In its relaxed, unhurried way, it is exactly what it claims to be—the national "pastime" rather than an intense, sustained game crammed with action. Born in a rural age, it offers still the appeal of an untroubled island where, for a few hours, a pitcher tugging at his pants leg can seem to be the most important thing in a fan's life.

Football's attraction is more contemporary. Its violence is in tune with the times, and its well-mapped strategic war games invite fans to become generals, plotting and second-guessing along with their warriors on the fields. With its action compressed in a fairly small area and its formations and patterns relatively easy to interpret, football is the ideal television spectacle: it belongs mostly to that loyal Sunday-afternoon viewer. Other sports have similar, if smaller, primary audiences. Golf and tennis belong first to country club members, horse racing to an enduring breed of gamblers, auto racing to throngs of Middle Americans who thrive on its violent roaring machines and death-defying vicarious risks. And basketball belongs to the cities.

The game is simple, an act of one man challenging another, twisting, feinting, then perhaps breaking free to leap upward, directing a ball toward a target, a metal hoop ten feet above the ground. But its simple motions swirl into intricate patterns, its variations become almost endless, its brief soaring moments merge into a fascinating dance. To the uninitiated, the patterns may seem fleeting, elusive, even confusing; but on a city playground, a classic play is frozen in the minds of those who see it—a moment of order and achievement in a turbulent, frustrating existence. And a one-on-one challenge takes on wider meaning, defining identity and manhood in an urban society that breeds invisibility.

Basketball is more than a sport or diversion in the cities. It is a part, often a major part, of the fabric of life. Kids in small towns—particularly in the Midwest—often become superb basketball players. But they do so by developing accurate shots and precise skills; in the cities, kids simply develop "moves." Other young athletes may learn basketball, but city kids live it.

This book is a study of the basketball life of New York—the most active, dedicated basketball city of all—from the asphalt playgrounds to the huge modern arena that houses the professional basketball champions of the world.

The New York Knickerbockers, champions of the National Basketball Association, are not direct products of the city's playgrounds. Like all professional teams, they have been assembled by drafting and trading to amass the best available athletes from across the country. Geographically and socially, they could hardly have more diverse backgrounds. The coach, Red Holzman, was a pure New York ballplayer; the captain, Willis Reed, is from the black rural South. The other stars include black products of city streets and the white son of a bank president. Yet as they rose to the summit of basketball, the Knicks became inextricably identified with the city they represented.

The media, based largely in New York, fell in love with the Knicks and with basketball, giving the sport its first taste of heavy television coverage, national magazine cover stories, and all forms of advertising and promotions. New York's rich citizens also joined the love affair, and the traditionally scruffy pro basketball audiences were replaced by a chic new breed in the bright new Madison Square Garden. And in the playgrounds, the kids too responded to the Knicks, acknowledging that a New York team was at last bringing a rare playground art to new levels of perfection. The Knicks seemed ideal symbols of the traditions of New York basketball, and if the media portrayed the Knick stars as larger than life, the playground kids understood that, too. In New York City, great ballplayers have always enjoyed that heroic stature: in the grimiest of parks, in the simplest of pickup games, they could momentarily be larger than life.

Basketball has always been something special to the kids of New York's bustling streets. Two decades ago, it fed the dreams of the Irish athletes on famous playgrounds such as the one on 108th Street in Rockaway, Queens. Those playgrounds produced Bob Cousy and Dick McGuire and other superb playmakers and brilliant passers; they also spawned countless athletes who were almost as accomplished but never made it to college and didn't achieve public recognition. On Kingsbridge Road in the Bronx, tough, aggressive Jewish youths grew into defense-minded, set-shooting stars; some led the colleges of the city to national prominence in the 1940s, but still others faded before the public ever learned their names. With money available for cars and stereos and surfboards, the hunger vanished from many white playgrounds, and so did the top-caliber basketball. But the blacks of Harlem and Bedford-Stuyvesant more than filled the void. Some made it to colleges and into the pros, helping to reshape the game with their flamboyant moves. Many more collapsed, victimized by drugs or the lure of the ghetto streets. Still others failed to find a niche in college or the pros, but endured as playground heroes, facing the challenges of the best of each new generation of players, occasionally proving themselves against pro players who return to the parks for summer games.

Each ethnic group and each generation of street ballplayers produced its special styles and legends, and each left its colorful brand on the sport. But more than that, each built a distinctive kind of pride—partly ethnic or racial, partly athletic, but much more than the sum of those parts. Veterans of playground ball describe it in terms of individuality, status, manhood; they also talk of the way it brings kids together. If the Knicks brought a special pride to all New York, they were only multiplying the feeling that the playground kids have always understood.

Occasionally the two distinct worlds of New York basketball converge. A playground idol such as Connie Hawkins joins the Phoenix Suns and comes into the Garden to challenge the Knicks; Knick stars like Bill Bradley and Willis Reed appear at 155th Street and Eighth Avenue to enter Harlem's most prestigious summer competition, the Rucker Pro Tournament. Such confrontations are always electric. Hawkins may pack the Garden, while a Reed or Bradley will add hundreds to the overflowing crowds at a Rucker game. And if a playground star like Herman "Helicopter" Knowings or Harold "Funny" Kitt goes up to block a pro's shot or stuff a basket over a pro defender, he creates myths that endure long after the score of the game is forgotten.

In general, however, the two spheres remain separate. One is enclosed in the glare of the Garden lights, celebrated by enthusiastic media and enjoyed mainly by those who can afford and find the increasingly scarce tickets. The other sprawls over countless playgrounds in every corner of the city, all but unknown to the media and enjoyed only by those who are part of the basketball-mad life of the inner city. The gulf between the worlds is as wide as the one between the beautiful people in the $12.50 loge seats at the playoff games and the kids who grow up thinking the world is bounded by 110th Street to the south and 155th to the north.

Yet there is a bridge: a mutual appreciation of a game that projects a significance, a sense of magic, to those who have known it, understood it, lived it. This book is not an attempt to equate the two worlds or weld them together; it is an attempt to describe the magic that they share. It is the saga of demigods like Willis Reed and Walt Frazier and Bill Bradley, and how they battled for the Knicks' first championship last year. But it is also the story of Earl Manigault, who became a playground idol only to be dragged to the streets and to prison by drugs; of Funny Kitt, another star of that world, still at a crossroads in his life, trying to find himself; of other stars who flashed briefly across the ghetto playgrounds before disappearing. It is the story of the affluent fans and the suddenly awakened media that glorified the Knicks—and also of the black youths who build their own glorious legends watching the weekend games at the parks of Harlem. It is, simply, the story of the city game, as it is experienced in the city that knows and loves it best.

"You make a few steals or work a few good plays, and you have the feeling that it's going to be one of those nights. The whole team gets into it, and then the crowd picks it up, and you come to the sidelines for a time-out and listen to that standing ovation, and it just makes you jingle inside."

—*Walt Frazier, New York Knicks*
Madison Square Garden

"There's a love of the game in this city that is very difficult to put into words. You start off when you're very young and you never get it out of your system. You might get married to a woman, but basketball is still your first love."

—*Willie Hall, a playground ballplayer*
135th Street park, near Lenox Avenue,
Harlem

BOOK I

The Knick Phenomenon

1

Two Games: The Challenge of Basketball

A MORNING rain had left wide shallow puddles in the undulating asphalt and some of Saturday night's litter had washed down from the corners of the small park, giving the basketball court a grimy and abandoned look. The green- and red-tinted glass of discarded wine and whiskey bottles glinted dully in the sunlight that was just breaking through; the surrounding wire fence was scarred every few yards by unrepaired holes that had been yanked open by countless basketball-hungry kids over the years. Within hours the court would be fairly dry, the debris would be kicked aside and the games—raucous, exuberant pickup affairs or perhaps even full-scale epic battles featuring local titans—would fill the Sunday afternoon with clamorous excitement. But for the moment the playground, set back from Seventh Avenue near 130th Street, seemed silently evocative of its illustrious past. Walking across it, Pat Smith was lost in thought.

Smith, who played for several seasons at Marquette University in Milwaukee, is twenty-four years old now, and years of studying in a less basketball-oriented city have rendered him out of shape for the highest caliber of playground competition back home in Harlem. Yet for two reasons he remains a cultural hero on the streets. For one thing, he was a classic Harlem product, a six-foot-three-inch center who spent his college career outleaping and outfighting six-foot-ten-inch rivals. He had never harbored illusions about his basketball future: very weak eyesight made him a terrible outside shooter and limited him to center, and six-foot-three-inch centers—regardless of their jumping ability—are not sought after by the pros. But at Benjamin Franklin High School in Harlem and then at Marquette, Smith had used moves and muscle and a fierce instinct for domination to delight his Harlem followers.

The second reason for Smith's stature was equally important: He had "made it." Like most ghetto youths, he had faced tremendous adjustment problems when he arrived on a predominantly white campus. In his first months at Marquette, he had fought everyone who seemed unable to understand his ghetto jargon, his racial pride, or his competitive fury. He was so combative that teammates and friends nicknamed him The Evil Doctor Blackheart. The name stayed with him, but the attitudes that produced it began to change. He became extremely popular on campus, did well scholastically, and developed a deep bond with his coach, Al McGuire. In Smith's senior year, that bond faced its ultimate test. For reasons that neither man has ever confided, McGuire suspended Smith for most of that season—and, incredibly, the two men grew closer than ever. Most black athletes who encounter such crises and find their basketball eligibility running out, drift back home, feeling lost and exploited—and lacking a college degree. Smith stayed at Marquette through the suspension, and remained two more years before earning his degree in June 1970. The reasons for his remarkable determination are as shadowy as the man himself sometimes seems; but it made the Evil Doctor a figure to be respected back home. And though he is intent on building a future outside Harlem, Smith returns home often, to be troubled once again by friends who have succumbed to drugs, to be enraged by conditions, and to remember some of the good things about growing up.

"The old Rucker Tournament was held in this park," Smith said, gesturing to one of the trees alongside the court. "When I was a kid I'd climb up into that tree. I'd stake out one of the branches early in the morning and just sit up there all day. A guy with a cart would come by and I'd yell for him to hand me up some lemon ices, and I'd eat one after another. There was no way anyone could get me to come down while the games were going on. I was in a world of my own, sitting up above the crowd and watching the great ones come in and do their thing. . . ."

The Rucker Tournament is actually not a tournament but a summer league in which teams play one another through the weekends of July and August. Established in 1946 by a remarkable young teacher named Holcombe Rucker, it was originally intended mainly to keep kids off the streets and in school by encouraging them in both studies and basketball. Rucker's idea was to give dignity and meaning to pickup games by adding referees, local publicity, and larger audiences; it worked, and gradually the Rucker Tournament expanded to include divisions for young athletes from junior high school through the pro level. A project that had begun with four teams and one referee began to offer basketball from morning until dark in various Harlem parks, before crowds estimated as high as five thousand. When Rucker died of cancer in 1955 at the age of thirty-eight, a well-known Harlem player named Bob McCullough and pro guard Freddie Crawford, now with the Milwaukee Bucks, took over the direction of the tournament. It remains the pinnacle of playground ball in New York, annually attracting stars from both pro leagues, members of touring teams such as the Harlem Globetrotters, as well as the best players of the regular pickup games of the city.

The pro section of the Rucker Tournament had long since been moved to another storied playground, at 155th Street and Eighth Avenue, but the lure of a decade-old game remained in that Seventh Avenue park for Pat Smith. Outside the ragged fences, the quiet Harlem Sunday was interrupted by the sounds of the women on the ubiquitous church steps, straightening uncomfortable dresses and pushing veils away from their faces as they chatted feverishly, in the weekly ritual escape from rat-infested kitchens and endless labor. Near the knots of women, grown men in boys' uniforms joined small children in formation for one of the minor parades that still serve some Harlemites as straggly symbols of unity and pride. Young, educated, and militant, Pat Smith had very different ideas about black dignity; moments earlier he had been depressed

by the Sunday delusions of some of his people. But under the tree
that had once been his reserved seat, he occupied his mind with
loftier drama, recalling a game of street basketball at its best.

"It was the kind of game that established citywide reputations.
Clinton Robinson was playing. Jackie Jackson was there. So was
Wilt Chamberlain, who was in his first or second year of pro ball
at the time. . . ." He savored each name as he spoke it; this was a
very special honor roll. Some of the names, like Robinson's and
Jackson's, would be familiar only to the ghetto kids who once
worshiped them; others, like Chamberlain's, would be recognized
by every basketball fan. But to Smith and many others they were
all gods, and their best games were Olympian clashes.

"Chamberlain and Robinson were on the same team along with
some other greats, and they were ahead by about 15 points. They
looked like easy winners. Then, up in the tree, I heard a strange
noise. There were maybe four, five thousand people watching the
game, and all of a sudden a hush came over them. All you could
hear was a whisper: 'The Hawk, The Hawk, The Hawk is here.'
Then the crowd parted. And the Hawk walked onto the court."

The Hawk was Connie Hawkins. When you ask ghetto basketball fans to cite the very best players ever to come out of New
York, you find much disagreement; but a few names are invariably
included, and one of them is The Hawk. Yet for years he seemed
fated to become one of those virtually forgotten playground stars
who never earn the money or fame they deserve. Connie made his
reputation at Brooklyn's Boys High in the late 1950s, but when he
was a freshman at the University of Iowa in 1961, he was linked
to a gambling scandal. His chief crime had been naïveté in talking
to glad-handing gamblers, and he had never been indicted or even
accused of trying to shave points or fix games. But his college
career was shattered and for almost a decade he was an outcast,
barred from the NBA, laboring in the short-lived American Basketball League and then in the American Basketball Association as it
struggled for survival.

In 1969, after a prolonged legal battle, Hawkins won a million-
dollar lawsuit and readmission to the NBA as a member of the
Phoenix Suns. He quickly justified everything the playground kids

had been saying about him for years. At the time of the game Smith described, Hawkins was a year or two out of Boys High, a man without a team or league. Yet he was the most magnetic star in Harlem.

"The crowd was still hushed as they called time out," Smith continued. "They surrounded the man. They undressed the man. And finally he finished lacing up his sneakers and walked out into the backcourt. He got the ball, picked up speed, and started his first move. Chamberlain came right out to stop him. The Hawk went up—he was still way out beyond the foul line—and started floating toward the basket. Wilt, taller and stronger, stayed right with him—but then The Hawk hook-dunked the ball right over Chamberlain. He hook-dunked! Nobody had ever done anything like that to Wilt. The crowd went so crazy that they had to stop the game for five minutes. And I almost fell out of the tree.

"But you didn't get away with just one spectacular move in those games. So the other guys came right back at The Hawk. Clinton Robinson charged in, drove around him, and laid one up so high that it hit the top of the backboard. The Hawk went way up, but he couldn't quite reach it, and it went down into the basket. Clinton Robinson was about six feet tall and The Hawk was six feet eight—so the crowd went wild again. In fact, Clinton had thrown some of the greatest moves I'd ever seen, shaking guys left and right before he even reached The Hawk.

"Then it was Chamberlain's turn to get back. Wilt usually took it pretty easy in summer games, walking up and down the court and doing just enough to intimidate his opponents with his seven-foot body. But now his pride was hurt, his manhood was wounded. And you can't let that happen in a tough street game. So he came down, drove directly at the hoop, and went up over The Hawk. Wilt stuffed the ball with two hands, and he did it so hard that he almost ripped the backboard off the pole.

"By then everybody on the court was fired up—and it was time for The Hawk to take charge again. Clinton Robinson came toward him with the ball, throwing those crazy moves on anyone who tried to stop him, and then he tried to loft a lay-up way up onto the board, the way he had done before. Only this time The Hawk was up there waiting for it. He was up so high that he blocked the shot with his chest. Still in midair, he kind of swept his hands down across his chest as if he were wiping his shirt—and slammed the ball down at Robinson's feet. The play seemed to turn the whole game around, and The Hawk's team came from behind to win. That was The Hawk. Just beautiful. I don't think anybody who was in that crowd could ever forget that game."

The crowd of spectators was much larger on the night of May 8, 1970, when the New York Knicks faced the Los Angeles Lakers in the final game of the National Basketball Association playoffs. There were 19,500 people in Madison Square Garden and thousands more in front of television sets in the homes and bars that were hooked up to the Knicks' cable-TV network. All—from the chic celebrities and silk-suited gamblers in the Garden's courtside seats to the cheering beer drinkers in the taverns—shared an experience as communal as that of the smaller, blacker groups at long-ago Rucker confrontations.

The first week of May had been a brutalizing, feverish ordeal for most New Yorkers. United States troops were slogging into the mud of Cambodia and a shocked young girl was screaming silently from the front pages of newspapers and magazines, in terrible, haunting testimony to the four murders at Kent State University. Anguished demonstrators were assembling near the United Nations and in the Wall Street area, pleading almost hopelessly to a government they knew wasn't listening, fully aware that the cab drivers who cursed them from behind flag decals on dirty taxi windshields were now the voice of their administration. Then the city's darkest fears took shape, as mobs of Wall Street construction workers unleashed the small hatreds and resentments that had been building within them for years, and descended on the young people whom their President had reassured them were merely bums. For two days the workers were content to rain beer cans and insults on the demonstrators. Then, on the afternoon before that final Knicks game, the workers came down to bully the kids at close range. Aided by Wall Street clerks, they went on a sickening spree, ganging up on the kids, kicking them when they were on the pavement, and leaving scores of bloody victims while policemen stood placidly by.

The politics of hate and polarization had thrust deep into New York's guts, and few people on either side could relish the sight of open war between Nixon's newly unleashed Silent Majority and the young, the poor, and the black. Countless people groped for sanity in the wounded city, and wondered if it would be sundered irreparably. Some of the spectators who came to watch the Knicks that night may have wondered just how much they could still care about a game. Then the Knicks showed them. They didn't solve the world's problems, any more than playground games cure the ills of the ghetto. But, like a ghetto game, the Knicks and Lakers did offer a moment of high drama, a brief and necessary escape from reality—a transcendent experience, which, in the end, is all anyone can ask of a great sporting event.

Fittingly, the drama began in much the same way as it had in that Rucker game for Pat Smith. The Lakers were at one end of the floor, gaudy in their purple and gold warm-up jackets, crisp in their practice shots, and dominated by the same seven-foot-two-inch figure who had dominated the Rucker scene, Wilt Chamberlain. Wilt was thirty-four now, struggling courageously to come back from a crippling knee injury; but he remained an imposing figure, a towering complement to the other Laker superstars, Jerry West and Elgin Baylor. At the other end of the court, the Knicks appeared ill equipped to challenge him; their own big man, Willis Reed, was not among them.

Reed, the center and captain and the Most Valuable Player in basketball, was back in the locker room, stretched out motionless on the training table as Dr. James Parkes, the team physician, injected 200 milligrams of a pain-killing drug called Carbocaine into his right hip. Reed had strained the muscles in the hip four nights earlier in the fifth game of the championship series. As he had toppled to the floor, New York fans had seen their cherished hopes fall with him. Because they were in New York, the big league of basketball and the citadel of national media, the Knicks had been christened early in the season—admittedly prematurely—as one of the most remarkable teams of all time. Logic had dictated that they would have to win championships before they deserved such accolades; but the spectacle of their superb team play and their fervid rapport with the crowd had not been conducive to logic—and New

Yorkers had confidently assumed that the Knicks' prowess would be rewarded with a title. Then Reed's painful injury had rudely shattered that confidence.

The Knicks had won the fifth game without Willis, but in the sixth game, in Los Angeles, Wilt Chamberlain had crashed over and around Reed's replacements for 45 points and the Lakers had won handily. There was still a chance that a delirious home crowd could inspire the Knicks to win again without Reed. But the crowd itself seemed to sense that the odds were very slim. The repeated chant of "We want Willis" contained a note of fear; plaintive signs were draped from the balcony to express the desperate hopes of the fans: REED, WE NEED YOU.

At seven-thirty-four, his lips pursed and his face intent as he forced himself to walk stiffly erect and hide his limp, Reed finally appeared. The crowd greeted him with the most deafening standing ovation of the season. For one hundred games the fans had poured out their love for the Knicks in countless bursts, hailing steals by Walt Frazier and passes by Bill Bradley and shooting sprees by Cazzie Russell. Yet in the hundred and first game they seemed to call on special reserves of emotion, in direct response to the reserves of courage that Reed had found within himself. Their voices rose in a two-minute crescendo as Willis strode to the foul line and took a few practice shots. The roar faded, then rose again when Reed was introduced with the other Knick starters—and then the Garden exploded when Willis made the first two shots of the game.

He would not score another point, and he would barely be able to run or jump; but his physical limitations scarcely mattered. Reed's mere presence had swept a city of basketball fans to a new exultation, and his psychological effect on his teammates ignited them toward their sweetest victory of all. Listening to the ovation when Willis appeared, Bill Bradley said later, "I felt as if I should have stopped warming up and joined the cheering myself."

On that night and on scores of others last season, the Knicks gave New Yorkers much more than a championship. With their rotating cast of heroes and their seemingly unending supply of dramatic feats, they provided the most varied entertainment a sport can offer. By winning the first title in the club's twenty-four years of existence, they represented the culmination of the city's basketball tradition. They wrote a glorious climax to the fascinating—and not always uplifting—story of basketball's role in New York City life. And they illustrated the quality that gives basketball its unique place in sport: the quality that makes a Bill Bradley want to stand aside from it all and clap, the quality that makes a Pat Smith almost fall out of his tree.

2

"It Makes It Fun": The Game as It Should Be Played

BOB SPIVEY spoke softly and thoughtfully, unconsciously shifting the cadence of his voice as he recalled the peaks and valleys of his brief career. Spivey was twenty-four but, in the manner of so many veterans of the Harlem streets and playgrounds, he sounded much older as he analyzed his past and his friends. "I grew up at 135th and Lenox, and I started playing organized ball at the Kennedy Center. Every year I played at the center, I must have won at least fifteen trophies. Then I played on the Benjamin Franklin High School team that lost to Boys High in the 1964 city finals in the Garden. Three cats off our team made all-tournament and two made all-city, and I guess some of us figured we had a lot to look forward to."

Spivey paused as he contemplated the dreams that had seemed so real to the dazzling stars on his high school team. Several of his teammates had pursued successful college basketball careers; others had lost track of their futures in a haze of drugs and veered toward prison. Spivey's path had fallen somewhere in between. He went with a handful of other New York stars to Ranger Junior College in Texas, seeking a basketball reputation as well as the academic improvement to qualify him for a major college. "We had fun down there, and we made that into one of the top junior college teams in the country. The school had never won a game, and we took them to the national tournament. We stuck together while we were doing it, too. We had seven guys from New York on the team, and we proved just how tough our brand of ball was." Afterward, however, Spivey had run into difficulty at Iona College. His coach had demanded slow, disciplined team play, and Spivey had insisted on maintaining his own free-lance style. Soon he decided to give up playing and concentrate on studying and earning his degree. Discussing his decision, he emphasized his need for individualism on the court. "Cats from the street have their own rhythms when they play. It's not just a matter of somebody setting you up and you shooting. You *feel* the shot. When a coach holds you back, you lose the feel and it isn't any fun anymore."

Spivey was talking about self-expression, not selfishness. His kind of individualism includes passing as well as shooting, and team attitudes as well as personal triumphs. It is ruled by its own form of discipline, the law of the playgrounds. "I'm not saying that college coaches shouldn't restrict their athletes, because some guys' games are so erratic that without restrictions they would ruin a team. They might go off and get 70 points or they might shoot one-for-thirty. But in the park it's different. If you get too erratic you lose your chance to play—and that's the supreme punishment you can suffer. There's nobody to tell you what to do, but you know that you're playing with five cats who are great individual stars. You don't need someone to order you to blend your game. You have to blend in to survive, and you do it by instinct. And it's the most beautiful thing of all when five cats really get their game together. It's spectacular to watch, the greatest entertainment there is, to see five guys doing their thing as a unit. That's when park basketball is really fun. People talk a lot about what the Knicks did this year, but that was nothing special to me. I've been watching it all my life."

What the Knicks did was undeniably something special, by any standard, and it was the result of long and arduous work. But Spivey's argument for rhythm and instinct curiously echoed the words of the most cerebral and least instinctive of Knicks. Bill Bradley, the banker's son and Rhodes Scholar, is the antithesis of the hungry ghetto player. He plays with studious concentration, as if he measures and evaluates each move a split second before committing himself; in his dedication to team play, he often seems doggedly determined not to "do his own thing." When the Knicks began to do their collective thing, however, Bradley said: "At times, we approach the ideal of how the game should be played. When one of us moves, the others adjust. We have unselfishness, cooperation, technique. We hit the open man, move without the ball, and help out on defense. Everybody's moving, taking part in every play. It makes it fun to play basketball."

The delight of the game was a constant theme of the Knick players during the first part of the season. They won eighteen in a row and twenty-three of their first twenty-four games, and almost every contest seemed to produce some new rapture for them and their fans. Defensive star Walt Frazier spoke of the fun of stealing the ball from helpless opponents, Bradley of the joys of teamwork, reserve forward Cazzie Russell of the special pleasure of improving the weakest facets of his game, most notably his defense. As the season dragged on through the relatively meaningless games after the Knicks had virtually clinched first place, the endless traveling and playing took its toll, and their statements began to sound less ecstatic. Then the playoffs presented a different set of challenges and pressures, and the players adopted fresh attitudes toward their situation. But through their dizzying early rise, the Knicks had as much fun as playground kids dazzling one another with their virtuosity and togetherness.

Reed was the boss, anchoring and shaping the aggressive team defense and serving as the hub of the offense while his teammates danced kaleidoscopic patterns around him. Frazier pulled the strings of the attack and filched countless balls from unwary defenders, bringing the Garden fans to their feet and sending his admirers in search of new apocrypha about his "fastest hands in the East." They claimed that he could steal hubcaps off moving cars, grab drinks that fell from bars and replace them without spilling a drop, snatch flies out of midair. Whimsically, Frazier fed the rumors: "I can catch two flies at a time. But the flies have heard about me now. They won't come near me anymore." With the spectacular *Bonnie and Clyde* era clothes that inspired his nickname, Frazier was the Knick with what an entertainer would have called star quality. But at his best, Clyde was as complete a team player as the stolid leader, Reed, or the self-effacing Bradley.

Alongside Frazier, veteran guard Dick Barnett sometimes appeared to be moving in slow motion, his eyes half closed and his expression almost bored. But Barnett was quietly and efficiently playing defense almost as well—though not as dramatically—as Frazier, and he, too, possessed a special weapon that could turn on Garden crowds: an implausible, gangling, fall-away jump shot that he hit with uncanny accuracy.

In the front court, Dave DeBusschere did the rugged and unglamorous work, guarding the opposition's best forward and helping Reed with the rebounding. Yet his battles along the baseline were never lost on the sophisticated Garden fans, who would cheer his rebounds as lustily as they did his frequently unerring bursts of outside shooting. Finally, there was Bradley, moving perpetually and adroitly around the perimeters of the action, then suddenly making a quick, calculated move to set himself up for a wide-open shot—the only kind he ever seemed to take.

On the playground level, this kind of spectacle would have transmitted waves of rumors and whispered exclamations of awe. Within minutes, cars would have been triple-parked on the street outside the court and hundreds would have been shoving against the wire fence for a glimpse. Soon spontaneous shouts would arise and enthusiastic appraisals would be rapidly exchanged in the growing crowd, not merely because this was classic basketball but because it had form, coherence, and a unique communal excitement—a form of joy that could be conveyed from player to player and then outward to the fans.

In the Garden, this phenomenon was expanded to embrace all of New York. Almost every fan in the city had played basketball when he was young, and even the nonparticipants had seen enough to develop an appreciation. When the Knicks began putting it all together in the spring of 1969, word spread quickly enough to make their tickets as valuable and chic as tickets to *Hair*. By last fall, the Garden was jammed for almost every game, and the fans came not only to watch but to share. The old-time New York enthusiasts, including the gamblers and the kids who have always populated the

Garden on basketball nights, were still there; but they were joined
by a shouting, chanting new breed that understood Bradley—and
would have understood a Bob Spivey—when he spoke of the joy
of the experience.

The Knicks compounded the fun with a series of surprises. Like
all fine entertainers, they varied their routines, yet always ended
on a happy victorious note. The five starters seemed to alternate
being stars, and when they slowed down, more fine players were
summoned from the bench. Cazzie Russell seemed to burst with
effusiveness merely in taking off his warm-up jacket. The crowd
responded in kind, and screamed more vehemently as he gunned
his shots into the basket and came down with fists clenched in delighted triumph. Dave Stallworth, a laughing, freewheeling forward, could replace DeBusschere adequately as a rebounder and
throw in some spectacular twisting, driving lay-ups. And guard
Mike Riordan, his jaw jutting and his face set as if he were looking for a street brawl, could pitch in with fifteen minutes or so of
pugnacious defense.

The presence of so many gifted athletes added an element of
playground-style hunger to the Knicks' play. When Russell, Stallworth, and Riordan entered a game, they wanted to use every
available minute to prove how much they could contribute. For
that matter, so did the clumsy, foul-prone Nate Bowman and the
seldom-used substitutes—Bill Hosket, Don May, and John Warren.
They never coasted or became sloppy in the final minutes of one-
sided games: it was too exhilarating to maintain the offensive pressure—and even more fun to hustle on defense, responding to the
crowd's pleas to keep opponents under 100 points. So even when
the Knicks were ahead by 30, the beat went on, and the fans stayed
to relish it. In the past, it would have been assumed that they remained solely to ascertain that the betting point-spread was safe;
but last year their motivations clearly were different. Knick basketball at its best was a sparkling extravaganza, and you don't walk
out on a peerless evening of entertainment just because you know
how it's going to end.

Bob Hunter, twenty-six, is a perennial Harlem playground star
who played at Tennessee State and is now with the Globetrotters—

and with any pickup team he can find on weekends in the 135th Street park. When he isn't playing himself, he stays at the playground to watch. "Look around here," he said, motioning toward a game and its hundred or so spectators. "You'll see many unique talents. That's what everybody is looking for—the unusual shotmaker, the great ball handler, the pinpoint passer. It may sound funny, but I feel that each player takes on a certain kind of dramatic character in this kind of game. He may be strong, aggressive, tricky, or whatever, and that character comes across to the spectators. It becomes like a Broadway play: The people look for a hero, supporting characters, a plot, punchlines, and finally a good finish; they get involved in the challenges and conflicts.

"Playing with the Globetrotters may be largely satire and slapstick, but it is still high-pressure entertainment. With the Knicks, it's a serious drama. And on the playgrounds you can get a little of both types of theater. But on all those levels, basketball is a form of dramatic art for me. And in places like this, it may be the only great drama the people ever get to see and feel and enjoy."

"The Knicks relate to everybody's basketball," said Joe Lapchick. "They are the meeting point of the old and the new in the sport. As an old-timer, I just sit at games and want to rip out the mooring of my seat at some of the plays they make. You really have to know and understand basketball to enjoy some of the things they are doing out there." No one knew and understood the game more thoroughly than Lapchick, who stamped New York basketball for three decades as the coach of St. John's University and the Knicks. A native of Yonkers and a member of the original Celtics, Lapchick had the perspective gained through half a century of observing and studying all levels of the sport. Yet the enchantment of the Knicks during their winning streak—like sublime theater achieving what Coleridge termed "suspension of disbelief"—blurred that perspective to the point where Lapchick gushed: "This is the greatest basketball team I have ever seen."

The fact that history and cold statistics may deny that statement is not relevant. What's important is that the Knicks in their supreme moments forced hardened observers to defy logic and history and statistics. Their achievements were meant to be savored immediately and viscerally, like the theater of the playgrounds. And no one could have reveled in that kind of experience more than New York fans.

As the Knicks winged through their first twenty-four games, they drew raves throughout the league, but some of the most direct compliments came, not surprisingly, from NBA coaches with the most experience around New York basketball. "They have five superb ball handlers," marveled Bill van Breda Kolff of Detroit, a former player and coach in the metropolitan area. "It's a forgotten art. People notice how much they steal the ball, but it's just as important that they rarely give it up." Former Knick Richie Guerin, the Atlanta coach, added: "The most impressive thing I've seen is that when they're up by 25, they work like it was a close game. They apply the pressure on defense and don't get selfish and they play team ball." Cincinnati coach Bob Cousy, the playmaker of the matchless Boston Celtic teams of the 1950s and early 1960s and another New York playground product, said: "If anything, they pass occasionally when they could shoot. And that's a fault every coach would love to worry about."

Unselfishness. If one word could have served as the Knicks' credo, that was it. Pro basketball players are gifted individual athletes by definition. In order to reach the pro level, all have been standouts in high schools and colleges; most are driven to continue to excel among the pros. But through coaching and experience and their remarkable personalities, the Knicks became willing to sacrifice that stardom in order to win. It wasn't easy; it never is, no matter how many clichés are mouthed about "teamwork." Self-sacrifice must be learned, often through laborious practice and occasionally through suffering. Those who have known the rigors and the suffering were fortunate enough to be able to appreciate the Knicks a fraction more.

Sonny Johnson works in one of the Street Academies operated by the Urban League in Harlem; his career at high school and prep school and at two colleges is a part of his past. Yet every few months one of the young guys around the academy needles Johnson, who is still in his early twenties, about being over the hill.

Then Sonny goes to a park near his apartment on Morningside Drive, works out in a few brief driving spurts, and promises, "I can still give you as great a five minutes as you've ever seen." Occasionally he does; and not infrequently, the timing that made him renowned in the playgrounds deserts him, or the young challenger proves a half step too fast. Johnson doesn't brood about it, but he can't help wondering where he might have been if circumstances had worked out a little differently. He played in 1967 at Gardner-Webb Junior College in North Carolina. The first black to attend the school, he made all-state, did well in class, but was depressed by the lack of social life. In the spring term of 1968, he went to the University of California, planning to sit out a year and then play for Berkeley. "People who saw me said I still had the stuff," he recalled, "but then my wife got sick. I had already left school twice in my career to come home and help my family out of financial trouble. That was the last time I came home to straighten things out. And they're still not straight. A lot of fine ballplayers got themselves strung out on drugs. I got myself strung out on poverty."

The memories, however, remain vivid. "I could call my own shots in a basketball game," Johnson said. "It made no difference what I did, because I always knew it would turn out right. I was always in a hurry, moving the ball around the court so fast that people would be yelling, 'Who is this guy?' Sometimes I felt that I could inspire my whole team. Other times I felt that, if necessary, I could do it all alone. Then I got a lesson."

The lesson was taught in one of the pickup tournaments that proliferate in Harlem. Many youth centers have teams of their own, and invite rival centers or individual youth workers to form teams for a tournament. This one was at Wagner Center; Johnson was playing on a talented squad organized by a worker named Bill Banks. Alongside him in the backcourt was Lonnie Robinson, a five-foot-ten-inch guard whom people described as "a pint-size Walt Frazier." Robinson was also called The Bandit, because he could reputedly steal the ball from anyone reckless enough to dribble it near him. Robinson was starring on defense, Johnson was leading the offense, and together they were shredding their opponents mercilessly. At half time in the first-round game in the tournament, they led by 20 points. Then Banks, the coach, suggested, "Sonny has 19 points already and a good chance to be the tournament MVP. As long as we're so far ahead, why don't you guys get him the ball as much as possible in the second half?"

"The hell with him," said Lonnie Robinson. "He got his. Let's the rest of us get ours." Johnson, a comrade of Robinson, thought Lonnie was kidding. But as the second half wore on, he realized how wrong he had been. Robinson didn't pass to him once and, incredibly, the team blew the game. Banks, who had put up the sum of twenty-five dollars to enter the tournament, stalked into the locker room, handed Johnson carfare, and told him to go right home. But Sonny lingered outside the door and listened to Banks read the riot act to his teammates. "He went on for about an hour, calling them every name in the book," recalled Sonny. "At first it was kind of funny to me. But then I realized that I probably deserved just as much of a lecture. I began thinking about my own style of play.

"I had never said to myself, 'I'm the star, I better get the ball.' But then I had never thought much about the other guys either. I had never said to myself. 'These guys may resent the fact that I'm the star.' I figured that from that point on, I'd better get the ball to the open man, and satisfy the other dudes on the court. That way instead of scoring 30 or 40 points, maybe I'd get 20. Guys would still tell me, 'Yeah, Sonny, you did a good job.' But then I'd be able to say, 'Yeah, you did a good job, too.' I hadn't had much chance to say that before. But I learned that it can mean a lot."

The Knick dressing room often showed how much it could mean. Individuals accepted congratulations on their own play and then, almost inevitably, began lauding the others. This wasn't false modesty; everyone *had* contributed. And as they praised one another, they achieved the harmony that Sonny Johnson found only after that lesson at Wagner Center. "We have unity and we're always helping each other out," said the captain, Reed. "The guys feel it. We might fall behind, but if we keep it going we just know we're going to put it all together sometime. We've got no superstars, but we've got something we never had before."

3

The Tradition: At Last, a Winner for New York

AL MCGUIRE is a product of the Rockaway playgrounds, a former member of the Knicks and the New York-bred coach of Marquette University. If Milwaukee seems far removed from New York, consider the fact that McGuire's team won the Garden's National Invitation Tournament last year with a team starring guard Dean Meminger and center Ric Cobb—both from Harlem. In the two previous years, Marquette had almost won the National Collegiate Athletic Association regional tournaments, with a team led by forward George Thompson—from Bedford-Stuyvesant—and center Pat Smith—from Harlem. There are perhaps a half dozen other college coaches who recruit as many New York stars or understand them as well as McGuire. But since Al, in his early forties, is the youngest, and the New York-oriented dynasty that he has built is one of the newest in college ball, his views on the past and future of city basketball are as clear and fresh as any in the game. When you seek to examine the traditions of city ball—the traditions that provide a prelude to the glories of the Knicks—Al McGuire offers some valuable starting points.

During the heyday of playground ball in Rockaway, Al's home court was the park on 108th Street; his constant teammates were his older brothers, John and Dick. John was the most flamboyant, and he became the boss, the unofficial captain of the family team. Dick had superb natural ability and instinctive knowledge of the

21

game. In high school, he was so shy that the coach hardly noticed him and he failed to make the starting team; but he went on to be a standout playmaker for St. John's and the Knicks. Later he coached Detroit and the Knicks, and he is now the chief scout for the New York organization. Al, the kid brother, had much of John's flair and a smattering of Dick's talent. Most important, he realized quickly that he could use the personality to compensate for whatever skills he lacked. When it appeared that better players might keep him out of the weekend games on the playground, Al simply got up two hours earlier, made friends with the kid who owned the only basketball in the neighborhood, and threatened to take the ball home if he wasn't invited to play. When he drew a tryout with the Knicks, he estimated that his ability would keep him around for approximately six weeks. So he promptly announced: "I can stop Cousy." And he did—just once; he picked a fight with Cousy, causing the Celtic star to be thrown out of the game along with him. But such antics prolonged his career beyond all reason, allowing him to state proudly: "I was the worst player ever to last three years in the NBA."

It was pure New York self-promotion, but Al found that it clicked almost everywhere. He began his head coaching career with seven years at tiny Belmont Abbey College in North Carolina, and eventually recruited so many tough city kids that the school outgrew its schedule and found itself without opponents. To correct that situation, he pulled stunts such as offering every fan in a rival arena a free ice cream pop if Belmont Abbey lost. They did lose, to a much stronger club, and Al anted up eight hundred dollars for the ice cream. But he was also rewarded with a lucrative return game the next year, helping to fill his schedule.

At Marquette, McGuire has kept up the verbal pace, alternately amusing, cajoling, and outraging his opponents, fans, and critics. "Al should be sent to Vietnam," commented St. John's coach Lou Carnesecca. "He'd talk the Vietcong into a helpless trance within two weeks." Others were less admiring; no less a personage than the venerable Adolph Rupp of Kentucky hated Al so fiercely that he helped arrange for Marquette to be bracketed in a division far away from Kentucky in the 1970 NCAA regional playoffs. McGuire responded by snubbing the NCAA altogether and bringing his team to New York to win the NIT. Amid the resulting furor, he also commented that Rupp had good reason to avoid Marquette: a year earlier, Pat Smith, the six-foot-three-inch center from Harlem, had outplayed Kentucky's six-foot-nine-inch All-American Dan Issel so thoroughly that Issel had managed only seven shots in the game as Marquette scored a smashing upset. "Naturally we stopped Issel," added Al. "We stop all stars. Our kids respond to that sort of challenge."

The challenges of city ball are embodied in an elaborate pecking order, one that has changed little in the transition from Rockaway and the Bronx to Harlem and Bedford-Stuyvesant. "Before we were big enough or good enough to get into the playground games," recalled McGuire, "we just nailed a hoop on a wooden light pole in the street. We'd scramble around underneath it in half-court games, and the big thing was to hit the hoop from all the way across the street. The kids who became the stars of those games soon felt entitled to try the playground, but they had to get there at about eight o'clock; on Sundays that meant going to seven o'clock mass. The littlest kids would get there earliest to get the court, and then they'd ask some older stars to join their teams so they could win and keep playing.

"Most of the games were three-on-three, and seven baskets meant a victory. It was also 'winners out'—which meant that you got the ball back after you made a basket. That forced us to learn defense, because if you couldn't steal the ball, the other team could make seven in a row and you'd be through for the day without taking a shot. As the day went on, more and more kids would be lined up against the fence, waiting to challenge the winners of the games, or to be invited to join a team that needed them. The good high school players could sleep later and go to ten o'clock mass, knowing they'd be asked to play soon after they arrived. When you got to college ball, you could wait until after eleven o'clock mass; and if you became a pro star like my brother Dick, you could go to twelve-thirty mass, come out and stand in the back of the crowd—and you'd still get invited to play right away. I'll never forget the first time I came home from my new job at Belmont Abbey. I slept late and went to twelve-thirty mass, then walked over to the playground. And nobody even noticed me. That's when it sunk in that my playing days were over—unless I wanted to start getting up for seven o'clock mass again."

The games in Harlem today are generally five-on-five, and they go up to thirty baskets instead of seven. But the principles of natural selection of teams have barely been altered through the years. "If you weren't one of the top players, the stars of the neighborhood wouldn't even want you on the court," said Jay Vaughn, who has never quite reached the top himself. Vaughn, now twenty-two, has always had ability, but admits that he can be moody and unpredictable. Against one of the playground leaders he can rise to spectacular heights; against moderate competition he can be sloppy and ineffective. At junior college in New Mexico he found no competition to stir him, and the coach dropped him from the first team. Then Vaughn decided to leave the team altogether; he is now concentrating on studying and working, hoping to find another way to complete college. But he has known high moments on the playgrounds, and he has become an articulate chronicler of the street basketball scene.

"If you hoped to run with the best players," he continued, "you had to get your own ball, get out first thing in the morning, and hope that somebody would say, 'Hey, can we hold your ball?' That meant you had a chance—if they had four great guys and thought they could afford one weak player, they might let you play one game. If you lost, you forgot about it for the day. And even if you won and had the right to keep playing, somebody like Herman the Helicopter might show up late, and they'd run you off the team to make room for him.

"There's a lot of humiliation on the playground. Before you finally establish your reputation, you have to suffer a lot. I was humiliated so many times that I got used to it. But it was one of those things. You either subjected yourself to the humiliation or left the park. And I didn't know what it was to stay out of the park. A lot of guys were even more hung up than I was. Basketball was their whole life."

The McGuire brothers went through a familiar routine at the weekend games in Rockaway. They would arrive in the morning arm in arm, gushing with brotherly love and loyalty. When they got their chance to play, Dick would go into his dazzling ball-handling act, drawing two or three opponents toward him and then threading perfect passes to his wide-open brothers. If Al got the pass, he would usually drive in for a lay-up—well aware that it was the only shot he could make. If John got it, he would shoot—no matter where he was. If John shot too often and too erratically, they would lose. And the brother team would suddenly dissolve. The McGuires would trudge home single file, Al and Dick in front with heads bowed, John in the rear, haranguing them for their mistakes that had cost them the game.

The ritual groomed John for an illustrious career as a New York City cop, a Queens nightclub owner, and one of the country's most famous gamblers. As a policeman, he never surpassed the rank of patrolman, partly because he broke all department records for absenteeism and partly because his superiors knew him too well. "We could make you captain," he was once told, "except you'd turn all of Manhattan Island into your own private parking concession." As a nightclub entrepreneur, John has been notably successful—and at the track, he can use every penny he pumps from his bistro. In fact, his business keeps him as trim and fit as he was playing street ball; he must be sharp for the daily race to the cash register against his partner and fellow horse player, Norton W. Peppis. At the track, John expends his energy chewing nervously on the corners of his programs; he saves his choicest tirades for errant jockeys and slow favorites. Yet he retains his innate sense of teamwork and sportsmanship. "Is anybody winning?" he often asks his friends. "As long as one of us is ahead, we're all ahead. Borrowing power is the key to this game." John's experiences with his brothers still serve him in many ways: after years of telling the unselfish Dick McGuire that he hadn't passed the ball enough, it became easy to look hurt and insulted and demand of bill collectors and bookmakers, "What do you mean, you want to get *paid?*"

Al McGuire has put the lessons of the street to more practical use, building a coaching style that combines elements of rich New

York tradition with a modern approach to city athletes. The Marquette offense is based on set plays and superb discipline, reminiscent of the patterns taught by premier New York coach Nat Holman during his tenure at City College. Holman's deliberate attack became synonymous with "eastern basketball," and it brought him hundreds of victories, climaxed by City's upset sweep of the NCAA and NIT titles in 1950. During the late 1940s college basketball was at its apex in New York, and Holman and his valiant City kids were its symbols.

Then the scandal hit. It began when a Manhattan College player reported an attempted bribe to the Bronx district attorney. Several Manhattan players were discovered to have accepted similar offers, and within a month an investigation by New York DA Frank Hogan had implicated athletes at City, Long Island University, and NYU. In the aftermath, it was also learned that the colleges in the city had used dubious recruitment practices to build their classy teams; rival coaches quickly exploded with self-righteous horror at the corrupting influences of basketball in New York and the Garden. Those same coaches were quieted abruptly some time later, when their own athletes—at schools such as Bradley, Toledo, and Kentucky—were also involved. But the damage had taken its toll in New York. The local teams would never recover, and college ball would never again be a surefire attraction in the Garden.

Holman had been dumbstruck at the suggestion of scandal, and until the last possible moment he resisted those who informed him. When at last he did face the grim reality, he was a sad and disillusioned figure. City College officials added to his grief by placing the blame squarely on him and suspending him. After a long struggle, he was reinstated in 1954, but by then he was an old coach of a minor league college team. Yet years after his retirement, Holman was still recognized as one of the colossi of New York basketball history. And as a monument to him, his techniques as well as his records were kept alive.

Holman's disciples have often been outnumbered. In recent years most colleges have emphasized fast-moving, run-and-shoot basketball, which is easier to coach and often more intoxicating to play. At the 1970 National Invitation Tournament, for example, Louisiana State coach Press Maravich chided McGuire for his old-fashioned style, in which, Press quipped, "the kids make forty passes to set up a thirty-foot shot." Watching Marquette play, Maravich added, "was like watching grass grow."

McGuire and his team quietly bore the criticism until after they had routed Louisiana State, all but shutting out record-breaking scorer Pete Maravich, the coach's son. Then the Marquette players shouted jubilantly, "We mowed his lawn tonight."

While some modern players have rebelled under old-fashioned "eastern" coaching, McGuire's athletes have adapted well to his disciplined style on offense—while fitting eagerly into his dynamic defense. Their team-defense approach is not unlike that of the Knicks, with an extra dose of playground incentive thrown in. After thoroughly balking superstar Maravich, for example, McGuire commented: "He's good, but I'd take Dean Meminger against him one-on-one up in Harlem any day." Added Meminger: "There are a lot of cats in the parks that are just as tough as Maravich."

Others may have been surprised, but McGuire understood what made Meminger outplay Maravich or Pat Smith whip Dan Issel— just as he understood what drove his other New York athletes to their finest performances. For one thing, unlike most white coaches, McGuire has made a genuine effort to communicate with black athletes on every level. And they are also from his city, his tradition. "In New York," said McGuire, "you can always search and find a player better than you are, to push you to greater things. It is an entire subculture built on competition."

"There's a large percentage of brothers who can really play ball," said Jay Vaughn. "But somehow they get sidetracked by problems and don't quite make it. Then they go the opposite way, messing with drugs and getting hung up. They're what you might call used-to-bes. I feel very sorry for those brothers. But I guess we can't all go the same way. The competition is just too intense.

"From the day you start playing ball in the parks, you know that under the quota systems used by college and pro teams, you're not going to make it if you're just as good as some white guy. If you're just good enough to be a seventh or eighth man on a college team, you can forget it, because they'd rather give that spot to some white kid. So you always know that you've got to be the best. You can never let up. You've got to be a *starter all your life*. People outside the city may not understand that kind of competitive pressure."

"You never get a breather playing ball in New York," added McGuire. "The best kids keep playing for fifty-two weeks a year. In Christ Lake, Wisconsin, a good athlete who's six feet four will play center on the basketball team, end on the football team, pitcher on the baseball squad; and in his spare time he'll be the town's leading water skier. In New York, there are very few three-letter men. It's basketball all the time, with the toughest ball of all played in the so-called off season, the summer tournaments."

In the winter, some of the time has always been reserved for merely watching the sport, and the pro and college athletes have contributed richly to the city's traditions. One generation of fans passed down the names of Holman and Lapchick and other early stars, and another generation went to cheer Lapchick's Knicks or Holman's City College boys, as well as the emerging stars of the new pro league that had been born shortly after World War II. First it was called the Basketball Association of America and soon it became the National Basketball Association; it was beset by countless problems, but in fits and starts it grew. In the late 1930s and the 1940s, the pro players developed line-drive, low-trajectory jump shots, because many of their games were played in dance halls with low ceilings. In places like Renaissance Hall in Harlem and Smyth's in Rockaway, the shots had to be low to avoid deflecting off ceilings. And during the second half, the players had to aim those shots while slipping and sliding on a floor that had been used for dancing at half time.

During the early years of the Knicks, the pros were still rated below the colleges as an attraction, and the club played many of its home games in the five-thousand-seat 69th Regiment Armory while the college teams occupied Madison Square Garden. But when the Knicks did perform in the larger arena, the kids crowded into the old building at Eighth Avenue and Fiftieth Street, climbing so far into the upper reaches that they got nosebleeds, then squinting down through the smoky haze to glimpse such idols as Bobby Wanzer and Harry Boykoff. The side balcony jutted out so far over the arena that part of the court was obscured from view, and entire segments of game action were hopelessly lost to the kids. Yet for fifty cents and their school identification cards, they got their money's worth, in dreams as well as basketball. "We could look down far below and see the cigars being lit by the people in the courtside seats," recalled McGuire, "and we'd always wonder if the day would come when we'd be down there."

They also had good reason to wonder if a truly great Knick team would ever play down there. The Knicks should have been the elite of New York ball, the epitome of all the city's playground excellence. Instead, they were often disorganized, laughable, pitiful—or simply a losing team to be largely ignored. People paid to see them because they would pay to see any form of basketball in New York, and the Knicks almost always led the league in attendance. But the arenas were seldom filled, and those who did come felt no special allegiance to the home team. For New York also led the league in gamblers, and the men with the cigars in the courtside seats bet against the Knicks almost as often as they bet on them. Yet if the "home-court advantage" never boosted the Knicks or intimidated referees as it did in Rochester or Syracuse or Fort Wayne, the fans could hardly feel guilty. For every game the Knicks might have lost due to lack of devout aficionados, they lost scores of others through front-office bickering, inept trades and draft choices, and constant executive meddling.

The man in charge was a stubborn, aloof, yet foresighted promoter named Ned Irish, who had made the Garden the center of big-time basketball in 1934 when he staged the first college doubleheader there. Irish had begun promoting the doubleheaders on his own, paying rent to the Garden, but the crowds were so huge and the profits so enormous that the Garden soon took him on as director of basketball. Irish became without question the most powerful man in the financial structure of the sport. When a group sought to establish a new pro league in 1946, they naturally approached him; he agreed, with some reluctance, to start the Knick franchise. For several seasons he continued to think of his pro team as a poor relation. This was unfortunate, because it relegated the Knicks to playing in the old armory. But it was also beneficial, in restrospect, because Irish cared little enough to allow Joe Lapchick, brought in as coach in 1948, to build one of the league's better clubs.

The dominant team of the early years was the Minneapolis Lakers, led by the first great big man, six-foot-ten-inch George Mikan from De Paul. The Rochester Royals were probably the second best; although they could seldom overcome Mikan's height, they offered fans a small, balanced team sparked by guards like Wanzer, Bob Davies, and a tough little City College product named Red Holzman.

The Knicks generally ranked in the next group of teams along with Syracuse and Boston. But in several ways, Lapchick was constructing a club that was a forerunner to future successful teams. He had eight men who shared playing time almost equally, shuffling in and out of the lineup in order to keep up the fast pace, to put pressure on opponents—and to compensate for their own lack of size and strength. Along with Boston's Celtics, the Knicks played the spirited, running basketball that would become a necessity after the twenty-four-second limit was instituted in 1954. In fact, the Knicks finished first in 1953–54, the last season before the owners decided to end slowdowns and deliberate fouling by forcing teams to shoot within the twenty-four seconds. Despite a pitiful playoff performance in which they lost four straight games, they had some reason to anticipate a bright future under the new rule. But behind the scenes, disaster had struck: Ned Irish, once the cool and disinterested businessman, had become a fan. And like all fans, he thought he knew how to run his team better than the professionals did.

The scandals of the early 1950s had robbed Irish of his booming college business, and suddenly the Knicks were the most important asset of the "mecca" of basketball. Irish had been widely reviled for his role in fostering the climate of big money and overemphasis that gave birth to the scandals, and the Knicks were all that remained to serve as his vindication. So he plunged headlong into the management of the club, and brought on an era of ineptitude.

The first casualty of the new policy was Lapchick, who became steadily disenchanted with Irish's meddling, and, early in 1956, finally quit. The Knicks skidded out of the playoffs that season, and made it back into the postseason games only once in the next decade. A parade of coaches came and went as the situation worsened. The front-office scene became so chaotic that at one point general manager Vince Boryla operated as an absentee executive from his Denver home, while Irish second-guessed beleaguered coach Fuzzy Levane at close range. As a legion of new stars helped NBA popularity to soar, the Knicks kept wasting first-round draft choices on people like Paul Hogue and Darrall Imhoff and Art Heyman—college darlings whose press clippings had seduced Irish while more hardened scouts for other clubs were singling out lesser known but more capable players.

At times during the endless bleak years it appeared that New York would never get a worthy representative in the NBA. But in 1964, for a combination of reasons, subtle changes began to occur. Eddie Donovan, who had been no more successful coaching the undermanned Knicks than his recent predecessors, was elevated to general manager—and somehow began to exert control. Irish may have been mellowing with age, or the growing conglomerate that was Madison Square Garden, Inc., may have been pressuring him to leave the Knicks alone and let them build; in any case, the club finally abandoned its traditional makeshift, stopgap tactics and looked toward the future. The Knicks started four rookies for most of that season, including Reed, the second-round draft choice from Grambling who was voted Rookie of the Year. The following year they gambled on Bill Bradley as their first draft choice even though he was planning to spend two years at Oxford as a Rhodes Scholar; it was, for the Knicks, a rare sacrifice of present gain for possible future value. The next two drafts brought the Knicks Cazzie Russell of Michigan and Walt Frazier of Southern Illinois, and trades secured Dick Barnett from Los Angeles and the big, moody, and occasionally brilliant center Walt Bellamy from Baltimore. The Knicks spent money freely to acquire

such a lineup, and by the end of the 1967–68 season it was clear
that they had purchased respectability. They had qualified for the
playoffs for two years in a row.

Still there was no magic in the Knicks. Bellamy remained the
most frustrating enigma in the sport. An All-American at the
University of Indiana, he had been drafted as a premium choice
in 1961 by the Chicago Packers (who later became the Baltimore
Bullets), and had been second only to Chamberlain in scoring
during his rookie year; then he had gradually slipped into moodi-
ness and inconsistency. If anything, his 1965 trade from Baltimore
to New York seemed to make him more unpredictable. Placed
under extreme pressure by demanding New York fans, Bellamy
would outplay Chamberlain one night, then wander trancelike
through the next two games. In addition, his large presence at
center kept Reed out of position and slowed the hard-working
Willis' own development. The starting guards, Barnett and
Howard Komives, were sparkling shooters but modest playmakers;
they gave little motion and fluidity to the attack. Russell, under
tremendous strain because of his lavish publicity and $200,000
contract, had trouble finding himself and his niche with the
team. And so for all their ability, the Knicks were in last place
on December 27, 1967, when Red Holzman replaced Dick Mc-
Guire as head coach.

Holzman immediately installed a pressing team defense that
altered the character of the team. Like most pro clubs, the Knicks
had been accustomed to playing defense by reacting; suddenly they
were told to instigate the action. Instead of waiting for opponents
to make moves and hoping to stop them, the Knicks took charge,
picking up rival dribblers at all areas of the court and leaving
their assigned men to help double-team men with the ball. The
tactic was exhausting and demanded a strong bench; but depth
was one commodity the Knicks enjoyed at the time, and they
made the press work. Keeping their rivals off balance throughout
the second half of the season, they hustled their way into third
place.

They also waged a formidable battle before losing to Philadelphia
in a bruising playoff series; but doubts remained about the future.

Holzman's all-out defense had worked marvels over the short run, but could the Knicks sustain it over entire seasons without succumbing to injuries and fatigue? The press was, after all, a device to hide weaknesses; would some of New York's more glaring faults remain submerged forever? As the 1968–69 season began, the worst fears of the cynics were realized. The Knicks got off to still another dreadful start.

Sophisticated Garden fans were well aware of the catalyst that was needed. New York was steadily destroyed by high-scoring forwards such as Billy Cunningham of Philadelphia and Elgin Baylor of Los Angeles, who were far too tough for most New York forwards, and a step too quick for Reed. The Knicks were also woefully inconsistent at center. To many fans the answer seemed obvious: trade Bellamy for a top forward and move Reed back to his natural position. Accomplishing this, however, was not simple. Standout forwards were scarce on the trading market, and whatever his flaws, Bellamy was still one of the game's ranking big men. General manager Donovan didn't want to give him away without receiving real value.

On December 19, 1968, Donovan's patience was rewarded. The Detroit Pistons were also floundering, and they were finally willing to relinquish their veteran local hero and former coach, Dave DeBusschere. The Knicks sent Bellamy and Komives to Detroit for DeBusschere. Donovan had showed courage by making the trade just as the Knicks were starting to win. And the next night, as if in instant vindication, DeBusschere helped New York rout the Pistons. The Knicks would never be the same.

Other trades have had more long-range effect on the balance of power in the NBA. Wilt Chamberlain has altered that balance each time he has been traded—first in 1965 from San Francisco to the Philadelphia 76ers, then in 1968 to the Lakers. And certainly the most far-reaching deal in league history was made in 1956, when Red Auerbach of Boston sent Ed Macauley to the St. Louis Hawks in return for draft rights to a young center named Bill Russell. But no transaction has ever had quite the instant, clear-cut results of the DeBusschere trade. Dave was valuable in himself, but he also represented an entire change in the makeup of the club. It was as if an incredible burden had been lifted, and every man on the Knicks was at last allowed to be himself, to function as if he were part of an exuberant and near-perfect playground all-star team.

Back at center, Reed asserted himself as a hulking, dominant force in the game. With Komives gone, Frazier got a full opportunity at guard and developed into Dick McGuire's successor as New York's favorite kind of player, the playmaker. And the entire defense grew more aggressive and confident, armed with the knowledge that DeBusschere could almost always neutralize the opposing team's star. The trade was undeniably the turning point, the single bold stroke that consolidated Donovan's achievements with the Knicks and made the years of patient building worthwhile. Yet one more step remained in the development of a champion—and ironically, it took the form of a crushing setback.

At about the time that DeBusschere arrived, Cazzie Russell was coming into his own. His defense still posed problems, but his offense was electrifying. Driving boldly and hitting sharply from outside, he was averaging over 18 points a game and threatening to get even better. Then, on January 21, 1969, he tripped during a scramble for a loose ball and broke his ankle. He was through for the season, and his absence could have been catastrophic. Added to a serious back injury suffered by reserve forward Phil Jackson, Cazzie's misfortune deprived the Knicks not only of a potential star but also of one of the commodities they had prized, their depth.

Bradley moved in at forward in place of Russell and the Knicks became, in essence, a five-man team. The reserve guard behind Frazier and Barnett was rookie Mike Riordan, who until then had been used only to come off the bench and "give" fouls. The substitute forwards were seldom-used rookies, Bill Hosket and Don May; behind Reed there was only the journeyman Nate Bowman.

It was a supreme challenge to the starting five. They faced thirty more games in the season, some against teams who could throw relays of reserves at them; and they knew that they would have to play almost every minute of those games. It was an arduous task that would force them to look very hard within themselves—

and at one another. If they could master that challenge they would know that as a team, they were special. If they failed, there would be only the excuses and laments that Knick fans had heard for too many years.

The Knicks lost their first game without Russell, in double overtime in Philadelphia; the next night they lost by a point in Detroit. Then they returned home and began an eleven-game winning streak that answered all the questions. The indomitable Reed showed just how high he could rise to an occasion. De-Busschere never ceased hustling, while Barnett, then thirty-two, found new strength in his old legs. Frazier became a more astute quarterback with every game. And Bradley, who had been having difficulty finding himself as he switched between guard and forward, filled the gap left by Russell and became the complete player that his fans had dreamed he would be. The Knicks finished a strong third, then routed the first-place Baltimore Bullets in four straight playoff games. The Bullets had entered the series with a pair of all-stars in Earl Monroe and Wes Unseld, backed by a half dozen able major leaguers. The Knicks had countered with only five men, but it had been enough. The skeptics were converted. The cynicism that had been a justifiable product of years of disappointment was erased. The standing ovation in the new Garden after the final victory over Baltimore bore a clear, strident message: "We believe." And nobody believed more firmly than the five players themselves.

In the next series, against Bill Russell and his old but wily Celtics, the Knicks ran into another club that could rise superbly to an occasion, a club on its way to its eleventh NBA championship in the thirteen proud years of the Bill Russell era. They also ran into the one obstacle they feared most, an injury to one of the starting five. In the fifth game, with the series tied, Frazier pulled a groin muscle and the Knicks lost. Frazier tried gamely to return in the sixth game in Boston, and somehow managed to limp through twenty-nine courageous minutes and score 17 points. Then, when Frazier was slowed to a painful walk and Barnett's shooting was hampered by a bruised knee, Riordan kept the Knicks in contention with clutch baskets.

The heroics were not quite enough to stave off the Celtics. But the five starters had grown too close and too proud to feel truly defeated, and they were young enough to know that time was on their side. The Celtics would own the title, but the Knicks would own the future. "We've got great young talent," said Frazier. "We've been forced to learn to play together in these last months. And next year Cazzie will be back, and who knows who else might help us? We're on our way."

"It's over for us now," echoed DeBusschere, "but there's next year. We're in the process of building a dynasty." The process had been initiated by Donovan and nurtured by Holzman, and the arrival of DeBusschere had brought the goal within reach. But it was the emotion of those final months of the 1969 season that had laid the foundation for the next incredible season. Five athletes had been forged into a team, and even in that moment of defeat, an electricity flowed among them. The Knicks, and all of New York, had indeed found "something we never had before."

4

Winning Streak

THE TEAM was called Young Life; it was sponsored by the Urban
League and it drew outstanding players from throughout Harlem,
and for several summers in the mid-1960s it did not lose a game
in the parks or youth centers. The team won largely on its ability,
but its streak was also attributable to a special sense of community
and competition. By nature, playground stars tend to think as
individuals; Young Life thought as a team. "We had a tough
troupe," said Sonny Johnson. "We had about ten of the best
ballplayers around, but more important, we were real competitors.
If somebody told us that a team down in Brooklyn was supposed
to be good, we'd be on our way to Brooklyn, yelling, 'Let's see
who's the best.' And with that attitude, we were always the best.

"You don't see the same competitive feeling much today. We
used to challenge anybody we heard about, no matter what park
they made their reputation in. The attitude was: 'You've got
a rep, now let me test it.' Now ballplayers have more distractions—
drugs, political action, other things both good and bad. So the
scope has narrowed. Instead of going out to Queens looking for
a game, kids are satisfied when they just prove that they're better
than the other kids on the same block. So I guess you won't see
another team dominate the parks the way we once did. It just
doesn't seem to mean as much to them anymore."

Six of the Young Life athletes shared a sprawling two-apartment complex on Manhattan Avenue near 120th Street. Earl Manigault, from Benjamin Franklin High, was there, still the most heralded player in Harlem even as he began to experiment with drugs; he was flanked by a kid known simply as Onion, who also had ability but an inclination toward the streets. Then there were Sonny Johnson and Bob Spivey, Raymond Holmes and Keith Edwards— all of them pushing toward diverse college careers, all of them absorbed in their team. "We lived together, we ate together, we partied together," said Edwards. "And the way we played ball, showing what we could do together on the court, kept us all close. You could say that we were just six young individuals trying to find ourselves. But we were deeply involved with one another, too.

"Things that nice can't last, though. Gradually those of us who wanted to get into the college thing got a little farther apart from Earl and Onion, who were into the drug thing. Earl was a beautiful man. Even when the drugs began to change him a little bit, my love for him never deteriorated. But the drugs had to pull us apart. Some of us were going our separate ways toward different schools, too. So pretty soon that period of our lives just ended. Looking back on it, I think we had something pretty special. I'd like to think that those experiences and challenges and victories gave us something to hold on to, something to remember."

"The kids who played, the kids who watched," said Sonny Johnson. "They'll remember."

Nobody in Harlem is sure how many games in a row Young Life won, and in a few years people will have to consult record books to recall that the New York Knicks won 18 straight games last season, breaking open the Eastern Division NBA race and establishing a new pro record.

The Knicks' streak began in Detroit on October 24, 1969, and ended with a loss to Detroit in the Garden on November 29. These dates and figures will define the Knicks' remarkable achievement for years to come, but in a sense they are meaningless. Would it really have mattered if the streak had been chopped at 16 games, one short of the old record, or if it had endured through 25—the number Bill Bradley had hoped for, "just on a whim, because it sounded like a good number"? It would not have mattered, of course, any more than it mattered whether Young Life won another half dozen games before Earl Manigault began to lose interest. Statistics won't be needed to recall how the Knicks enriched and enlivened the sport and the city. Those who played, those who watched: they'll remember.

Perhaps the most exhilarating aspect of the Knicks' streak was that it lacked the one quality that makes some sports' winning streaks almost boring—a sense of invincibility. No one is invincible in the punishing framework of pro basketball; when you are not confronting the hazards presented by the other top teams, you are facing physical and emotional fatigue. Long plane trips, travel delays, and back-to-back games in distant cities can make the Seattle Supersonics look every bit as fierce as the Los Angeles Lakers; to a team caught weary and unawares, an unknown like Dale Schlueter of San Francisco can become as menacing as a Lew Alcindor. So every Knick and every sensible fan knew that no matter how good they were, they were eligible to lose at any time; and such knowledge only added to the tension and giddiness as the streak remained intact.

The first six games of the season served as a fitting prelude to the streak. The Knicks won the first three easily against weak members of the NBA, then met the first two major challenges of the season before sellout crowds in Madison Square Garden. First came the Lakers, the team that still appeared strongest in the league on paper. Chamberlain, Baylor and Jerry West, the three superstars, were all healthy for one of the few times during the season—and West was at his peak form, scoring 42 points. But the Knicks mustered a superb defense and subdued them, 99–96; the dreams and the preseason predictions began to seem tangible to the cheering crowd.

Then came The Hawk, Brooklyn's own Connie Hawkins, waving the ball in his massive hands, twisting his supple body in the moves that have turned on so many Rucker crowds, drawing De-Busschere off balance and into early foul trouble. The crowd hailed Hawkins when he was announced and responded to the magnetism that many had not felt since his banishment years before. But the Knicks responded, too, and drove over and around The Hawk's Phoenix teammates to build a huge lead. Trying desperately to rally his team, The Hawk occasionally appeared hesitant and indecisive; he passed off when he could have shot, some of his trickiest passes left teammates as befuddled as the fans—and The Hawk's homecoming was spoiled by a 24-point Knick triumph.

Two nights later, the Knicks reminded the fans how human they were, and how fragile any streak could be. Having disposed of Chamberlain and West and Hawkins, they succumbed to Dale Schlueter. Nate Thurmond, San Francisco's powerful center, was injured midway in the game, and New York appeared set for a cinch victory. "An injury like that can make a team fall apart," Willis Reed said later, "or it can pull them together. Tonight I guess it pulled them together, and we were the ones who got careless." With Schlueter, an obscure second-year man from Colorado State, filling in for Thurmond, the Warriors stunned the Knicks and the incredulous Garden crowd, 112–109.

These, then, were the Knicks: a very good club, as everyone had hoped, but one that could ill afford carelessness or letdowns. A team that could not fall back on one star, a team that would have to depend on unity, on bench strength, on hard work. A first-place finish and even a championship appeared well within reach, but an eighteen-game winning streak seemed almost as unlikely as a loss to Dale Schlueter. The stage was set.

The streak began the next night in Detroit and continued at home against Baltimore, as substitute Bill Hosket played his longest stint as a pro and helped hold off a Bullet rally. It had reached four games when the schedule forced the Knicks and their fans to face a more distant threat. Lew Alcindor, the towering talent who was expected to dominate the pro game for years to come, made his first Garden appearance with the Milwaukee Bucks. Lew was listed at seven feet one and one-half inches on the program, but looked taller; Reed was listed at six feet ten, but was at least an inch shorter than that. As they lined up for the tap, there was a slight gasp from the huge crowd. If this was the matchup of the future, the duel that would determine titles the way the Russell-Chamberlain battles had determined them for so long, then the Knicks' star appeared hopelessly overmatched. "He's bigger than Wilt or anyone else I've played," admitted Reed. "I'd have to guess that he's more like seven-four than seven-one."

Lew smiled when he heard the remark. "You mean Willis is really jealous of my tall?"

Soon Reed was impressed by more than Lew's height. Alcindor was still learning, feeling his way, making mistakes. But he played with amazing agility for his size, and with a few deft moves toward the hoop, he got Willis into foul trouble. Reed sat down and in came Bowman, gangling and enthusiastic, as apt to foul out in five minutes as he was to score a basket. The first round of the Alcindor-Reed match appeared to be Lew's.

But then the fans got a glimpse of the Knicks' strange spell. Bowman was a man possessed, leaping higher and playing more intelligently than he had ever managed before. He snared eight rebounds from Lew, won a tap-off from him, and even blocked one of the big man's shots. Alcindor, perhaps from the sheer shock of it all, suddenly appeared distracted and confused on the court. His statistics were impressive, 36 points and twenty-seven rebounds, but Nate won the hour and the Knicks won the game.

Nate enjoyed it to the hilt, chatting with reporters as calmly as if he stopped Alcindor every night, while his effusive roommate Dave Stallworth, shouted, "That's The Man. Look at them surround The Man." Was it Nate's finest game? The answer seemed obvious. "No," deadpanned Bowman. "I played a better one in Detroit a year or two ago."

Reed, as usual, was more thoughtful, talking quietly and analyzing just what Alcindor would mean to him. "I don't think," he said, "he knows just how good he is. He's going to make things interesting around here." The two teams would meet again the next night, and Reed's mind was obviously jumping ahead. "He's getting ready," drawled Barnett in his deep, knowing voice. "Our man will be ready the next time."

In the Bucks' locker room, Alcindor smiled when Reed's compliments were repeated to him. Then he listened with quiet impatience to the reporters' questions. Yes, it was good to be back in his home town; no, he wasn't too pleased with his performance.

Even answering the most mundane questions, Alcindor seems tossed by inner storms. He has not yet learned to hide his feelings as Chamberlain often does, or to marshal them in the manner of Bill Russell. But then he may have more emotions to cope with. Even when he tries to be sullen and guarded, Alcindor projects a massive sensitivity and a powerful intellect. Like so many black products of New York, he is a very old man of twenty-two. Was he eager for the rematches to come with Reed and the Knicks? "Sometimes I feel very young and eager. Other times I feel like I was here before Buddha."

Reed came back with a vengeance the next night, and the Knicks whipped the Bucks in Milwaukee. For the moment, at least, the threat of Alcindor was put aside.

The win in Milwaukee was the first of five games on the road, including four on a swing through the West. It was the kind of trip that equalizes NBA teams, making even the strongest men vulnerable through sheer fatigue. The Knicks survived the grind in Phoenix and San Diego, but early in the third period in Los Angeles, apparent disaster struck. Playing without Chamberlain, who was thought lost for the season with a knee injury, the Lakers were hanging on with hustle and defense when Wilt's replacement, Rick Roberson, went up for a rebound and threw an elbow into DeBusschere's nose. Dave hit the floor hard, his nose broken; the Knicks' luck in avoiding injuries appeared to have run out. But Dave Stallworth replaced him and contributed 11 points and seven rebounds as the Knicks broke a deadlock and spurted to a 10-point victory.

Two nights later, DeBusschere was back in the lineup, his nose protected by an other-worldly white mask. And in another example of the way the Knicks were streaking, Dave broke out of a shooting slump and appeared more accurate with the cumbersome mask than he had been without it. In that game in San Francisco, however, a new challenge came up; guard Jeff Mullins, always dangerous, got hot in the first half with 24 points and led the Warriors into a 5-point lead. Red Holzman turned to Mike Riordan at half time. "Forget about scoring, forget about doubling up and helping out on defense," Holzman said. "Forget about everything but sticking with Mullins." The feisty Riordan cherishes such assignments. During the second half he smothered Mullins. Jeff managed only 6 more points as the Knicks pulled away to win by 13. The western swing was over and the Knicks were unscathed; the streak had reached ten straight games.

Four of the next five victories were at home, and as the Knicks sustained the tempo, all of basketball seemed swept along with them. Even to the most casual fans, the game was no longer simply a matter of running and shooting and scoring the most points. "Hitting the open man" and "team defense" became household phrases in New York; a sport that had once seemed shapeless to many fans now offered intricate patterns and fascinating techniques to the transfixed observers. There seemed to be an aesthetic attraction for almost everyone. Some still savored the theatrical drama of the games; others pointed to the balletic fluidity of the action under the backboards; still others responded to the orchestral balance of the Knicks, whose overall achievements became so much more than the sum of their parts.

As usual, Holzman became totally carried away with the euphoria. "It's nothing special, just a philosophy of working together. It just amounts to hard work."

Although his doggedly low-key manner was often deflating to psyched-up athletes and Knick historians alike, Holzman had a point. Beneath the explosive magic of the Knicks at their best, there had been long hours of labor on basic and demanding techniques. The Knicks were not performing miracles and they were not inventing new ways to play the game; they were simply doing what countless athletes had done before, but bringing it at times to new levels of perfection.

The concept of team defense, for example, was hardly original. A number of coaches in both college and pro ball had subscribed to it for years, and Holzman merely refined it a bit, emphasized it a little more, and found eight athletes willing to work tirelessly to execute it. "Hell, nobody invents anything anymore," he snarled when people tried to give him too much credit. "We're all borrowers. Everything in this game has been done before. When something succeeds, it's usually because you worked a little harder at it."

Actually, almost every Knick play could be examined through several layers of reality and complexity. Nothing was ever quite as simple as Frazier could make it look or Holzman could make it sound. A classic example was the stolen pass—the play that so often set up quick New York baskets, robbed opponents of momentum and poise, and brought thousands to their feet, filling the Garden with the chant, "De-fense, de-fense."

On the surface, the play was instantaneous and electric, a flash of eyes and hands and feet, a panorama of apparently instinctive reactions. But beneath it lay a conscious plan, a pattern of play that had been drilled into the Knicks since the opening days of an arduous training camp.

The theory of team defense can best be outlined in terms of options: The more options that can be closed to an attacking team, the better the chance for disrupting the offense. When an offensive player brings the ball upcourt, the Knicks take positions designed to force him in a proscribed direction, thus limiting the amount of the court that he can work with and cutting his alternatives. In most cases, the ball is forced toward one side of the court; once the offense is committed to that side, the Knicks gang up on the man with the ball.

This triggers a delicate chain reaction. When two Knicks surround the ball handler, it naturally leaves one offensive player unguarded. Both offense and defense are aware of this. The man with the ball automatically looks for the man who has been left open; but the Knicks are also conscious of that open man, and a third defender is moving toward him. Just as the harassed ball handler releases a pass toward the "open man," a Knick arrives and he is no longer open. The result is a stolen pass.

In practice, of course, this kind of textbook play seldom works out. Every defensive move must be made with care and superb balance, so that a defender can suddenly reverse himself if a pass is aimed for the man he has just left unguarded. Double-teaming and leaving men open are essentially gambling moves; unless they are executed with great quickness and precision, the gambles can backfire more often than they work. But as confidence mounted and the winning streak grew, the Knicks seldom seemed to lose a gamble. Holzman's defensive theories were translated into dazzling moves that turned defense into an offensive weapon, unsettling countless rivals and convincing everyone who watched it that Holzman was merely being modest when he kept insisting, "I'm no genius."

A hypothetical situation can illustrate the theory in more concrete terms: Laker guard Dick Garrett brings the ball across the midcourt line, with Frazier guarding him and forcing him to his left. Suddenly Barnett leaves his man, Jerry West, and helps Frazier to double-team Garrett. Now four of the fastest hands in basketball are surrounding Garrett, probing at the ball and obscuring his vision; but concurrently, the dangerous West has apparently been left wide open. Garrett's natural reaction is to force the ball somehow to West. But by the time he finally gets the pass off in that direction, DeBusschere has left his own man, Elgin Baylor, and darted toward West. The ball is grabbed or deflected down the court, and Barnett and Frazier, reacting instantly to the steal, drive down for a lay-up.

In another variation on the theme, assume that Garrett is able to see the direction of the Knicks' defensive flow. He holds the ball rather than passing toward West, and looks for another open man. Again his options have been severely reduced. The safe, orthodox passes for a guard bringing the ball up the left side are toward the other guard, the forward on the same left side, or the center; the most unnatural move is toward the forward on the other side. Yet the Knick defense has left just that forward—Baylor—wide open, inviting Garrett to attempt to thread a long pass toward him. If he accepts that invitation, the Knicks couldn't be happier. First Bradley and Reed have chances to slap at the crosscourt pass; then DeBusschere, with ample time to react to such a long pass, has a final shot at it. A high percentage of Knick steals occur when opponents succumb to that temptation to hurl the ball crosscourt into traffic.

These were only two of many defensive plays that fueled the winning streak and elevated team defense to an almost religious plane for Garden fans. But the key to it all was personnel and depth. It took eight hustling, tireless athletes to keep the defense functioning at full speed—and Holzman had them. The Knicks at their best were sometimes compared to the great Boston Celtics defensive teams, but there was a distinct difference. The Celtics could afford to take reckless gambles, in the comforting knowledge that the catlike, ubiquitous Bill Russell was behind them to rectify their mistakes. As they aged, the Celtics could also afford to pace themselves on occasion: even if a man slipped past the outer lines of the defense, he could take no liberties driving toward Russell and the basket. The Knicks did not enjoy the same luxury. Reed anchored the defense, but he did not carry it. If the Knicks gambled and lost too often, Willis could not always save them— and he was likely to get into foul trouble trying. So the Knicks had to be alert at all times, aggressive and yet ready to retreat to their positions at a moment's notice. The bench, which gave the starters important rests during almost every game, enabled them to maintain that edge.

Offensively, the early-season Knicks seemed to dance to secret communal rhythms, moving and flowing without the ball as well as with it, then unfailingly locating the open man, who usually made his shot. But again, the apparent free flow was largely illusory; what looked like extrasensory communication was more often the product of long drills and solid discipline. The seemingly random offense was really carefully programmed. The Knicks scored not by sorcery but by near-perfect execution of about a dozen set plays and several dozen variations.

Like all fine quarterbacks, Frazier constantly probed the rival defenses and took advantage of his own club's strengths. When opponents had difficulty adjusting to a certain maneuver, Holzman and Frazier would use it over and over. When one of the Knicks' streak shooters—Bradley or Barnett, Russell or DeBusschere—indicated that he was hot, Frazier would direct the action toward him as often as possible. So at their best, the Knicks would not only seek the open man but also ascertain that the open man was their hottest shooter of the moment.

It was not unusual, for example, to see Barnett make his first few shots, and then get the ball on six of the next eight or ten offensive plays. He might drill all six shots into the hoop, then cool off; and he wouldn't take more than a half dozen shots for the rest of the game, as Frazier turned to his other weapons. The effectiveness of the entire routine, of course, was based largely on unselfishness. Since the Knicks never worried about individual scoring totals, they seldom forced their shots; each man was perfectly willing to let one of the others have his turn at getting hot.

For all the success of the intricately planned, balanced offense, however, the plays that did the most to turn on the crowds were the bursts of inspired improvisation: Frazier or Bradley driving down the middle toward the hoop, drawing defenders—and then flipping the ball at the final moment to a wide-open Reed or De-Busschere for an uncontested lay-up; Reed planting his body as if to block out a defender with one of his massive "picks," then slipping away from the man he is blocking and taking a pass near the rim for a dunk; or in the fans' favorite move, Frazier and Bradley working their back-door play.

The back-door is one of the oldest and simplest of playground tricks, a sudden maneuver that not only produces two quick points, but also leaves a defender flatfooted and embarrassed. In the parks, it is one of those plays that buy respect; once an opponent has been burned by it, he must be a shade more hesitant, a step less aggressive—and thus a fraction less effective. The gambit is seldom seen in pro ball, partly because most offensive stars are so attuned to one-on-one moves that they never develop the sensitive two-man communication that triggers the play. The back-door is never called or set up in advance, but both Frazier and Bradley are always alert for opportunities to use it. When a defender shows that he may be vulnerable, they wait for their chance to burn him.

Usually, it begins when Frazier feeds the ball to Bradley and then moves toward him as if he is going to screen out the defender so Bradley can shoot. Bill moves behind the screen. If the defender remains blocked, Bradley is wide open to shoot. But if the defender "reads" the screen and anticipates a shot, he is inadvertently opening the back door. The second that Frazier senses the defender committing his eyes and body toward Bradley, he breaks around him and flies toward the basket. Without pausing or telegraphing the pass in any way, Bradley shoves the ball to Frazier, who is breaking down the lane at top speed for the lay-up. It happens so quickly that the slightest hesitation or flaw in timing would ruin it; but when it works, it's as striking as it is simple. And its very simplicity adds to the crowd's appreciation, because, in a sense, the back-door is a microcosm of the sensitive and selfless play that distinguishes the entire offense at its best.

The Knicks had fifteen triumphs in a row when they survived one of their closest calls. The game was reminiscent of their only defeat of the young season, when the injury to Thurmond had induced them to relax against the Warriors. This time the opponents were the Lakers, and they brought enough injured stars to entice anyone into complacency. Chamberlain was on his back in a hospital, recuperating from knee surgery. The tape and wires that held Elgin Baylor's thirty-five-year-old body together had given way once again. Starting forward Keith Erickson and Chamberlain's replacement at center, Rick Roberson, were also out of action—leaving coach Joe Mullaney with West and only six spear carriers available. The Knicks led by 9 at the half and figured to pull away as their bench wore down the undermanned Lakers. But no team with West can really be considered undermanned, and as the Knicks seemed to drift and lose their motion, Jerry fired the Lakers into a 2-point lead after three quarters. The sellout crowd drew a collective gasp. The tough game in the streak was supposed to come the next night in Atlanta, where the Knicks would try to tie the record against the rugged Hawks; the Laker game had been counted as a pushover—and now it seemed on the verge of slipping away.

Finally, in the closing minutes, the New York depth did wear down the Lakers, and the Knicks escaped with a 7-point victory. But the game had again pointed out the emotional ups and downs that affect every NBA team—the unpredictable factors that would haunt the Knicks again when they entered the playoffs as favorites.

If the Laker game had represented a "down" moment, however, the next evening's game in Atlanta was probably the pinnacle of the Knicks' performance during the streak. The first half was free-scoring and wide open; at half time the Knicks led, 68–61, but both teams were hitting so precisely that the result still seemed in doubt. Then the Knicks exploded; what happened in the first ten minutes of the second half gave new meaning to the idea of defense in the NBA. The Hawks literally could not bring the ball up the court. Frazier and Barnett interrupted their dribbles, Bradley and DeBusschere grabbed the few passes that eluded Clyde and Dick, and the Knicks careened down the court to convert one steal after another into contemptuously easy lay-ups.

They might have been playing against high schoolers. Yet the club they were humiliating was not one of the weak, easily awed members of the NBA. Atlanta was in first place at the time and destined to finish first in the Western Division. They possessed big, extremely physical forwards and an all-NBA guard in Lou Hudson; in fact, they were to finish the season with victories in their next four games against New York. But on that night they were reduced to standing helplessly and watching the Knicks race away from them with the ball. During that third-quarter streak the Knicks outscored Atlanta, 32–5; it was a breathtaking reminder that their record-tying seventeen-game streak was no fluke.

The Knicks had become the most glamorous team in NBA history, not merely with their streak but with their wardrobes, their fans, their big, shiny arena. Their feats had been splashed with theatricality from the start. Everything had seemed to happen almost on cue, under the brightest spotlights in the most auspicious surroundings. Yet, as the rest of the league knew, all is not glamour in the NBA, and most games are not played in Madison Square Garden, or in the magnificent Los Angeles Forum, or even in the new Philadelphia Spectrum. And so it may have been poetic justice—a way of reminding the Knicks of their own lowly beginnings and long struggles—that the ultimate achievement, the game that would set a new record for NBA winning streaks, should take place in Cleveland.

The Cincinnati Royals, who were not drawing impressive local crowds anyway, played four home games last year in Cleveland; one of them happened to be on the night the Knicks sought the record. The attraction drew an ample Cleveland audience of 10,438; as the game began, it appeared that a large percentage had come to root not for the Royals but for the record.

The Royals were in a state that could be described, depending on one's point of view, as one of flux or of desperation. Rookie coach Bob Cousy, lured away from Boston College by the challenge of building a top pro club, was trying to remake them in his image—fast-moving and well-balanced. The growing pains had already been considerable. Cincinnati fans had howled when Cousy traded away star forward Jerry Lucas in order to inject more speed into the lineup; it was no secret that superstar Oscar Robertson was not enchanted with a system that did not give him the ball in countless one-on-one situations. And Cousy's entire renovation project was not aided by the fact that nobody came to the games in Cincinnati.

Yet the young Royals at their best played aggressive defense and maneuvered the ball deftly. They already had battled the Knicks ferociously in one game in Cincinnati; they were the kind of team that could break the streak, if the Knicks were not at their best.

The Knicks definitely were not at their best. The offense was torpid and the defense failed to discompose the Royals. De-Busschere and Barnett suffered miserable shooting nights and except for Frazier, the others did little to compensate. Robertson, meanwhile, in the manner of all competitors, rose to the challenge: putting aside his differences with Cousy, he concentrated on destroying the Knicks' streak—and scored 33 points before fouling out in the final seconds.

But if the Atlanta game had marked the technical pinnacle of the streak, the highest drama had been reserved for the game in

Cleveland. With sixteen seconds remaining, the Royals led, 105–100. And the man protecting the lead, making the plays, was the great backcourt man of another era, forty-one-year-old Cousy himself. Cousy had activated himself only days before; since he was admittedly out of shape, the move seemed designed more to stimulate attendance than to aid the Royals. But when Robertson fouled out, Cousy peered down the bench for the right man to remain cool in the face of the desperate final efforts of the Knicks —and chose himself. In thrusting his presence into the confrontation, Cousy spanned a generation of basketball and added an historical element to the script. In 1959, the Boston Celtics had tied the existing records of seventeen wins in a row. Cousy had been their playmaker. And when they had failed to reach eighteen, the team that thwarted them had been the Cincinnati Royals.

Cousy had entered with a five-point lead; then, before the unbelieving crowd, he had made two foul shots to apparently clinch the game. With sixteen seconds still showing on the clock, Reed made two of his own, but the Knick hopes were dim. The Royals had only to hold on to the ball for sixteen seconds; the Knicks, still 3 points behind, somehow had to steal it and score— not once but twice. Cousy called time out to regroup his forces, then prepared to put the ball in play at midcourt. "We had known that we couldn't keep it up forever," DeBusschere said later. "And at that moment, it looked like it was all over."

"I was already thinking," said Frazier, "about starting a new streak."

But there was still a slim, improbable chance, and the Knicks gathered themselves for a last desperate effort. The team defense that had been static all night suddenly came to life. Frazier's hands were all over as Cousy peered around him, trying to pass the ball inbounds; Cousy's first target, Norm Van Lier, was blanketed by Barnett. Desperately, Cousy looked elsewhere; if he held the ball for five seconds, he would give it up to the Knicks. His second choice was forward Tom Van Arsdale. But as Cousy's eyes flashed toward Van Arsdale, DeBusschere sensed the pass and took a daring gamble, diving between Cousy and Van Arsdale. His timing was perfect. He stole the pass and drove for a lay-up. Only three seconds had been consumed. It was 105–104, with thirteen seconds to go.

After the basket, Cousy put the ball in play. Van Arsdale brought it into the forecourt, killing time. Now it was Reed's turn to gamble. Leaving his own man, he swatted a big hand at Van Arsdale's dribble. For a split second the ball was loose. Then it was secure in Frazier's quick hands, and Clyde was driving for a final shot. Frazier missed, but Van Arsdale, in desperation, had fouled him from behind. With two seconds remaining, Clyde had three chances to make two shots. "If I'd missed them," he said, "I wouldn't have had the nerve to come back to the locker room." His first two shots swished cleanly through the hoop, and the streak had reached its extravagant climax.

Psychologically, there were no more heights to scale. The Knicks came home the next night to play Detroit, and the fans welcomed them with a lengthy standing ovation. But it was their last tumultuous moment; they were spent. As they dropped behind quickly, they appeared ragged and weary, physically worn and emotionally drained. For three periods they kept the game even. Then they slowed to a halt and the Pistons—who had been the first victims of the streak—pulled away. The Knicks played without flair. With nothing left to prove, they had nothing left to give. But twenty seconds before the end, the crowd rose again, and with one more impressive ovation, thanked them for the streak.

The defeat marred Holzman's twenty-seventh wedding anniversary; the coach reacted with the same unbridled fervor he had shown during the streak: "In this league, any team can beat any other team." The players also spoke philosophically, as if they were still happy that they had postponed the inevitable the night before. "It only proves we're human," said Reed. "We don't depend on any one guy, but we do count on some of the group giving us a lift. Tonight wasn't our night as a group. We should have stayed home."

Once it had ended, you had to wonder just what the streak had meant. Could its emotional peaks ever be recaptured? In a few months, would it seem as monumental a feat as it had seemed in

Atlanta and Cleveland? "It was good for the team," said Holzman. "The guys wanted it. The record was nice."

"It always means something," said Frazier, "to accomplish what nobody's ever done before."

Yet only moments after the end, Bradley was placing it all in perspective: "It's the regular season race and the playoffs that count. Intermediate records don't mean too much. In that sense, the streak was superfluous."

It had its material benefits, however. The streak had brought on an unprecedented wave of media attention, giving new status to the team and the sport. In a general way, it would be a spur to league attendance, television revenues, possibly even expansion. More specifically, it would open countless financial opportunities to the players. And, of course, its effect on the Eastern Division race had been anything but superfluous; only a catastrophic slump could now rob the Knicks of the huge lead they had built. The streak, then, had represented their initial response to the first of the two major challenges of the season. It would be months before they had to call up a new series of responses—with a whole new range of dramatic possibilities—when they faced the greater challenge of the playoffs.

BOOK II

The Cast of Characters

5

A Matter of Respect:
Willis Reed

PAT SMITH was sitting at a bar called The Gym, in Milwaukee, Wisconsin, sipping a Scotch and looking up at the color television set. Around him, the room was crowded and noisy. The patrons had just watched their home-town team, Marquette University, win the National Invitation Tournament in New York, and now they were drinking beer and cheering the second televised game of the afternoon. UCLA was facing Jacksonville in the 1970 National Collegiate Athletic Association final.

For three years UCLA had dominated college ball, largely because of the massive, intimidating presence of Lew Alcindor. But in their first title game without Lew, the defending champions seemed to be in trouble. Artis Gilmore, the seven-foot-two-inch Jacksonville center, was towering over the action almost the way Lew had once done; and he was surrounded by other tall rebounders and artistic playmakers. Soon Jacksonville opened up a 10-point lead. In The Gym, the kids from Marquette were wondering if the UCLA era was at an end. "Better wait," said Pat Smith. "It's not settled yet."

Then UCLA forward Sidney Wicks did what Pat Smith and every other playground ballplayer in the country knew had to be done. He challenged Gilmore. Wicks was more than half a foot shorter and fifty pounds lighter, but now those statistics didn't matter. It was pride, not size, that had to be tested. Gilmore took a pass, turned toward the hoop, and began to toss up one of the short jumpers that were his most effective weapons. Wicks, his handsome, striking features contorted with the effort, went up to block the shot. He went up the way Herman the Helicopter or Funny Kitt or another playground star would have gone up: not jumping but soaring, taking the crowd and his teammates with him on a heart-grabbing trip. Gilmore released the shot. At the apex of his leap, Wicks blocked it and slammed the ball down into the bigger man's chest.

Wicks held his fist aloft in momentary triumph. Gilmore shook his head. And the most important college ballgame of the season had been turned around. Jacksonville still held a solid lead, and most fans were probably anticipating a long, unpredictable struggle. Only a few knew better. Connie Hawkins, preparing for his own game the next day in San Diego, knew what had happened. So did Funny Kitt, watching in Sheridan, Wyoming, where he was in junior college, and Herman the Helicopter, at home in The Bronx. And so did Pat Smith, watching quietly and appreciatively amid the noise of The Gym. Moments after Wicks' play. Smith sipped the last of his drink and got up. "I'm going home now," he told his roommate, Fat Jack Rusnov.

"How can you leave?" asked Rusnov. "This is a great game."

"This game's decided," said Smith. "UCLA can't lose."

"But they're still 8 or 10 points down."

"It doesn't matter," asserted Smith. "They've got respect now."

Smith walked home, leaving the others to watch the scenario that he knew would unfold: Gilmore growing a fraction of a second more hesitant; Wicks and the other UCLA forward, Curtis Rowe, sailing higher and moving faster; the entire UCLA team realizing that its bigger opponents could be handled—and drawing away to a convincing triumph. The others had to doubt Smith's prediction and see for themselves, and Smith understood that, too. They were not black and they were not from New York. It would be hard to explain to them what he meant by respect.

Alcindor understood, of course. And in the final game of the playoff series between Milwaukee and New York, he put the question of respect in bold relief for the 19,500 people in Madison

Square Garden. The Bucks were floundering, showing their youth and inexperience in countless damaging ways; trailing by 10, Alcindor went up for a flat one-hand jumper—and Willis Reed timed it perfectly and blocked it. Muttering to himself, Lew came back down the court. He knew what had to be done. A Knick shot missed, and the Bucks started a play. Lew took his position in the low post, looking almost plaintively for a pass. At last he got it, whirled, and went up. For a moment he hung suspended, far above Reed and far above the basket, as if waiting for everyone around him to sense the full impact of what he was about to do. Then, with both hands, he stuffed. The ball whooshed down and through the hoop, shaking the backboard and the spirits of all who watched.

All but Reed. Willis knew what Alcindor had sought to accomplish and he knew that in some games it could have worked. But Reed understood respect, too, and perhaps that understanding was the most important of all the factors that made him the Most Valuable Player on the Knicks and in the NBA. So there was no pause, no moment of admiration for what Lew had tried to achieve; there was only the answer to it. On the next play Willis beat Alcindor down the court and stuffed. Seconds later, he found Bradley alone underneath with a perfect pass. The Knicks were in charge again, but even that was not quite enough. Thus, the next time he got the ball in close, Reed turned instantly and drove, gaining a half step on Alcindor. Then he went up over the big man and stuffed again. The flurry had been swift and decisive. The Knicks' 10-point lead had blossomed to 22, and the question of respect had been settled. They won by 36.

"The great ballplayers were kings," said Sonny Johnson. "Their summers were luxurious. You would come home from school and everybody would be waiting, to see how you had improved and changed. Then there were the challenges from the new stars of the parks. And when you overcame those challenges, the respect was deeper than ever. You'd feel it when you talked to the younger kids. You'd feel it when you went to the parties and talked to the women. Sometimes it took the form of kidding. Pat Smith, for example, could hardly see, even after he got contact lenses. Everybody knew he had no outside shot, and they would call him Ray

Charles. But they wouldn't have bothered to call him anything if they didn't appreciate what he could do when he drove for that hoop. Even during the kidding around, you couldn't mistake the attitude toward him.

"Part of it meant being rough. When you got shoved and jostled too much, you had to use an elbow once in a while. Sometimes you really had to work on a guy. But not often. You wanted to keep control of things, but you didn't want to be known as a nasty ball-player. You wanted to be admired, an All-American type. You knew how many people were looking up to you. That was one of the great aspects of being a king."

Willis Reed is a king. When the stars of the parks talk of respect, they are defining Reed and his effect on the men around him. His physical attributes, as important as they are to the Knicks, are only a part of his contribution. And though he is their captain and occasionally arouses them with his words, he is not an inspirational leader in any traditional mold. Instead, Reed leads quietly: with unflagging enthusiasm even when the schedule grows too long and the games become meaningless; with surpassing courage in the face of pressure and pain; with what Bill Bradley called simply "his stature as a man—his great dignity."

To portray Reed's impact on his team is difficult, because so much of it is spiritual, and because Willis is a paradoxically elusive personality. Answering questions, he is direct, articulate, and courteous; and yet he always seems to conceal an inner being, as if by preserving a part of himself away from basketball, he can better hurl all of himself into the action on the court. For that is the essence of Reed: the totality of his commitment to his sport.

The athletes in the parks may express it best. "You see so many great players," said Charley Yelverton, a Harlem veteran who plays for Fordham University. "And yet only a few seem to know the whole principle of being an athlete—the principle that makes you dig your guts out, no matter what kind of game you're in. Earl Manigault was the best player I ever saw, but he didn't have that principle. Neither did a lot of other great ones, even ones who went on to college. But the players who did have it, you couldn't forget. Jim McMillian was one. Most guys would sort of go through the motions, turning it on only when the game got interesting. But McMillian would be running at full speed, battling on every play, even when it wasn't interesting or challenging. And sooner or later when he was in a game, he would inspire everyone else to run just as hard and stay with him." McMillian's attitude helped make him an All-American at Columbia; he was drafted by the Lakers.

"One thing about the top players in Harlem," said Sonny Johnson, "is that even a 30-point pickup game is a serious thing. You don't just play the game for the hell of it. It's an ego thing: an I'm-better-than-you-are thing, and also a personal thing. You want to prove to yourself just how much you can do, how much you're worth."

Reed used the same words early this year, talking to a magazine writer: "The ego is involved. The game is a challenge and an experience. When a man accepts a challenge and sets out to prove himself, he can get an evaluation of himself."

With the ego at stake, commitment naturally increases—for a Sonny Johnson or a Willis Reed—to the point where the material rewards for victory begin to seem minor. Johnson is broke; Reed's career has brought him substantial wealth. Yet when you spend time around Willis and begin to comprehend his priorities, you become convinced that he would agree with Johnson's summation: "Basketball has always meant something to me that is beyond money. If I got one contract that covered the cost of all the sneakers I've worn out, I'd put it in the bank and call everything straight."

"As the big man," Reed says frequently, "I have to be the boss!" He asserts that sense of authority in everything he does on the court. It is not enough for Reed to score points and grab rebounds and play defense. He seeks to control a territory, to enforce a discipline on teammates and rivals alike. He is the hub around which the New York attack spins; he gives it solidity while Frazier and the others give it motion and flair. Defensively, Reed punishes any rival who would infringe on his territory; he makes full legal use of his elbows and hands and 250-pound bulk. He guards his man as closely as any center ever has, locking a knee inside the other man's leg, cutting off a path to the basket with a leg or a shoulder. By playing such close defense, he is virtually daring his rival to try to break around him. Yet he is also agile enough to flash off his man on a moment's inspiration to slap the ball away from an unwary forward who strays too near him.

Because his style is so physical, Reed has been in his share of fights. The most famous came in the opening home game of his third season, in 1966. Playing forward, Reed was matched against Rudy LaRusso, the rugged Los Angeles forward. The two men jostled and shoved all night, and suddenly LaRusso whirled and swung at Willis. Another Laker grabbed Reed's arms, and LaRusso landed a second punch before he realized that Reed had been held back. That brought out the deepest anger in Willis— and before it subsided, he had taken on every Laker who dared to test him. First he knocked down LaRusso. Then he flattened six-foot-ten-inch center Darrall Imhoff. Then six-foot-nine-inch rookie John Block got up from the Laker bench, and Reed turned and broke Block's nose. It was one of basketball's most clearcut boxing victories.

In recent years Reed has seldom allowed himself to fight, partly because he knows how much he will be missed by his team if he gets thrown out of a game. But his control over his smoldering anger only makes it more fearsome. After one midseason shoving match with Milwaukee forward Greg Smith, an aggressive rookie, Willis glared at Smith and said, "I'm the king bee around here." Smith didn't argue. He learned respect.

Tom Meschery, the poet who plays forward for Seattle, wrote of Bill Russell as "an eagle with a beard." And truly, as a man and a competitor, Russell seemed to fly above mere mortals, at peace with himself and yet militantly intent on his goals. As an athlete, too, he played with a lofty splendor. Occasionally he allowed himself to glide while others exhausted themselves in battle. But when the big game or the ultimate play was needed, he would swoop into action and execute it.

Reed demands a different metaphor. His is a more down-to-earth style, full of grimaces and deep breaths, suffering and sweat; perhaps it will never evoke poetry. In fact, the best capsule description of Reed so far has come, suitably enough, from another day-to-day workingman, New York *Post* columnist Larry Merchant: "Reed plays basketball the way long-distance runners are supposed to run: dropping dead at the finish line. Whatever he has he gives."

That, succinctly, is how Reed remains the boss. It is how he wins respect and how he keeps it. When people dissect the components of the game's great centers, Reed comes up short of Russell in defensive genius, of Chamberlain in strength, of Alcindor in grace. So he gives more. "The game is my life," he says. "I owe it to myself to put everything into it, all the time."

This quality in Reed begets clichés, some of them meaningless and others degrading to his teammates. To say that Willis "always comes to play" is to imply that the other Knicks sometimes come to watch. If that were true, obviously, there would have been no championship. But Reed's commitment seems subtly different from that of his teammates. Bradley devotes a certain amount of his life totally to basketball; but other parts are drawn just as single-mindedly into intellectual exploration and self-examination. De-Busschere psyches himself sky-high for games, then drinks beer and jokes with friends and worries about the stock market. Frazier loves basketball and clothes and beautiful women; Barnett loves the game and freely admits that he loves the paychecks even more. Reed's life is also full of women and money and outside interests. But when you speak of him, none of those things seems to fit into the same sentence with basketball. The other things may produce pleasure or comfort or satisfaction. Only basketball seems to enflame Reed's ego.

He grew up in rural Louisiana. He has been asked so often about his early life that he prefers to toss off the answers in glib phrases, quickly passing on to what interests him—his sport. His birthplace, Reed recounts, was Hico, Louisiana, "so small it had only one store." Most of his youth was spent in Bernice, "a much bigger place; it had two traffic lights." With those details established, Willis usually goes on to the events that seem important: the first time he dunked the ball, his early development as a player, his high school career. The rest of his background may seem less important; or he may just feel that it is his own business.

Reed likes to retell the story of his coach finding him in a gym, teaching older boys how to dunk. "You can't even walk right yet," the coach yelled, "and here you are showing off." Reed concludes with the moral: "From that day on, I resolved to learn to do everything with the ball that a smaller man could do."

The anecdote is dramatic and to the point, but it hardly sums up eighteen years of a proud young man's life, as Willis might have you believe. There were other forces driving Reed. The only son of a warehouse foreman, he had to work hard, sometimes picking cotton and watermelons. And so he got a fast look at what life might have offered him if he hadn't happened to be six-feet-five when he reached high school—and if he hadn't made full use of his talents. That glimpse undoubtedly kept him going at times when basketball practice grew frustrating or schoolbooks became a bore.

When the scholarship offers began to arrive, Reed considered schools in both the North and the South, finally selecting Grambling, the black Louisiana college that is famous for producing football stars. He was recruited for both football and basketball but decided to stick with basketball. Although Grambling was not known for that sport, he was confident that the school had wide enough national reputation to attract ample attention. And though he failed to get the recognition of some of the stars of his era, he did interest several scouts, including New York's chief scout at the time, Red Holzman.

The Knicks chose him on the second round of the 1964 draft. Reed wasn't flattered. "I thought I should have gone in the first round," he admitted. "I couldn't believe that there were eight players better than me in the country. So that was the first thing I had to prove—that I had been underrated." He righted that wrong with a vengeance, stepping in opposite the best centers in the game and scoring and rebounding well enough to be named the NBA Rookie of the Year. Unlike most young players, he refused to be awed by stars like Russell and Chamberlain—and he stood his ground in the most violent of clashes. "I played as if every game were a war. Let's face it: if I didn't make it here, where would I have gone?"

Walt Bellamy arrived in a trade the next year, and suddenly

Reed faced an entire new range of mental and physical challenges. As a forward, he had to improve his already effective outside shot; he also had to learn to defend against much smaller men, players with quick, deceptive moves that would sometimes leave him standing behind them, fighting embarrassment and rage. And during that first season at his new position, he had to play on an injured foot that became more painful with every game. It was a difficult season, but Reed never complained. When it ended, surgeons removed a bone spur from his instep—and found a second one beneath it, pressing against a nerve. It had been remarkable that he even survived the season; yet somehow he had learned a new position, earned a spot on the all-star team and indicated to people close to him just how special he was to become.

For two and a half seasons more, Willis labored tirelessly at forward. Then, at last, he was liberated, when Bellamy was traded for DeBusschere. "It's like coming home," he exulted, "like being in a foreign country for a long, long time and then coming back to your old home town." He was back "in the hole," directing things and taking charge. "The trade showed the management's confidence in me," he said. That confidence, added to the painful lessons of his years at forward, drove him to assert himself at once as both a superb center and a leader. He was, in every sense, the boss.

"Ever since I'd been a little kid, I'd dreamed of being like Bill Russell, leading a team to a championship," he said. "And when we started to roll last year, I realized that I could do it—we could do it. As captain, I could help by burning some of the guys once in a while, keeping them up. But it was more important to do it by example. Some nights I wouldn't even feel like suiting up. I'd be hurt and feeling low, and I'd wish I could just relax for a while. But if I didn't keep myself going, what could I expect the other guys to do? They respect me. I can't let them down."

Off the court, Reed is a man apart from his teammates. Unlike some athletic clubs, the Knicks feel no compulsion to stay linked when they leave the court; they seldom frequent the same places or organize group activities. This is, in part, a natural result of their widely variant backgrounds and interests, but it is also a desired state. For eighty-two games and countless practices during a season, they work consciously and intensely to blend into a unit, a family. Constant socializing off the court might produce friction or boredom, thus disturbing the blend. So the Knicks go their own ways, eschewing possible close friendships in favor of a more important quality, mutual respect. Reed sets this pattern for them.

Reed's financial enterprises reveal much about him. He has a hamburger place near the Garden, a clothing store in Grambling, and several endorsement contracts; but he gives little of himself to these ventures, leaving them largely in the hands of advisers and managers. He also has a basketball camp for boys twelve to eighteen; and he plunges himself into that. The Willis Reed All-Star Camp is not one of the many summer camps that give kids a few weeks in the country and an occasional visit from a hero. Reed spends weeks there, living with the kids, instructing them, even driving them hard, in a small reflection of the way he and his teammates approach the game.

But the most significant fact about Reed's business life is a negative one. He is not writing a book. DeBusschere kept a diary of last season for publication; Frazier wrote his autobiography. And as the star player in the publishing capital of the country, Reed was naturally approached with half a dozen lucrative offers. He considered them, then politely turned them down. "If I did a book about myself," he explained, "I'd want it to be completely open and honest. And I'm not ready to be that open and honest about everything, just to make some money. There are some things that I believe I should save for myself. I don't want to share them."

So Reed remains, a kind of everyman to Knick fans and yet a man with a deep private existence. And perhaps his carefully guarded individualism adds to the dignity that teammates admire, while the blurred details of his inner self only augment his larger-than-life impact on the fans. Like the playground stars, Willis enjoys the All-American, good-guy image, and the admiration of women and kids; he is happy when teammates look up to him and opponents speak of his skills and sportsmanship. But he makes certain that all those reactions to him are qualified. The primary reaction—the only one that he demands in a total, unqualified way —is respect.

6

The Backcourts of New York:
Walt Frazier, Dick Barnett, and
Lesser-Known Stars

THE KID would come onto the court with a slow, languid walk, looking around almost sheepishly at the taller athletes he wanted to play with. He was only an inch or two over six feet, and he didn't talk much, and the expression on his face told the onlookers nothing. In fact, he would sometimes have to shove his way through the crowd around the park gates, because he failed to impress them as a ballplayer they should make room for. Then he would start to warm up and the spectators would become even more skeptical. His dribble was high and jerky, an apparent invitation to the quick, deadly ball stealers of the playgrounds. There was no way, it seemed, that Clinton Robinson could survive in pickup games against Harlem's top players.

"Then you watched him and watched him, over a period of years," said Pat Smith, "and suddenly you realized that nobody had ever taken the ball away from him. One guy after another would wait for the right moment, take a well-timed run at the ball—and find that it was gone. And when a guy tried to steal and missed, he was dead, because Clinton would have the ball in the net before you could recover."

"He had a game like Earl Monroe's," added Bob Spivey. "Except Clinton's passes were better than Earl's. He could do more things with the ball."

Monroe, of course, came out of the Philadelphia playgrounds to star at Winston-Salem College in North Carolina and then become the leading scorer for the Baltimore Bullets. There were moments in last year's playoffs when he left thousands gasping at his moves, his shots, his artistry. But nobody from Harlem or South Philadelphia or Brooklyn gasped. They had seen it all too many times, when players like Clinton Robinson "did it" to the Chamberlains and Hawkinses and the other playground heroes.

"Clinton went up against the best, dudes that were really big and strong and fast," said Smith. "And he did it to them with consistency. I watched him for years before I even knew his name. But I could have spotted him anywhere, the minute I saw that high dribble and that beautiful shot. He was the kind of player you really appreciated on the playgrounds, because he wasn't just a great leaper or a great athlete. He was an all-around backcourt man."

No phrase rings truer in New York: the all-around backcourt man. Anyone with ability could shoot and score, but New Yorkers have always appreciated the man who could do more: the one who could weld a group of individuals into a smooth team with his playmaking, the one who could turn defense into an offensive weapon with his steals. "When we were growing up," said backcourt man Sonny Johnson, "we saw playmakers who might have challenged Oscar Robertson, shooters who hit the basket without looking at it, like Monroe, defensive players who might have equaled Walt Frazier. But the escape routes from the ghetto were narrower then, and the incentives to finish high school often weren't there. So the great ones would show off for a while in the parks, and then they would be gone, and we'd have to look somewhere else for the new stars."

For many years, all New York could look toward the Garden, where Dick McGuire was mesmerizing opponents with his passes and the kids on the best college teams were imitating his style. Then McGuire departed and the college game succumbed to the scandals, and a long drought set in. The Knicks had fine guards in Richie Guerin and Carl Braun, but to many fans, it wasn't enough to watch them set scoring records. As the losing years continued, the crowds longed for a great all-around backcourt man, and they punished those who couldn't measure up. Nobody suffered more than Howard Komives, who arrived as a rookie from Bowling Green in 1964 with a deadly shooting eye and unlimited hustle—but lacked the ability to run the team. The fans booed Komives until he left in the DeBusschere deal; then, at last, they could begin to yell the way only New Yorkers yell for backcourt heroes. Replacing Komives as a starting guard, second-year man Walt Frazier rapidly developed the consistency he had lacked. Within weeks the fans had the man they had waited for.

As with so many aspects of the DeBusschere deal, Frazier's emergence as a star had a multiple effect on the team. Taking charge of the offense and setting fire to the defense, he brought out the best in his teammates. And nobody benefited more than the sleepy-eyed, high-dribbling, awkward-shooting Dick Barnett. Dick had always had a deadly shooting eye; Frazier's passes found him open so often that his shooting became a far more potent weapon. In his quiet, workmanlike way, Barnett also had been an outstanding defender; but Frazier's flamboyant defensive play provided a perfect complement to his own steady guarding, and made more people aware of the job Barnett could do on his man. As each game passed, Frazier and Barnett seemed to develop a keener sense of one another—and Garden crowds developed a deeper love for them. They marked the end of the seemingly endless wait, the arrival of a truly superior backcourt team in New York. Watching them work, Garden fans could not only anticipate a title; they could look back on the richest of all New York basketball traditions.

Clinton Robinson never heard the full-throated cheers he deserved. He played briefly with the Globetrotters and he dazzled some of the turnouts at the Rucker Tournaments, but he never found one of the escape routes from the streets. "I watched him one summer, scoring on the best of them and getting six or seven assists in every game," said Pat Smith. "Then I went away and came back, and he was gone. The next time I saw him, he was on a street corner, nodding." Soon the drugs had robbed him of the delicate timing and the sudden explosive shots and the last germs of incentive, and Clinton Robinson was just another lost part of the tradition.

That tradition is so rich that, in the parks, it is broken down into geographical categories. "The great Brooklyn backcourt men are usually outstanding jump shooters," explained Spivey. "The dudes from Harlem tend to drive to the hoop more." The players who made it provide eloquent testimony to the depth of the playground talent. A glance at the pro rosters reveals Em Bryant and Freddie Crawford and, from Boys High in Brooklyn, Seattle player-coach Lenny Wilkens. Yet behind those who escaped, there were countless others on the ghetto playgrounds, refining and perfecting the treasured backcourt skills, only to disappear.

The veteran observers talk of Willie Parker, whose jump shot would have made Barnett's appear orthodox by comparison. "He fell back so far," they insist, "that it was impossible to stop the shot. You just had to keep hoping that he'd lose his balance completely—but he never did." They recalled Joe Lewis, The One-Armed Man, who got his nickname because he made his moves only to the left. "Everyone in the park knew it, and everybody was overplaying him to that side—and still nobody could stop him." And they speak with reverence of Pete Williams, a six-foot-six-inch guard with the quickness of a smaller man, and a lethal shot that earned him the tag Peter Gunn.

"Pete was beautiful," said Pat Smith. "He could pass and jump-shoot with the best, but his lay-up was even greater. He would begin his drive and then jerk his head away from the hoop, and you'd be standing there wondering what he was looking at, while he was getting two points. He was clever, too. Once he stood out past the foul line and pumped in about five jump shots. Then he turned to a guy and offered to bet fifteen dollars that he could make ten more shots in a row. The guy assumed that he meant ten more of those jumpers, and even though he knew Pete was a great shot, he couldn't resist the odds. He made the bet, and then Pete dribbled in nice and easy and made ten lay-ups. What could the guy do? He had to pay.

"But maybe Pete had too much luck with stunts like that. He

was definitely smart enough to handle school, but he just never bothered with it. He never got strung out on drugs or wine or anything, but he became a kind of superhustler. Any kind of deal that could be made on the streets, Pete was there to make it. He wound up in jail for embezzlement."

The two backcourt men with the widest reputations of all, however, were Pablo Robertson and James Barlow. Robertson is only five-feet-eight, and doesn't bear comparison with the pro guards, who must combine talent with size in order to survive. Yet Pablo, who now plays occasionally for the Globetrotters, is hailed as one of the great "fancy players" of all time, a guard who could ignite playground crowds in a way that no bigger man could match. One observer after another tells his own favorite story of Pablo "shaking" defenders, weaving around and through entire teams and then flipping behind-the-back or between-the-legs passes to teammates who were waiting for easy dunk shots. To "shake" a man is not merely to elude him, but to tantalize him, to throw him off balance and leave him helpless as you drive by. The ultimate "shake" was performed on a drive along the baseline: nothing humiliated a big man more than a little man who could challenge him underneath the basket and execute a move that would "shake him into the pole."

The only man who could "shake" with Pablo was James Barlow, who played with current Detroit Piston ace Jimmy Walker in prep school at Laurinburg Institute in North Carolina and, according to many, "made Walker the star that he was with his incredible passes." Barlow went to college in Frankfort, Kentucky, but died in an auto accident before the rest of the world could see his act. Sonny Johnson, who grew up near Barlow around 155th Street, insists that he was the greatest backcourt man ever to come out of the neighborhood; others claim he would have ranked second best. But hardly anyone disagrees with Johnson's estimate: "Barlow and Pablo were the two baddest players for their size that anyone ever saw."

Two years younger than Barlow, Johnson became his most ardent fan, and he still talks of him with relish. "James was not a great shooter. He was mainly a ball handler, a dribbler and a passer.

And most of all, he was a smart player. He knew more about ball than the average player would ever dream about knowing. He knew exactly where and when to throw a pass and how to hit his man just as he broke for the hoop. And he knew when to take his man to the basket and just freak him off. Sometimes a guy would be guarding him tight, standing his ground, thinking he was doing a hell of a job. And then suddenly James would be gone, driving toward the basket to lay it up or flip it behind his back to somebody else. He did it so fast, it could really take the heart out of a cat. And he made it look so simple."

When Barlow faced Pablo, the word would spread quickly. Within minutes the park would be crowded, and to most of the fans, the other players on the court would be all but forgotten. They would catch the tricky passes and score the points, but they were little more than stage props—a backdrop to a classic showdown. "The best duels were up at Rucker," said Pat Smith. "Pablo would shake Barlow and Barlow would come right back, and soon they would both be spinning, dodging, driving both left and right, doing everything that could be done with a basketball. The park was at 155th and Eighth, not too far from Yankee Stadium, and on some days when there were ballgames there, people would leave the Stadium and triple-park outside the playground to watch. One Sunday night Pablo and Barlow got into a duel that neither one could break open. Every time one of them would make a sensational move, the other would match it. It went on until it was nearly dark, and then it started to rain, so they agreed to come back the next Sunday. And every one of those fans seemed to come back, too, because there was a mob out there. Then the two guys did it all over again, maybe even better, and I couldn't even describe the excitement of that crowd. I don't even remember who won. Watching that much talent in action, it didn't seem to matter who won. . . ."

It mattered very much who won the opening game of the NBA playoffs last spring; a defeat could have signaled the beginning of a nightmarish end to the Knick season. Yet, watching the game, there were moments when it was easy to forget the high stakes, the dire possibilities, even the running score. Earl Monroe and Walt Frazier were locked in a transcendent backcourt battle, a confrontation between the most exciting offensive star in basketball and the game's premier defensive player. The floor was filled with talented athletes and each of them had his own effect on the outcome, but as the game approached its pulsating conclusion, the other actors were inevitably thrust into supporting roles. The stars were Earl the Pearl, doing his whirling, twisting, unbelievable playground thing—and Frazier, the only man who could possibly stop him.

The wildly partisan Garden crowd was rooting desperately for Frazier, and some of Monroe's artistry undoubtedly went unappreciated in the frenzy. But at his best, The Pearl seems to defy time and space and noise and reality. Again and again he moved into the forecourt, backing warily toward Frazier, dribbling high, sneaking glances toward the basket with darting eyes while feinting away from it with twitching shoulders. Then he would turn suddenly, unpredictably, and the shot would be in the hoop.

"I'd reach for the ball and he'd be up shooting," said Frazier. "The next time I'd say to myself, 'Wait, don't reach for it'— and he'd be driving past me. Sometimes he would shoot and hit without even looking at the basket and I'd think, 'He's shooting best when I'm all over him.' So then I'd give him a little room— and he'd hit that way, too. He was just unbelievable."

Frazier never let up, but for the forty-eight minutes of regulation play he was beaten badly, as so many had been beaten by The Pearl, from the South Philadelphia parks to the NBA arenas. It was a dazzling, unforgettable backcourt show, one that seemed to demand a new range of superlatives. "If the old-time members of the Hall of Fame could have come out of their graves and seen Monroe," said Joe Lapchick, "they would think that they never played the game of basketball." Added Ray Scott of the Bullets: "God couldn't go one-on-one against Earl Monroe."

But somehow the Knicks stayed close, offsetting Monroe's individual genius with their balance. As the seconds ran out, the game was tied. The Bullets got the ball with time left for one final shot. Monroe would take it. Frazier would have to stop it. Now the rest of the night-long duel didn't matter. It was almost as if it had rained and the two stars had gone home, returned, and started all over. Frazier was given a chance for revenge in the *mano a mano* conflict. The pressure on him was greater than ever. "I wouldn't," said Clyde, "have it any other way."

Monroe came down the middle of the court, his head bobbing as he looked for the opportunity to shake his man. Frazier overplayed him slightly to one side; Barnett glided over from the other side to help out. "Dick told me that he'd come over to help at a certain time," said Frazier. "But in the end, I knew I had to do the job myself." The crowd noise reached a shrill pitch and seemed to hold; the seconds passed with excruciating slowness. Then, suddenly, The Pearl was in motion, spinning off the dribble, sailing upward and forward toward the foul circle. But this time Frazier refused to be shaken. His reactions were instantaneous, his positioning perfect, and the best Monroe could manage was a forced shot, a desperate heave across his own body and over Frazier's outstretched arm. The Pearl had made similarly "bad" shots all night, of course—but this one stayed out. The game went into overtime.

The two teams struggled, exchanging fouls under the boards, missing as many foul shots as they made due to the intense pressure. Yet their sweaty ritual still had the quality of a chorus, a backdrop for the titanic duel that would inevitably decide the game. Within a minute remaining in the five-minute overtime, it began again: Monroe brought the ball up, shielding it with his lean body, watching for his opening, protecting Baltimore's 2-point lead. But this time it was Frazier who found the opening, timing his lunge perfectly to slap the ball away in mid-dribble. Barnett grabbed it, drove, and drew a foul; he made the two shots to tie the game.

Now twenty-three seconds remained. Time for one more battle, Monroe on Frazier, one-on-one with the game at stake. Frazier had stopped him twice, but he had to do it once more or all would be for naught. To many, the feat seemed all but impossible; but Clyde was just starting. "The longer it went on," he said later, "the more confident I felt. He burned me all night long, but at last I knew it was my turn to burn him." Again his hand reached past Monroe, slapped the ball to Barnett to set up a drive. This time, however, rookie Fred Carter, a magnificent six-foot-three-inch leaper, jumped high on the backboard to block Barnett's lay-up—and the game went into a second overtime.

But time and emotion were at last on Frazier's side. Monroe was exhausted, worn down by his physical heroics as well as the pressure of taking all the big shots. And Clyde, shaking off the puzzling demons that sometimes slowed his offense and slackened his defense, was finally asserting himself. He held Monroe to one basket in the second overtime, and with twenty-eight seconds left he hit Reed with an adroit pass to set up the basket that clinched it. The Knicks won, 120–117.

It had not been a demonstration of the Knicks at their best, and it had definitely not been one of Frazier's superior overall performances. The marvelous Monroe had given the game its character; his feats were the ones that would be recalled after even the result had been forgotten. Yet the game and the backcourt duel had been revealing about Frazier, the man whose moods and cycles often defied prediction or definition.

Clyde is a special breed of star, an athlete who conveys a wide range of deep and perplexing emotions to teammates and fans alike. He can be prodigious or strangely lackadaisical, totally involved or unexplainably removed from the action, the ultimate team player or one who dribbles too much and slows down the entire attack. He is good far more often than he is ineffective—and the biggest challenges are almost sure to turn him on the most—but at times his quality of inconsistency makes him all the more fascinating to watch.

Frazier is not a leader by nature. He likes to dine and relax alone, away from his teammates, and even in the locker room he rarely joins in the banter and mutual congratulations that are often touched off by Dave Stallworth or Cazzie Russell. Yet his role as quarterback is so essential that he must be a leader on the floor. When he drifts off into one of his private worlds, his teammates are frustrated, almost helpless; when he comes to life, his rapport with both the Knicks and the fans is electric. "If I make a few steals, get a few passes going really well, hit a few jumpers," he says, "I get that feeling that it's going to be one of those beautiful nights. We all start moving in the right groove, the fans get behind us, and something really special happens out there. After a while, I feel I can do anything."

Reed and Frazier are an interesting pair of leaders. Reed's role can be compared to that of pitcher Tom Seaver as the Mets won the 1969 world championship: Both provided not only brilliance but also dogged consistency and conscious leadership. Frazier is more akin to Joe Namath when he quarterbacked the Jets to a world title: Both were capable of dreadful moments—five interceptions or a dozen errant shots and passes—but only in games that scarcely mattered. In the big games they exuded confidence and took charge. Both were apt to lose statistical battles—as Namath did to Daryle Lamonica of Oakland in the 1968 AFL title game, as Frazier did to both Monroe and Jerry West in the playoffs. But when the game-saving plays were required, they made them. And then they talked about them, freely and candidly, playing the starring role to the hilt.

Of all the postmortems on the Jets' Super Bowl triumph, the one that remains most vivid is Namath, gloating not so much for himself as for his entire underrated league, taunting those who had underestimated him—and then listening to an NFL writer ask if he didn't feel sorry for Earl Morrall, the Baltimore quarterback who had been so badly humiliated in the game. Joe's answer was quick: "Better him than me."

Then there was Clyde, not gloating as much as exulting, hearing a similar question about Monroe. "I do feel compassion for Earl, because he did so much," he said. "But better him than me."

Frazier, however, was always a more likable hero than Namath. His exuberant postgame comments never had Namath's cutting edge, and he never resorted to making petty distinctions among reporters of whom he approved or disapproved. He genuinely enjoyed finding new ways to express the Knicks' magic in words; his wit was sharp and spontaneous. "Fast hands, fast feet," he would say when things were going well. "Sometimes I'm so fast, it scares even me."

There are nights when he can scare everyone, scoring 25 or 30 points, running the attack and leading the defense. Yet as the long season wore on and the most important playoffs arrived, he couldn't risk trying to do all three—and possibly faltering. He had to establish his priorities, and both he and Holzman agreed that the first concern was defense. "Against the great ones like Monroe and the Lakers," he said, "I've got to give defense my full concentration. When we're going right, defense is all the team needs from me. The other guys have their things. Defense is mine."

A native of Atlanta, Frazier was a typical flashy young backcourt man when he arrived at Southern Illinois; but when academic ineligibility kept him on the sidelines for one season, he took the opportunity to develop a new specialty. Every day he scrimmaged against the starting team, defending against their best players. He studied offensive moves and defensive reactions, learned to look at a man's eyes as well as his feet to sense where he is going to move. "Defense is instinct and reflexes," he says—but he goes on to describe it as much more. "You've got to anticipate, to feel your man out early, to find out his habits and tendencies. When you can sense what's going to happen, you can gain a split-second edge. Then quickness takes care of the rest."

New Yorkers first saw Frazier's quickness in the 1967 National Invitation Tournament. Southern Illinois, it turned out, outclassed the field; the starting guards on the club were Frazier and Dick Garrett, last year's rookie star for the Lakers. But Southern Illinois played a balanced offense and tight defense, and the stars had not piled up any impressive statistics; Frazier came into the Garden with little advance billing. Then he put on one show after another, climaxed by the final game against Marquette. Southern Illinois trailed by twelve points at half time in that game, with Marquette playing well-drilled ball and shooting precisely. But Frazier had done his studying, and he had found the small chinks in the Marquette armor. The Marquette guards were hard-working and scrappy, but they were not superior ball handlers. Clyde realized what he could do to them, and in the second half he did it, again and again. Soon the harassed Marquette team couldn't get the ball across midcourt. Frazier was stealing, whipping the ball downcourt, running the offense. Southern Illinois pulled away to a convincing victory. A few months later, the Knicks chose Frazier in the first round of the draft.

Because of his year scholastically *hors de combat* Frazier had another season of eligibility remaining in college. But he also had financial difficulties and an impatience to make it big in New York. After his NIT performances, there was little left to prove at Southern Illinois, and the Knicks had no trouble luring him into pro ball with a lucrative contract. For a year and a half, Frazier's talent came across in short bursts, with long lulls between. When the DeBusschere trade opened things up for him, however, he emerged quickly as a star. The crowds fell in love with him, and the feeling was intensely mutual. "When I hear all those people screaming," he often said, "it really gets the adrenaline pumping. They make the game fun, because they appreciate everything you're doing—not just scoring, but also defense and passing. When we call a time-out and go to the bench, and I hear that ovation, it makes me jingle inside."

Responding to the jingling, Frazier unabashedly plays to the crowd, both on and off the court. His sense of image has produced an interesting split in his personality. For though he prefers, for example, to do most of his socializing away from teammates and fans, after each game he makes it a point to stop in at the crowded Harry M. Stevens bar beneath the Garden, armed with a smashing outfit and even more smashing women—as if to keep the swinging image intact before pursuing his own pleasures. Frazier lives in an uninspired little room in an uninspired hotel called The New Yorker, across from the Garden. But that room is bedecked with sensational clothes, and every time he ventures outside it, Clyde is the epitome of sartorial splendor.

Nate Bowman gave Frazier his nickname because his wardrobe was modeled largely on that of the Barrows' era. The fans picked it up immediately, partly because Frazier steals basketballs with the flair Clyde Barrow brought to banks. And from the top of his wide-brimmed hats to the tips of his alligator shoes, Frazier gives New York fans what he knows they want—not merely an athlete but a personality. Alone, Clyde often loses himself in his own quiet musings. But when it is time to talk, he is effervescent, making certain that he sounds as much like a star as he looks. "At first I enjoyed being compared to Oscar Robertson," he says. "But in the final analysis, I'd like to have an identity of my own." Then an impish grin lights Clyde's face as he enjoys the put-on, the self-confidence, and the entertainment quality in what he is saying. "When people speak of me in the future, I don't even want to hear Oscar's name mentioned."

Bob Hunter is a member of the Globetrotters and a veteran of thousands of playground contests. He is a fancy player, a six-foot-five-inch guard with a dazzling eclectic style that is a composite of the great shots and moves of many of his boyhood idols. But Hunter's philosophy is far more down to earth than his style of play. He expresses it in slow, deep, thoughtful tones as he reminisces on his development.

"I remember when I was about twelve years old, I'd go over to my school, PS 68 on 128th Street, in the wintertime and shovel away the snow so I could use the court. I practiced all the time, and when bigger players had the court I watched them and tried to imitate them. I remember Carlos Williams, who had a jump shot right off his ear, looking at the hoop out of his right eye; I copied that. Then I learned John Harris' way of dribbling and driving, because it was very forceful. Then there were players like Bill Clark, who played at Kennedy Center; he had a strong, bold game like Elgin Baylor's, and I imitated that, too.

"I shoveled snow, I played in the rain, I never stopped. Because this was the only thing in the world at the time. It was the only outlet I could understand. I simply had a ball and there was a basket. That was all there was to it. I became obsessed. And through the fifth, sixth, seventh grades, I saw myself improving and learning.

"I went downtown to high school, to Seward Park on the Lower East Side, because I was interested in art and wanted to take a fine arts course. It was predominantly Jewish. I didn't know just how well I could play until I got there and started doing it to guys. As each game went on, I noticed players drawing back from me a little more. The rumor would spread—Hunter is coming— and guys would lay back on defense, so I couldn't use my tricky drives on them. Soon I had to develop a whole new attack. They were so conscious of my drives, I had to master the jump shot and shoot over them. I could already play forward and center, but I began to realize that I was never going to be tremendously tall and I'd better learn to play guard. Holcombe Rucker, who coached me in Harlem, said, 'Yeah, that's about where it's at for you— guard. Just keep working, it will come to you.' And as usual, he was purely right.

"In those days the flowout from Harlem wasn't as good as it is now. Only black schools and a few white ones were open to the black athletes, and there wasn't much incentive to prepare for college. For a kid twelve years old, for example, college was just something that he heard some cousin or friend went to. It wasn't a tangible reality. I was approached by Loyola, one of the white schools that were opening up, but I just hadn't prepared myself enough. When I wasn't in the schoolyard, I had been home with a pencil, sketching. So my marks were terrible. Rather than go to a prep school to make up a lot of work, I decided to go on to a black school, to Tennessee A&I. As far as ball went, it proved a greater challenge, because it was simply the best of the black.

"The first day there, I walked into a gym full of distinction—a gym full of stars. There were high school all-Americans, and there were all-Americans from a year or two before, who had tried white schools, failed or dropped out, and turned up at Tennessee A&I. So it seemed as if after all my work, I had managed to find a new challenge, and my first thought was: 'I don't know how much more I can do.' But once again I found out that when necessity requires it, you can come up to a challenge.

"Everyone there had a trick, a move, a system. Everyone had been a star someplace or other. And soon I learned that the flashy stuff wasn't as important anymore. The most necessary quality was consistency. Everybody had the game, but the guy who really made it was the one who could get the most out of his game all the time. It was a matter of discipline, of confidence. If you were steady, producing all the time, then when the chips were down you already had a pattern, and you wouldn't have any problems rising to the occasion. . . ."

Dick Barnett left Tennessee A&I—now called Tennessee State—in 1959, then spent a decade bouncing around four pro teams in two leagues. His trademark was his shot, a twisting, gyrating, lovely thing that floated softly into countless hoops over the years. Yet over those same years, as a sixth man coming off the bench, as a jumper to the ill-fated American Basketball League for one season, and finally as a gracefully aging veteran, Barnett developed less obvious attributes. Steady and smart, he became the compleat ballplayer, working both ends of the court and contributing to every aspect of his team's play. As a pure shooter, he ran in streaks. But as an all-around player, he developed a rare consistency. So when the playoffs arrived—with their pressure and their back-to-back games that were expected to drain an old man of his energies—no one rose more impressively to the occasion than Barnett.

In the religion that some New Yorkers built around the Knicks last year, Barnett was inevitably one of the lesser deities. His face was too sleepy, his voice too soft, and his moves too economical to inspire fervent hero worship. "He's too much of a paycheck guy," explained one season ticket-holder. "The other guys seem to be chasing a dream. Barnett's chasing the money that goes with a championship."

Barnett didn't bother to deny it. "Let's admit it," he said. "Pride and talent are a large part of winning, but money is a big part of it, too. This is a business." Even in the final moment of triumph, Barnett remained poker-faced and cool. The rest of the championship team was spraying champagne, shouting with joy, but Barnett was dressing slowly in a corner of the locker room, with only a thin smile to distinguish the moment from the eight hundred–odd other games he had played for his paycheck. "It's relative," he said of Frazier. "It was the title game, so of course it seems bigger than if he had done it another night."

But what about Reed, limping into action to set fire to his team and the entire Garden?

"I knew he'd play," drawled Barnett. "It was no surprise. The crowd was more emotionally involved than I was."

This downbeat approach naturally aligns Barnett more with Coach Holzman than with most of his teammates. And understandably, Holzman is his biggest fan. Red shrinks from expressions of excitement or praise for most of his remarkable athletes. "I don't have to add anything to what you see," he tells reporters. "You guys write enough superlatives as it is." But not enough of the writers praise Barnett, so Holzman deviates from his style and makes a rare declaration: "He is one of the great backcourt men in the recent history of the NBA."

While Frazier plays to the crowd, rising and falling and jingling inside with the flow of the game, Barnett plays only to himself. He studies, he works, he runs faster than thirty-three-year-old legs should let him; his bland expression and his matter-of-factness hide the fact that he is obsessed with perfecting his game. If Barnett prefers to see himself as a laborer among entertainers, a wage earner among star-touched dreamers, then he has at least committed himself to being the ultimate laborer. "People think this is a two-hour-a-day job," he says. "It's not. It's a twenty-four-hour-a-day job. I think about basketball all the time."

As a result, Barnett is an ideal steadying influence, a man who can do whatever the Knicks need at a given moment. When Frazier had to devote all his energies to defending against Monroe in the Baltimore series, Barnett assumed the quarterbacking, bringing the ball up and whipping passes that kept the attack in high gear. When Frazier returned to offense against Los Angeles, Barnett inherited the task of defending against Jerry West—and did it as well as anyone could have asked. When the playoff schedule stacked up games on consecutive nights, Holzman fretted about Barnett's endurance. But on the second nights Barnett, who keeps in superb shape, somehow drove himself to play longer and better than ever. And when the situation looked bleakest, Barnett always maintained his frigid poise. In one playoff game in Los Angeles, he watched sleepily as his first eight shots missed the target, then forgot all about it and made nine straight points and the winning basket.

Barnett has written no books, opened no restaurants, and endorsed few products. His clothes are smart, but conservative by comparison to Frazier's or Stallworth's. His narrow, goateed face peers out from no color spreads in magazines. He is articulate and analytical in his approach to the game, but he keeps his interpretations largely to himself. On a team of celebrities he is a non-celebrity, and he likes it that way. "As long as management and the other players appreciate me," he says, "I'm satisfied. I don't go overboard about the publicity stuff."

Holzman tries to go overboard for him: "Dick has raw talent, brains, desire, and coachability. It's a pity more people don't recognize how outstanding he is." It may also be significant that Holzman does recognize Barnett's special genius. Since Eddie Donovan departed to take over the expansion team in Buffalo, Holzman has served as both coach and general manager. He will continue in both capacities for at least a year, but then he may want to relax a bit as general manager and expose someone else to the rigors of coaching. Two candidates seem most logical for the job. One is Al McGuire, a pure showman, a pure New Yorker, probably the most dynamic coach in college ball. He would be a brash and colorful leader for a colorful team. But he would also be a radical departure from the Holzman style. If Red seeks a successor in his own image—a stoical, dedicated student of the game, a consciously flat personality who lends poise and advice while letting the players bask in the publicity—then the most obvious choice of all will be Dick Barnett.

Interestingly, Frazier does not touch a basketball during the off-season. He exercises to keep in shape, but he shuns the game, marshaling his emotions, holding himself back so he can burst into each new season with freshness and enthusiasm. Barnett, on the other hand, seizes every opportunity to play summer ball. "It revives me," he has admitted. "When I start to play, nothing else exists. Call it an escape from reality if you want." Barnett feels no need to conserve his emotions; he doesn't believe a man can really psyche himself for games. There is a ball and there is a basket. People pay him important money to put that ball in the basket. For Dick Barnett, that's all there is to it.

7

In the Glare of the Media:
Cazzie Russell and Bill Bradley

By MIDSEASON, the Knicks were seeing more tape recorders than basketballs; a player couldn't toss a pair of dirty socks to trainer Danny Whelan without providing a new tidbit for a book, a television special, or a major-magazine piece. The national media, based largely in New York, had discovered what the city's kids had known all along: basketball at its best had rhythms and heroes and dramas that were worth exploring—and exploiting. The Celtics and 76ers and Lakers had proved the same thing to their own fans many times before, but their fans did not run television networks and news magazines and book publishing companies. So until last season, basketball was widely dismissed on Madison Avenue as a sweaty, undershirt game to be left to the provinces and the playgrounds; compared to other sports, it didn't even sell all that many tickets, to say nothing of books, hair tonics, and deodorants.

The Knick streak altered the picture drastically. Those people in the courtside seats were Dustin Hoffman and Robert Redford and John Lindsay. Suddenly the game was declared to have class. The athletes on the court were distinctive personalities. And most important, they wore the words NEW YORK on their chests. The phenomenon may be unfair, unrealistic, and undesirable, but no one can deny its existence: the Boston Red Sox or the Saint Louis

Cardinals can have exciting pennant victories; only the New York Mets can fashion a full-scale, dozen-book, living-color miracle. So the Knicks picked up where the Jets and Mets had left off, and the hyperboles flowed freely. They had not yet won their first NBA title, but the Knicks were named the Now Team, the Team of the Seventies, even the Dynasty.

The players reacted well to the onslaught. Less sophisticated in high finance than some of their sporting colleagues, they settled for endorsement money that a Tom Seaver or Joe Namath might have scorned; but by pro basketball standards, some did very well indeed. And they carried their sudden fame with aplomb, laughing quietly at some of the more frantic adjectives, joking easily about swelled heads, keeping things in fair perspective. It was inevitable, however, that when slumps occurred, the media would be blamed by some observers. And as the Knicks held their lead and seemed to answer the question of whether they would win their division title, critics posed new queries: Would the Knicks soon lose the hunger that great teams need? Would small resentments develop when competitive books and diaries were displayed in bookstore windows? Would the Knicks pay for their instant fame with quick defeat at the hands of resentful rivals— men who felt they had done just as much on the courts, without endorsing a single product or nibbling one publisher's lunch?

Certainly there was considerable resentment among opponents. But it was seldom directed personally; no one could logically blame the Knick players for the fact that they were operating in New York. Most rivals limited themselves to some pregame needling of the Knicks, and nursed the hope that they could grab a bit of reflected glory by knocking them out of the playoffs. More intense antipathies tended to be balanced by the knowledge that the Knicks' orgy of exposure was an aid to the entire league. To cite the most tangible bit of evidence, the American Broadcasting Company contract with the NBA was multiplied seven times over. The Knicks weren't solely responsible for the increased revenue and higher ratings, of course, but they certainly didn't hurt.

The other questions can be answered only by time. The Jets seemed to suffer somewhat from their post–Super Bowl bonanza.

Elevated to unreal heights by the media, they seemed to grow less tolerant of criticism, routine problems, and even bad luck. Several opponents were surprised at their lack of poise in the face of everything from poor play to referees' decisions during the 1969 season. The Jets acted as if they couldn't quite accept the fact that things could turn against them. The Mets also showed minor signs of a championship hangover the next spring: Tom Seaver grew petulant when his stuff briefly failed him; other players' wives bugged their husbands a bit about why Nancy Seaver got to spend so much time on television. Such matters are small and they can be overcome; but one wonders if the Knicks will have to overcome them in the future.

The Knicks seem to possess safeguards against such annoyances. They have shared fairly equally in the spoils. They have a self-less and dignified captain to hold them together. And unlike some of the Jets and Mets, several Knicks have a broad understanding of the media—in all its fickleness and impatience as well as its hero worship. No one understands more fully than the two college superstars who were once hailed as instant saviors of the Knicks—and then roundly scolded for being merely human—Cazzie Russell and Bill Bradley.

Cazzie Russell has been overrated by extravagant publicists and then burned by unfair critics when he failed to live up to his billing. He has been burdened with great pressure because of his college reputation, his role in the Knicks' hopes, and the then record $200,000 contract he signed in 1966. Some athletes would have withdrawn from the media that created such problems. But Cazzie grows even more effusive than usual when he talks of media and communications. For Cazzie's most cherished dream is to reach people: as a broadcaster and as a messenger of Christ.

In practices, on buses, and during pickup games, Russell loves to break into a burst of staccato announcing, pulling images out of the air to depict imagined baseball or basketball encounters. Occasionally the feeling even carries over into games. After one of the Knicks' more miraculous victories, he said, "It was like in a playground, when you make a move and yell, 'He drives, he shoots—he scores!' I was out there myself, but in a sense I felt like I was watching it, describing it into a mike. It was almost a dream, an imagined thing. Then when I glanced at the clock and realized it was almost over, I turned to Barnett and said, 'Hey, we're gonna win this thing.' "

Most of Cazzie's pro career has been far less euphoric. As a rookie he was discouraged and largely ineffective. When he finally seemed to find himself in his third season, he broke an ankle and lost the starting job he had finally clinched. And even as the Knicks drove to the top last year, Cazzie spent the majority of his time sitting restlessly on the sculpted plastic chairs that serve as the Knick bench. Once hailed as one of the game's emerging superstars, he played an average of twenty minutes a game; determined to make himself into an all-around player, he knew that he was falling short in his defensive play. But Russell never allowed himself to feel discouraged; on the bench he led the cheering and when he did enter a game he seemed to burst with spirit. Only rarely did he admit that he would prefer to play more, and even then he would emphasize that he was basically happy. After all, he was contributing to a winner—and he still had his dream to hold aloft.

"My ambition as a professional is to eventually broadcast baseball and basketball games," he said. "My ambition as a man is to serve Jesus Christ."

The other Knicks sometimes joshed Russell about his piety, nicknaming him The Reverend. To some, his religious fervor seemed as odd as his fascination with health foods and the unusual calisthenics that he invented to strengthen his body. But Cazzie shrugged off the wry remarks with a tight-lipped grin and went on with his doctrine: "Man today disturbs me, because he changes his laws to fit his needs. I believe in an immutable law, the Bible. I don't believe in the kind of religion that sends you running to Christ for help. I believe in letting him know that I know his goodness before I get in trouble and ask for his aid."

Cazzie's Baptist convictions sometimes led him into tortuous philosophical theorizing. When Bradley was injured, for example, giving Russell a chance to start, Cazzie rejected the idea that God had arranged it; but then he concluded, "God works in strange ways. Maybe he broke my ankle last year to give Bill his

opportunity to sail." Despite such moments of tenuous logic, however, Russell's beliefs helped him to climb out of Chicago's South
Side ghetto—and they made the disappointments and setbacks of
his pro career much easier to bear.

Among other things, religion gave Russell a sense of proportion
—a realization that basketball was not the only important thing
in his existence. Bradley also approached the game with a broad
perspective. Bill's was based on a long-range, intellectual view of
life, a knowledge that, whatever happened during the years he
gave to basketball, it would eventually be overshadowed by the
happenings of the rest of his life. If Bradley and Russell rooted
their perspectives in different philosophies, however, they may
well have enjoyed the same benefit: an ability to shake off the
wild predictions as well as the harsh criticisms of fans and media,
and to find the niches in which they could make valuable contributions to their team.

The son of a steelworker, Russell was a freshman at George
Washington Carver High School before he ever thought that
sports might propel him out of his South Side environment. Then
a gym teacher singled him out of a physical education class and
encouraged him to throw his remarkable, still-growing body into
sports. Cazzie credits that teacher and subsequent coaches with
helping him to develop, but he saves most of his gratitude for
his religion. "In sophomore year I could hardly make a lay-up.
By the time I graduated I was the most valuable player in Illinois.
I recognized God's will in that, and when I got to Michigan, I
studied public speaking so that I could be a better messenger for
him."

Russell had scarcely any social life at Michigan, in part because
he didn't drink or smoke and wasn't particularly interested in
partying. Instead, he filled his life with preparations for his various
missions in life. Dreaming of announcing, he worked for the
campus radio station. He also founded a chapter of the Fellowship
of Christian Athletes. And of course, he worked endlessly, with
unflagging enthusiasm, to forge himself into the finest basketball
player alive. "The difference between Caz and the rest of us,"
said a teammate, "was that we all had full schedules and didn't

have much time for extra practice. Caz had a schedule just as full, but he made time for extra basketball."

As a result, Michigan, once a perennial loser, swiftly became the most powerful team in the country. In his junior year, Russell was generally recognized as the best player in college ball, with one possible exception—Princeton senior Bill Bradley.

The two stars met twice that year, kindling arguments that endured through their Knick days. Actually, it has always been fruitless to compare and rate the two men, because their styles are so different. Cazzie was the flashing, leaping, apparently instinctive leader of a Michigan team that might have come off the best of playgrounds. Its stars were tall and physical; their best game was to drive an opponent to death and whip him close to the basket. Bradley, on the other hand, was the leader of a band of Ivy Leaguers—by definition, supposedly, a team that would have to win by finesse, if at all. Bradley seemed to weave his team into intricate, fast-moving patterns, setting things up with guile rather than force; then he would ignite the attack with his marvelous shots and perfect passes.

Fittingly, the first and most dramatic meeting of the two stars was in the old Garden, in the semifinal round of the midseason Holiday Festival tournament. For thirty-five minutes and thirty-three seconds, Bradley owned the night. Responding to the partisan crowd, trying to carry his undermanned teammates to an incredible upset, Bill scored 41 points, set up countless others—and showed that he could muscle his way through the bigger Michigan forwards to snatch key rebounds. Princeton was leading by 12 points when Bradley fouled out, on a tired man's foul, grabbing an arm in a meaningless situation.

Then Bradley sat helplessly on the bench as the inevitable ensued. Russell had suffered through a ghastly first half, caused in part by a damaged sneaker, that slowed him badly. But with Bradley gone and some new footwear added, Cazzie and his teammates asserted themselves; the lead shrank with every agonizing minute, and with three seconds remaining, Cazzie drilled a jump shot for the winning basket. The night and the crowd belonged to Bradley, but the game was Michigan's. "I never realized how that game would stay with people," Russell said last season. "But in New York, I still hear it mentioned all the time."

Michigan thumped Princeton more convincingly in the NCAA tournament that spring, but again Bradley enjoyed a share of the glory. The following night, hours before Michigan lost to UCLA in the championship game, Bradley set a tournament record with 58 points in the third-place game—and again emerged as the individual star of the tournament. The verdict of the two confrontations seemed to favor Bradley. But Russell's supporters pointed out that Cazzie had another year in which to improve, and they insisted that his more physical style would make him a better pro. The entire argument made at least one thing apparent: Russell and Bradley towered over college ball, and a pro team that could lure both would anticipate a superb future.

When Bradley delayed his pro career to pursue his studies at Oxford, Russell became the first of the two heroes to arrive in New York—and the first to encounter the problems and pressures of joining the Knicks. After a decade of suffering with the Knicks' ineptitude, New York fans were anxious for an instant solution; but Cazzie was not the man to provide it. The Knicks of that era had ample talent and scoring punch, but glaringly lacked cohesion, defense, and consistency. Cazzie, ironically, offered only more natural talent and scoring. He could not step in as a playmaker, he was weak on defense, and as a rookie, he could hardly promise consistency. Consequently he had trouble breaking into the lineup and fretted on the bench; and when he did play, his bold, driving style grew tentative and confused. The season was an ordeal. Some observers loudly berated coach Dick McGuire for not using Russell more; others cited Cazzie as a gargantuan flop. Russell averaged a paltry 11 points a game, and his detractors noted that Dave Bing—the Syracuse player the Knicks had passed up in order to draft Cazzie—had quickly become a star for Detroit.

Certainly Cazzie was confused, frustrated by not playing and aware of the pressures generated by his salary and public acclaim. But he was undoubtedly victimized even more by a basic technical problem—one that, in another parallel between their careers, would also handicap Bradley. Cazzie is six feet five and a half inches tall; Bradley is a half inch shorter. According to a theory in vogue until very recently, they were the "wrong" height for pro ball, too small to battle six-foot-nine-inch forwards under the boards and too large and slow to defend against smaller, quicker pro guards. The pros tended to make such athletes into guards, apparently on the premise that, whatever the problems, it was preferable to go in with a height advantage than to take the worst of it at forward. History, unfortunately, lent flimsy support to this proposition. Only one such "big" guard has stepped into a lineup and become an instant success—and that is the incomparable Oscar Robertson.

In recent years, in fact, several "wrong-size" players have succeeded at forward. The idea that a hulking front line is indispensable has gradually been debunked. Philadelphia's Billy Cunningham, at six feet six, struggled somewhat in his rookie season but emerged as one of the NBA's best-scoring forwards. John Havlicek, six feet five, fit smoothly into the Celtic machine at forward; Joe Caldwell, the same height, developed in similar fashion for Atlanta. And after serving their separate, painful backcourt apprenticeships, both Russell and Bradley at last found their way into the forecourt—where they were free to take advantage of their special skills.

Moved to forward in 1967, Russell became the team's third-best scorer; in 1968–69, as the Knicks began to pull everything together, he owned the second-best scoring average on the club. He still had defensive flaws but they were less glaring, and he was consumed by the desire to correct them. At last, Cazzie seemed on the verge of the starring role many had predicted for him. Then, on January 21, 1969, he broke his ankle.

"It seemed like the worst night of my life," he recalled. "As I lay in the ambulance, they had to prop my leg up in the air because I was too tall for the cot. The ambulance seemed to hit every bump there was in New York and with each bump, more pain shot into the leg. Then when the cast was on, it seemed to feel heavier every day. It was a very depressing thing to face, and I don't think I could have done it without God's help."

The Knicks and Bradley flourished without him, and Russell never retrieved his starting assignment. In fact, Russell averaged less playing time last year than he had as a rookie; but the effect on him was vastly different. Four years earlier he had watched in bewilderment as the coach chose much smaller, less gifted men ahead of him. Last year he refused to allow himself to feel cheated, telling himself and others: "No player likes to sit on the bench. But you can't have more than five guys on the court at a time, and we have some very good players. This is a great team, and I have to feel confident about my role on it."

His role was to jump off the bench, barely containing the energy that was pulsing within him, and dash onto the court to pick up the team and the crowd. Racing upcourt and shoving through traffic jams of defenders, Cazzie would shake free, take a pass and coil his carefully groomed, muscular body for the shot. The crowd roared as the ball left his fingers; then the low-trajectory shot was home and Cazzie's fist shot high in triumph. Four, five, six times he might hit, and a listless Knick offense would come alive. A close game might be broken open.

At times, of course, cynics noticed that while Russell was pumping his five quick baskets, his assigned man on defense was picking up a few for himself. And since Holzman's job was to notice such lapses, Cazzie's galvanic bursts were often brief. Then he would be back on the sidelines, leading the cheers and perhaps pondering the small imperfections that he knew he still had to conquer.

"My desire to become the complete player is as great as anything," he said. "I understand that I should be overplaying my man, boxing out under the boards, grabbing rebounds with both hands so they can't be stolen. I understand, I know what I must do, but I just don't have it all down. When I do, I'll run up and down Eighth Avenue, telling the world." When he does, Russell will undoubtedly do it in his best announcer's voice, echoing those Chicago playground dreams: "He drives, he shoots, he scores. . . . He blocks the shots. He grabs the rebound. . . . It's Cazzie Russell, the complete pro ballplayer at last!"

Bill Bradley circumvented many of the emotional ups and downs that battered Russell. Relegated to the bench, he was not tormented by a feeling that he should play. Besieged by the media, he did not feel a desperate drive to prove himself to everyone immediately. Armed with a $500,000 four-year contract that made Russell's seem almost meager, he did not feel that it burdened him with any special pressures. Or, more accurately, if any such problems or pressures did exist, Bradley was not about to share them with the world. Bradley had never asked peripatetic fans to hail him as an all-American boy and future presidential candidate—which they did while he was still a Princeton undergraduate. So when things became more difficult and his meteoric career seemed to level off, he certainly wouldn't have asked for sympathy.

Bradley joined the Knicks in December of 1968, amid even more fanfare than Russell had inspired the year before. In addition to the rookie problems that had faced Cazzie, Bradley had to overcome the rustiness of two and a half years away from highly competitive ball, the lack of preseason training—and the fact that many expected him not only to fit in but to take charge of the entire team. It took him more than thirteen months to find himself and his place on the club. At times his progress must have seemed excruciatingly slow, but whatever doubts or hopes Bill developed always eluded any glib description by the media. Even now, his position defies those who would like to pass quick judgment: he is neither superstar nor failure.

Someday, possibly, Bradley may write a book, and those who yearn for details of the inner struggles behind his progress as a Knick may rush to read it. They will undoubtedly be disappointed. Bradley will never write an as-told-to autobiography or a diary of a season; in fact, he will never publish anything in the role of an athlete who happens to be able to write. He writes a good deal in his small West Side apartment, working out personal and social ideas and keeping an informal journal. ("Doesn't everyone keep one," he asks, "in some form or other?") He is intrigued by journalistic techniques and various forms of expression and, for all his guarded attitudes, he sometimes gives the impression that he would eventually like to write for publication. But he also emphasizes that he would never think of publishing anything unless he felt it was worthwhile, in itself—not merely as the product of an athlete.

Bradley will never want to be the "athlete who also. . . ." Whether he goes into foreign service or business, social work or politics—it is very easy to think of him as a leader, very hard to equate him with the word "politician." He is not certain himself what he will ultimately do, but whatever he chooses, he will approach it as totally distinct from his basketball career. "At this point," he says, "I have committed myself to a certain number of years of basketball. I have made the game my first priority, and I am giving myself completely to it. Later something else will receive my first priority and I'll try to give myself just as fully to that. It would be a mistake to mix various goals and periods of my life. And it would be presumptuous to think of basketball as some kind of prelude to other things."

To keep his priorities in order and preserve what he feels is his integrity as an individual, Bradley has built as many barriers as possible between the public and his non-sports interests. He has spent summers working for the Urban League's Street Academy program in Harlem and for the Office of Economic Opportunity in Washington. When people ask why, he can't help showing that he thinks the question is silly; with controlled politeness, he answers, "I guess it's because it's important." When they press for details of his involvement, he winces, backs away from the question, points out how small his role has been and how he'd rather not talk about it. Some interpret his reaction as false modesty, others assume that he is anxious to shun the image of the white liberal do-gooder. The first response is completely wrong, the second somewhat inaccurate; if Bradley thought it would accomplish anything worthwhile, he would probably learn to live with any image. His real reason for shielding his commitment to the poor is simple and understandable: if he weren't an athlete, that commitment would go unnoticed—and that is the way he wants it.

Bradley explained his need for privacy most succinctly to Robert Lipsyte of the New York Times: "The things I do outside basketball are only of public interest because I'm in basketball. Saying that an athlete has outside interests, that he's a whizbang at business or knows a lot about something, that's hyperbolic. You do want to build something for yourself outside basketball, but to talk about it is hyperbolic. I've got to be allowed to develop those other pockets of my life without the unnecessary scrutiny of those people who are interested in me only as an athlete, and not as a person."

Knowing Bradley is a fascinating, perplexing, sometimes frustrating experience. He is immediately likable, for his thoughtful ways of expressing himself, his sincerity, and his genuine interest in other people. In the context of sports, he is a scintillating intellectual; in general, he is less easily typed, and therefore more interesting. He has a bright, searching mind, and he has used most of his twenty-six years probing new regions of himself and the world. Partly because he is still giving basketball priority, he has avoided rigid conclusions about other areas; thus he projects a sense of exploration, of unlimited possibilities. You cannot help but want to know him better.

But then you run into the barriers. A question ventures too far into his private sector, and suddenly Bradley cocks one of his high arched eyebrows, smiles thinly, and withdraws. There are hints of mistrust and arrogance in the gesture; you feel an uneasiness. The first instinctive response is personal: perhaps you haven't established the confidence you thought you had, perhaps Bradley still fears that if he says too much, you might betray him with one of those awful look-at-the-intellectual-socially-conscious-future-President articles.

Later, however, you see the withdrawal gesture time and again, with others whom you know Bradley trusts, and you realize that it is neither personal nor arrogant. It is the simple, inviolable insistence on privacy, and it has its undeniable logic. "The other aspects of my being are not in question now," the gesture seems to state. "I am devoting myself fully to a very public world. If you want to judge me, judge me by that."

And the public exposure of basketball reveals much about Bradley as a person. To begin with, he became a superb ballplayer without being an exceptional natural athlete. His shoulders slope, his muscles are unimpressive, he is a poor jumper, and he is not an unusually fast runner. He also lacks the element of hunger that was essential to the growth of so many stars; he is almost surely the only eminent basketball player who wintered in Palm Beach until he was thirteen. As the son of the well-to-do president of the sole bank in Crystal City, Missouri, Bradley grew up amid all the comforts that are supposed to distract potentially great athletes. Yet he began playing ball when he was nine, and within a few years he developed a deep fascination and love for the game, which he described almost poetically in the remarkable biography of him written in 1964 by John McPhee: "What attracted me was the swish, the sound of the dribble, the feel of going up in the air. You don't need eight others, like in baseball. You don't need any brothers or sisters. Just you. I wonder what the guys are doing back home. I'd like to be there, but it's as much fun here, because I'm playing. It's getting dark. I have to go back for dinner. I'll shoot a couple more. Feels good. A couple more."

Bradley played alone on Palm Beach playgrounds or with friends in Crystal City; seeing his obsession, his parents obligingly blacktopped the backyard and installed a regulation basket. But Crystal City is hardly a basketball hotbed, and Bradley, who was six feet three by the time he reached eighth grade, easily surpassed all available competition. So he developed his skills without the benefit of the one-on-one playground clashes, the fierce challenges to his manhood and identity from the highly rated kids from the next block or the next town. His improvement was a matter of self-fulfillment rather than proving himself to others. The amount of work he devoted to satisfying his personal goals and demands gave one early clue to his character.

Driving toward his self-imposed goals, Bradley developed a rigid Spartan streak. In high school and college he practiced long hours after teammates had gone home, and he eschewed pickup games or flashy, enjoyable drills in order to work endlessly and repetitively on the aspects of his game he felt were weakest. It is axiomatic, of course, that such practice is the best way to improve;

but precious few growing basketball players ever lived by the axiom as Bradley did. "I think," said Bill van Breda Kolff, who coached him at Princton, "that Bradley is actually happiest when he is denying himself pleasure." It is no coincidence that the very best phase of Bradley's game has always been the one that reduces itself most easily to long, boring practice—the shooting of free throws.

Approaching his college career, Bradley began contemplating the system of priorities that would guide his life. About seventy colleges eagerly attempted to recruit him, in a gaudy display of enticements that ultimately left him opposed to the entire practice of recruiting athletes. At the eleventh hour he chose to attend Princeton without a scholarship, and the decision was a fortunate one. The Ivy League in the early 1960s was a pleasantly and perhaps naïvely isolated enclave in which to work out possibilities and explore one's self. At faraway campuses like Berkeley, students were already noticing that universities might be twisted in purpose and too closely tied to a defense effort that was just raising its head in Vietnam. At Yale or Princeton, however, political issues still seemed more clear-cut. Students who were so inclined could march in the South or work in the ghettos with that heady, now distant knowledge that the government was also for civil rights; and whether one chose politics or sports, studies or fraternity parties, the universities seemed to provide a tranquil landscape in which to function.

In that controlled laboratory, Bradley was able to postpone some choices. He devoted time to both his studies and basketball, without feeling that he was cheating himself or others. He also found time for a satisfying if not dazzling social life, participation in the Fellowship of Christian Athletes, and work with youths in a church program. Clearly, he was shortchanging no one. A classmate was once quoted: "Bill Bradley is everything his parents think he is," and nobody ever came forward to disprove the theory.

His basketball career soared from one peak to another: the 1964 Olympics, the incredible near-miss in the NCAA tournament, almost every Ivy record there was—and general recognition as the finest player in college. But when, on rare occasions, his priorities clashed, Bradley leaned toward his studies; when necessary, he risked exhaustion on the court by staying up all night writing papers on the eve of a game.

On graduation, the priorities came into direct conflict, and Bradley chose his Rhodes Scholarship over a chance to play for the Knicks. "I had been to Europe the summer after high school," he said. "I enjoyed it immensely and I was really awed by England. I guess that's when I first thought about studying abroad. I also thought it would be beneficial to leave the States for a while. I had some personal questioning to do, I wanted to view this country from a different perspective, and I wanted to meet people with different viewpoints."

Oxford gave Bradley the luxury of contemplation. With his schedule no longer crammed to the breaking point, he was able to "indulge himself," as he puts it, in broader thinking and questioning. He shows a real joy when he speaks of his two years abroad, but as usual, he keeps the results to himself. He is determined not to use athletic exposure as a platform for ideas that he feels would be of no interest if he couldn't run the back-door play.

Bradley found time for basketball in Europe; he played informal ball at Oxford and joined the Simmenthal team of Milan, "only because I had to have physical activity at a pretty intense, competitive level." Most Americans who play in the bustling, wide-open Italian league keep their amateur status but accept fairly profitable and undemanding "jobs" offered by the promoters. Bradley refused the job and played in return for his air fare back and forth. His performance made him one of the country's most revered sports heroes, and as he led Simmenthal to the Italian title, Bradley admitted to himself that the sport was still more to him than merely a competitive form of exercise. "I had a number of alternatives after Oxford," he said, "but I think subconsciously I knew I would come back to basketball. I still had a great love for the game, and I wanted to test myself against the best."

His odyssey led him back to the Garden, then, and the priorities were rearranged once more. "Eventually I will be doing other things," he said, "but right now basketball must come first. So if I'm reading something fascinating and want to stay up all night with it before a game, I won't do it. I would be less than honest with myself or the Knicks if I didn't commit myself completely."

Like Russell before him, Bradley joined a troubled team that needed far more from him than he could give. He might have benefited from time on the bench to study his rivals and adjust, but Dick McGuire, his job in danger, was under intense pressure to use him. Attempting to learn while guiding an entire offense, Bradley suffered some uncharacteristic mental lapses. He threw passes to unoccupied spots, fell behind his men on defense, once blew a game by taking a shot when he could have run out the clock. Off the court, he even managed to get hit by a car on Eighth Avenue; the cuts and bruises forced him to miss six games, and in a black-humorous way, the bizarre incident only seemed to emphasize how lost Bradley was in New York.

When Holzman replaced McGuire, he used Bradley less. In his briefer appearances, Bill showed flashes of his old greatness and signs that he was indeed learning pro ball; but the progress was torturously slow. For the remainder of his first season and the first half of his second, Bradley was in an uncomfortable position, still garnering more public attention than most of his teammates, yet spending most of his time on the bench. To an outsider, the reason for his enduring appeal to the press was clear: the medium may be fickle but it is not color-blind; in basketball as in boxing, there is great demand for white hopes in the predominantly black milieu. "I never thought about that," Bradley insists, in a tone that makes you believe him. "I never felt embarrassed or pressured by people's attention. The only kind of pressure I feel comes from within. It's purely a personal thing."

Bradley's response to pro ball can best be illustrated by one development. In his early floundering days with the Knicks, most experts agreed that his two major weaknesses were his unimpressive defensive play and his difficulty in moving without the ball on offense. When Russell broke his ankle and Bradley moved in at forward, those had become his two principal strengths. Characteristically, Bradley had measured his personal shortcomings and overcome them.

Among the Knick starters last season, Bradley ranked fifth in scoring average and fourth in rebounding. Before less sophisticated fans than New Yorkers, his contributions might have been considered relatively minor. But Garden fans were well aware of Bradley's importance: more than anyone else, he put the flow into the Knicks' attack. Moving constantly around the perimeters of the action, he was always a potential target for Frazier's passes; and with his acute sense of where the other moving parts of the machine were, he would quickly move the ball onward to initiate countless plays. Left alone, he could hit his soft jump shots in game-breaking streaks; guarded closely, he could always find a free man—or open the back door for Frazier. And by his own penetration into all the areas of the court, Bradley forced the other Knicks to keep in motion, virtually assuring the perennial presence of that nightly Knick hero, the open man.

From above, the patterns woven by Bradley appeared artistic, almost delicate; he played the way coaches drew diagrams. But at closer range it became clear that his movement was not a simple textbook exercise. Professional defenders are large and have strong arms and elbows, and they do not let men roam through their territories without trying to slow them down. A move along the baseline from one corner to the other, for example, is a hazardous, bruising journey. And Bradley, once derided by some as an effete Ivy Leaguer who would never stand the physical battle, squirmed and hustled his way around many bulky defenders to set up key baskets.

Beyond that contact without the ball, Bradley did not feel impelled to prove himself physically under the boards; that job belonged to Reed and DeBusschere. But in the fifth game of the playoff series against the Lakers—the game in which Reed was hurt—Bradley showed another dimension of his talent. With Willis deactivated, moving without the ball became secondary. The Knicks desperately needed simply to get the ball, in rebounding battles against Chamberlain and another seven-footer, Mel Counts. So Bradley abandoned his deft patterns, left the perimeters, and plunged into the middle of the action under the boards. He came out with seven key rebounds; Russell, the other small forward who seldom rebounded, came out with eight, and the Knicks scored their most incredible victory of the year. "It was a matter of getting position and holding it, boxing people out," said Bradley with a smile. "I can't credit it to adrenaline. With all the juices flowing, my jump only improves from four inches to eight."

In case anyone had missed the point while he was playing, Bradley's importance to the Knicks became starkly apparent late in the regular season when he missed a month of action with an ankle injury. Since first place was safe and the playoffs impending, Holzman gave Bradley all the time he needed for a full recovery. But with every game he missed, it became more evident that the Knicks were something less than the super team of the early season. Minus Bradley, the Knicks seemed almost immobile. Frazier held the ball too long trying to find a man to pass to. As Bill's replacement, Russell scored more than Bradley would have and hustled tirelessly, if sometimes ineffectively, on defense; but he couldn't provide the same fluidity. "I'll give off and the man will stand there and bounce the ball," complained Frazier. "He'll give off and the next man will stand and bounce it. We have no continuity."

"When Bill isn't playing," added DeBusschere, "everybody dribbles more and stands around. Nothing gets done." Without Bradley the Knicks were a group of outstanding players; with him, they were a flowing, interracting, brilliant team. There may be no compliment he would rather take with him when he leaves professional basketball.

8

The Bit Players: Mike Riordan, Dave Stallworth, Nate Bowman

THE OPENING GAME of the Milwaukee–New York playoff series had been hard fought, and the struggle had gone down to the final buzzer, when substitutes were in the game and the Knicks were protecting their 8-point lead. One of those Milwaukee substitutes was Guy Rodgers, thirty-four years old and playing out the thirteenth year of a career as a superb playmaker, ball handler, and gut fighter. Opposite Rodgers was Mike Riordan, twenty-four years old and flourishing in an improbable NBA career of his own —largely because he approaches every game as if it were a street fight. Inevitably, there was a loose ball; just as surely the two men lunged for it, elbows flying, and came up glaring, ready for battle.

Then the moment passed and the game ended in a Knick victory. But Rodgers made it a point to shove through the crowd in the corridors beneath the Garden and visit the Knicks' locker room. Throughout his career, Rodgers has been described as everything from a dirty player to a fierce competitor. But age has mellowed him somewhat, and on that evening he wanted to smooth over any damaged sensibilities. Entering the Knicks' room, he asked someone, "Where's Riordan?"

Riordan happened to be sitting a few feet away. He heard Rodgers ask for him. He said nothing. Then Guy spotted him and extended a hand. "I didn't want any hard feelings about that play. When it's over, it's over. You know?"

"Yeah," said Riordan. His grin was tight. "I know."

Rodgers left and Riordan considered the matter. "He said it was unimportant, and I guess it is, in a way," said Mike. He paused and wondered whether he really believed it. "No, damn it. It is important. Everything's important. I've got to play that way."

Jut-jawed and intense, Riordan is the Irish kid you might meet in a bar on Queens Boulevard in Sunnyside, sipping beer and watching a ballgame. You might want to challenge him on the bowling machine for a few dollars, but you wouldn't want to try and hustle him. And you definitely wouldn't mess with his girl. He looks as much like Queens as Bill Bradley looks like Princeton —which means the imprint is unmistakable. So he has a large and warm following among New York fans, and that broad tough face is a welcome part of the Knick panorama.

If the Knick stars often made basketball seem a form of theater, the three reserves who joined Cazzie Russell in providing the club's bench strength were bit players straight from central casting. Riordan was the neighborhood brawler, complementing the subtler skills of Frazier and Barnett with his own bluntly effective style as the reserve guard. Forward Dave Stallworth, recovered almost miraculously from a heart attack, added an element of sheer melodrama. And awkward Nate Bowman, the six-foot-ten-inch center who spelled Reed for several tantalizing minutes in each game, contributed bumbling moments of un- witting slapstick. Their appearances were often brief, occasionally shockingly effective—and always invaluable. One tired man could destroy the motion of the Knicks' offense or the aggressiveness of the defense; the bench was the safeguard against that exhaustion, the transfusion that could revive the team and the crowd in times of stress.

In ten years, perhaps, Riordan will be an elder statesman like Guy Rodgers, capable of leaving his battles on the court and calming some new up-and-coming warrior. But it isn't likely. Riordan knows that he may not even be around pro ball in ten years, because his talents will never be compared to those of Rodgers or Frazier or the NBA's other prime guards. He's also aware that ever since he tried out for basketball as a high school freshman, people have tended to underrate him; and it could happen again. So he plays for the present, scratching and clawing for every basket and every loose ball. "If the coach told him to run through a brick wall," goes one standard Knick quip, "you'd have to feel sorry for the wall."

Riordan's career has offered him countless opportunities to abandon the idea of being a basketball player. At Holy Cross High School in Flushing, Queens, he was cut from the freshman team; the next season, he was not even invited to try out for the junior varsity. Then the varsity coach saw him shooting baskets alone in the gym, encouraged him—and promoted him to the varsity. He became a good player but not a star; he was overshadowed at Holy Cross by a player named Bob McIntyre, who went on to a fine career at St. John's. Riordan went to Providence College, where he became one of the spear carriers behind superstar Jimmy Walker. Providence coach Joe Mullaney, now with the Lakers, thought so little of Mike's pro prospects that he offered him a nice safe job coaching the Providence freshmen; in addition Riordan won a fellowship to study for his master's degree. His future seemed promising—away from basketball.

The Knicks drafted Riordan in the eleventh round of the 1967 pro draft—the round in which teams start throwing away choices on boys who show good manners and girls with accurate set shots. (San Francisco actually did draft a girl last year, but the NBA ruled that she couldn't play.) Riordan had no reason to suspect that he would make the Knicks and he didn't. But he spent a season commuting to Allentown, Pennsylvania, to play in the Eastern League; he averaged 20 points a game, and earned another try-out. Incredibly, he made the 1968–69 Knicks. He was promptly assigned the less-than-crucial duty of coming off the bench when the Knicks wanted to "give" a foul. Fouling people on purpose was almost his sole function, but he did it with an avidity that brought hallelujahs from the crowd every time he entered a game. As always, he took his job in grim earnest. "It was important and somebody had to do it. And it got me into the games, giving me experience."

He gained far more experience in practices, working tirelessly, emphasizing defense and mastering both his long-range shooting and driving to the hoop. In the final 1969 playoff game in Boston, when Frazier's injury forced Riordan into action, Mike amazed even his teammates by scoring 15 points. He earned his place, and last year he was usually the first substitute to enter each game.

Riordan has his limitations. As a shooter, he is not always dependable; as a defender, he is tenacious but not always quick enough. He lacks speed and consistency, and when he had to play long stretches during injuries to Frazier, he faltered. But in brief spurts, when he is not forced to conserve his energy, his battling style can be highly effective. On nights when Frazier was in one of his low moods or Barnett was acting his age, Riordan often sparked the Knicks with a half game or so of scoring and defensive steals.

And on those special nights when every part of the team was flourishing, when the Knicks were blowing some hapless opponent off the court, it was often Riordan who administered the coup, with a sudden, accelerating, implausible drive to the hoop. Mike seemed to live for the moment when he could get a step on a defender, turn toward the basket, and, at full speed, stare eye-to-chest at a giant like Lew Alcindor or Wilt Chamberlain. The mismatch was ridiculous, and the big man would prepare to smash the nervy six-foot-four-inch challenger to the floor; but more often than not, Riordan would somehow elude the defender's massive arms and score.

At first, such dives were side attractions, crowd-pleasing David-Goliath skirmishes in games that had long since been decided. But as the season went on, Riordan and the Knicks began to realize that he could actually pull off such dares with regularity. He helped win several playoff games with his moves to the hoop. "Sometimes you start to drive and say to yourself, 'I'm going in there if I have to jump over the big man and float in backward,'" he said. "Then your professional instincts get the better of you and you look for the open man to pass to. But if you don't see him, well, you just keep flying."

Before one early-season game against the Lakers, Riordan heard his old coach, Mullaney, call him from the Laker bench: "What are you doing playing in this league?"

"If you can coach up here," retorted Riordan, "I can play here."

Others kidded Mike the same way, asking how he spelled his name, who he was, how he could be competing in the NBA. But as the year wore on, there was more and more respect in the remarks about him. He and Mullaney needled one another right through the final playoff series, but it was always good-natured. And in a way it made Riordan's feats all the more satisfying because each time he uttered that one phrase, he could recall how many people had once refused to believe it: "I can play here."

Dave Stallworth seemed to play ball to the beat of the rock music that pulsed from his ever-present portable stereo. He was a big man, six feet seven, and unusually fast, and from the first days on his Dallas high school team he was able to dominate action on a basketball court with his constant, rhythmic moves. Basketball success tumbled toward him: all-state in high school, all-American at Wichita State, a first-round draft selection in 1965 by the Knicks, who enjoyed two first-round choices that year as a reward for finishing a dismal last—and who took Bradley and then Stallworth. Along the way, press agents nicknamed Stallworth Dave the Rave, and he lived up to the billing, not merely beating opponents but dazzling them with those high-speed, balanced playground moves. He was a fine pro rookie and an even better second-year player, seeing a lot of action as the Knicks' "sixth man" and then as a starter. Without the pressures that burdened his more publicized teammate Russell, Stallworth seemed to be building a solid pro career, and enjoying every minute of it. Then, abruptly, the music stopped, and his world came crashing down around him.

It began in March of 1967, with a stab of pain in Stallworth's chest. He left a game against the San Francisco Warriors in

Fresno and went to the hospital, scared and puzzled. He heard a doctor use the words "heart attack" and he shook his head. "I refuse to believe it," he remembered telling himself. "I'm too young, too active. I'm in such good shape. It can't happen to me." Then the electrocardiograph results came in. It was a false alarm. He could play the next night.

In the next game, in San Francisco, Stallworth injured a leg. In another game it might have upset him, but it seemed insignificant after the scare of the night before. He sat out most of the game, and when the team returned to New York, he was admitted to the hospital for further precautionary tests. "I shouldn't have been worried," he recalled. "I had felt no more pains in my chest. But deep down, I felt that something serious was wrong. I couldn't have told a doctor what it was, or pointed to anything that hurt. But I had a strange feeling that I had played my last game. It was really freaky."

The premonition came true. Stallworth was found to have suffered a heart attack. It was described as mild, by normal human standards; he had been in no danger. But by basketball standards, it meant the end. He could never risk subjecting his heart to the stresss of all-out physical competition. The music was subdued as Stallworth left his hospital bed. Around him teammates and friends reached out, feeling terrible, wanting to help. But what do you say to a twenty-four-year-old who has just been told that his career is over?

Stallworth went to his parents' home in Compton, California, to begin recuperating, but within months the pace became too slow for him. Picking up the beat, he drifted back to Wichita and took over as coach of an amateur team. The team compiled a 28–0 record and went all the way to the finals of a national tournament. Back in New York, people heard about it and sent best wishes to Stallworth in his new role. But Dave hadn't given up on his old one. Only eight months after his attack, he was jogging and shooting baskets. When doctors agreed that such limited activity wouldn't be too chancy, he sneaked onto the courts and pushed himself a little further, playing in pickup games. After a few months he dared to tell Knick general manager Eddie

Donovan what he was doing. Donovan had kept Dave on the payroll as a scout and kept in touch with him; but when he heard about the pickup games, Donovan scolded Stallworth "for taking chances."

For a full year Stallworth took calculated risks with his body, tentatively at first, then more boldly. The moves were still there, the stamina seemed to be returning. Stallworth tried not to build false hopes, but he could hardly contain himself. "At first it had seemed like it would be a major medical miracle to come back," he recalled. "But as the days went on, I felt it would just take a little good luck." Finally he put it on the line, conferring with Dr. Kazuo Yanagisawa, then the Knicks' doctor. On May 28, 1969, after several careful examinations, the word came down: "I feel that he can resume normal activity."

"I felt," said Stallworth, "like tearing out of the office and jumping over the Empire State Building."

Dave's return to training camp seemed like a glorious omen to New York fans. For years they had seen unforeseen disasters strike the Knicks just when victory appeared within reach. Yet last year, with a lack of depth at forward one of the few possible weaknesses facing the club, an unforeseen addition had suddenly arrived. Dave DeBusschere had been effective the year before, but his one foible had been a tendency to draw fouls; and there had been no one to back him up when he fell into trouble. Now Stallworth was a capable replacement, and DeBusschere would be an even better player for it.

The rock music began blaring again. Stallworth usually came off the bench early in the second period, his mouth open slightly in a grin that exposed the white star on his gold front tooth, his eyes flashing at his rival—the opposing team's champion, the man DeBusschere had been guarding. Stallworth could not quite match DeBusschere's consistent defense and rebounding—few NBA players could—but he provided a reasonable facsimile; nobody took advantage of him. And on offense, like Russell and Riordan, he could go on those bursts that recharged the Knicks.

If his medical history haunted him, Stallworth seldom showed it. Along with Russell, he was one of the locker-room cheerleaders, turning up the volume of his taped music, then shouting above it to celebrate the Knick triumphs. But if the season had a dream-like quality at times for many of the players, it must have seemed positively unreal to Stallworth, the man whose career had ended two years earlier. On the club's first trip to San Francisco, in the midst of the record winning streak, he was overwhelmed by the memory. "I started reliving it all over again," he said. "The games, the hospital, the way it stunned me. I even felt like I was getting chest pains again." After that, however, he seemed to put it all behind him; he was too busy enjoying the present.

The climax of his season came in the game that meant so much to all the Knicks, the fifth game of the championship series—the one in which Reed was hurt. First Nate Bowman and then Bill Hosket went into the pivot, trying futilely to stop Wilt Chamberlain from destroying the Knicks. As Los Angeles drew away, Holzman tried a desperate move and placed DeBusschere in the pivot. Dave held Wilt off well, then got into foul trouble. In the final period, Holzman turned to Stallworth.

To the fans, the idea of Stallworth clashing with Chamberlain may have seemed to be a hopeless mismatch. But Stallworth, more than any Knick, knew that nothing was ever hopeless. "Honestly," he insisted later, "I never thought that the game was lost. We shoot too well. If we could keep Wilt busy and let the rest of the guys play four-on-four, I knew we could win."

And as DeBusschere had done before him, Stallworth more than occupied Chamberlain's time. He slipped around Wilt, slapped away passes intended for him, and broke up the center of the Laker attack. Where DeBusschere had used muscle, Stallworth used finesse; but the result was the same. The Lakers grew more addled; Wilt became more frustrated and ineffective. The Laker lead, which had been about 10 points for much of the game, evaporated. In the final minutes, the Knicks pulled ahead. The disbelieving fans were beside themselves. Stallworth was exultant. Yet one gesture remained—a final challenge, a final definition of what basketball was all about to Stallworth.

With time running out, he took a pass and whirled toward Wilt. Chamberlain responded, moving to the baseline and block-

ing the path to the hoop. But Stallworth kept coming. In midair
he faked, twisted, and somehow slipped past Wilt. Still floating,
he went under the basket and lifted a perfect backward lay-up into
the net. It was one of those classic moves that stay frozen in the
memory, and it seemed a perfect symbol of the remarkable Knick
victory. In the locker room Stallworth was surrounded by reporters; it was the most postgame attention he had received all
year. Then they drifted away and Dave sat smiling to himself.
Someone came over and mentioned the shot, and he tried to
sound very matter-of-fact. "Yes, I challenged him. And I beat him.
I've done it before." Then his bright face exploded in laughter.
"It was kind of freaky, though, wasn't it?"

As backup centers go, Nate Bowman was a respectable one.
But then, backup centers don't go very far in the NBA. Few teams
are fortunate enough to possess even one outstanding big man;
hardly anyone enjoys the presence of two solid centers. The
Knicks were no exception, and they lived all year with the
knowledge that only one man would have been irreplaceable if
injured—Reed. But if Bowman's skills could never have enabled
him to fill in for long stretches, he did have a definite short-range
value, holding off the opposition as best he could while Reed
grabbed valuable moments of rest.

If such praise sounds rather backhanded, it is only in keeping
with Nate's faintly bizarre career. He left Wichita State with
Stallworth in 1965, and like Dave, he was drafted in the first
round. There the parallel ends. In the two years before he found
his way to New York, Nate belonged to four different teams—
Cincinnati, Chicago, Philadelphia, and Seattle—and played a total
of nine NBA games. Hampered by chronic ankle trouble and his
special brand of ineptitude, he disappointed every club that took
a chance with him, until the Knicks picked him up in 1967 to
back up Reed.

By last season, Bowman's role was well established in the nightly
Knick ritual. Near the end of the first half, Reed, drained by the
overwhelming effort he always expended, would walk slowly to
the bench. Nate would take his spot in the pivot. And most of

the fans in the Garden would glance up at the scoreboard and make an apprehensive mental note: "The Knicks are ahead by 12. If we're still ahead by 6 when Nate leaves, we'll be fine."

Bowman would often assert his presence with a quick offensive foul or an unsubtle chop on a rival shooter's arm, giving away the ball or 2 quick points on foul shots. Then the Knicks might set up a play, come upcourt, and begin to pass to Bowman on the right side of the key—only to find Nate over on the left. And eventually, he would give the crowd the ultimate adventure by attempting a shot. His nickname was Nate the Snake, and it described his shot well. His six-foot-ten-inch body would coil in strange configurations, his huge hands would seem to caress the ball lovingly, with palms as well as fingers—and Nate would let fly. Two out of five times, the ball would find its way into the basket; on the other shots, it was just as apt to fall three feet short of the rim. Either way, the crowd would roar its approval or dismay. And after particularly flagrant misses, even the Knicks might join in the reaction, awarding him the "game ball"—a traditional trophy for unusually terrible plays. Nate accepted such kidding good-naturedly: "I can miss by five feet sometimes, because I sort of palm the ball and then release it, and my hands are so big that when they get sweaty, I got my troubles."

Many times, of course, Bowman did a thoroughly workmanlike job, bulling his way into position and holding it, allowing the Knicks to function smoothly around him. But he was a victim of his own style: when he did things well, it meant that he was managing not to disrupt the attack—and so he was hardly noticeable. But when he did things badly, he did them with a flamboyant touch that nobody ever forgot. Holzman, who often yelled himself hoarse trying to get Bowman to remember the plays, also spent a good deal of time trying to correct the injustices that Nate suffered. Any time Nate put in a good performance, Holzman was quick to mention it to reporters after the game.

"I know my job," Bowman said simply. "I have to give Willis a break." Buoyed by the prospect of the championship spoils, he generally seemed content with that minor role. Yet there were moments when he chided reporters for ignoring him, and other moments when he revealed stronger opinions about his own ability. On the rare occasions when Reed would get into foul trouble and Bowman would have an exceptional night, Nate would greet the press expansively, recounting his expert plays in detail, making it clear that he felt he could really do the same things every night. On one such evening, a reporter glanced at a statistic sheet and said, "Pretty good, Nate, you got thirteen rebounds."

Nate noted surprise in the man's voice and stared balefully down at him. "You can't get thirteen rebounds every night," he said, "if you're not playing."

Bowman will undoubtedly get much more playing time in the future. He has been sent to the Buffalo Braves, a new NBA expansion team. The new club will provide the greatest opportunity he has known in his journey through pro ball, and perhaps Nate will live up to his proud opinion of himself. There is no doubt that Garden fans will be rooting for him. They owe him as much. In the most entertaining of seasons, he provided more than his share of the fun.

9

The Men Who Made It Jell:
Dave DeBusschere, the Catalyst;
Red Holzman, the Coach

SOME ATHLETES have the ability to expend tremendous amounts of energy in an economical way, conserving themselves during lulls in the action and then rising to every demand without apparent strain. It can be an attractive manner of playing, a translation of grueling physical exertion into what appears to be a facile, aesthetically pleasing form of action. Many ballplayers possess this quality to some degree; Dave DeBusschere doesn't possess it at all. DeBusschere is the kind of athlete who plays hard and looks it, during every second that he is on the court. Perspiration gushes off his face, his chest heaves as he races up and down the floor, his whole body strains and contorts as he elbows for position under the boards. There is no economy or sublety in the style, no sense that it all comes easily. You watch DeBusschere and you understand what hard work pro basketball can be—and what a job the man is doing.

DeBusschere, of course, was the catalyst that touched off the Knicks' explosion into a superb team. Without him, they had been a collection of outstanding talents; with him they became an outstanding team. A great deal of his effect was purely technical: he was a perfect addition to this particular club, fitting into their style of defense, moving aggressively without the ball on offense, and sending Willis Reed back into the pivot where he belonged. But to Garden fans, DeBusschere represented more than a missing piece to a jigsaw puzzle. His special approach to the game was as welcome as his rebounding and defense.

For years, New Yorkers had suffered with players who seemed unable to sustain their best efforts for more than a few games at a time. Inconsistency seemed to be the most chronic of Knick ailments. No one was sure why the Knicks seemed to rise and fall so sharply: perhaps they lacked concentration, or tried too hard to conserve their energies, or remained confused about whether the game was meant to be work or a form of play. Whatever the real problem was, DeBusschere offered a cure. From the moment he stepped onto a basketball court, he never wavered in his concentration, never held back, and never forgot that what he was getting paid for was hard labor. Consistency, the most elusive of elements in New York ball, was the heart of DeBusschere's contribution.

DeBusschere stands six feet six, a moderate height for an NBA forward, but coaches refer to him as a "tall" six feet six—he rebounds and handles his position with the effectiveness of a much bigger man. This is not simply a matter of jumping ability; Dave is a good leaper but hardly an acrobatic one. Instead, he adds imagined inches to his stature by steady physical exertion, fighting his way into the best position under the backboards and then holding that position against all onslaughts. To estimate the most advantageous place to fix himself, DeBusschere utilizes his keen basketball mind; to hold that spot, he employs his strength, his 220-pound bulk, and his sharp elbows. After some of his more heated battles, he comes out of games covered with bruises; but he usually leaves with more rebounds than any other forward on the court.

When other Knicks depart the Garden after their games, the kids awaiting autographs usually break into huzzahs. When DeBusschere makes his exit, they often switch to the chant: "Defense, de-fense." For while all the Knicks emphasize defense, DeBusschere seems to symbolize it. Every pro fan is accustomed to watching superstars take charge of games, carrying inferior teams to improbable victories. DeBusschere's task is to keep that from happening to the Knicks. The list of men he must guard begins with Gus Johnson of Baltimore, Elgin Baylor of Los Angeles, Billy

Cunningham of Philadelphia, and Connie Hawkins of Phoenix—and it goes on to include every top forward in the game. Any one of those stars is capable of breaking open a game, but they rarely managed to do it against DeBusschere last year. When the NBA coaches elected their all-defensive team, Dave easily outdistanced every other forward in the voting.

Like most aspects of his game, DeBusschere's defense is not an aesthetic spectacle. He rarely sails up above a rival to block a shot, or steals a ball with one graceful swoop. He defends by pressuring his man, keeping him off balance at all times. Rather than blocking shots, he prevents his opponent from taking a decent shot; instead of making clean steals, he forces his man into mistakes, then grabs the ball when it squirts loose. "There's nothing I can do to really 'stop' a player like Gus Johnson," he said. "I just have to lean on him and make him take the toughest shots possible. Sometimes, the way he shoots, the tough shots will go in anyway. But I just have to stay on top of him and hope he won't get too hot." DeBusschere's battles with Johnson often resembled Greco-Roman wrestling as much as basketball; both men used the word "vicious" to describe them. In several playoff games, Johnson seemed to defy gravity, reason, and every other force that should have been on DeBusschere's side; Gus made shots falling down, looking away from the hoop, and staring into DeBusschere's eyes, and he helped the Bullets make the series close. But Johnson's glorious feats came in spurts; DeBusschere, as always, maintained his pace. And when the series ended, his steadiness had been rewarded with the victory. "It was the roughest, most physical series I can imagine," said the battered DeBusschere. "And it had to be the most satisfying experience of the season."

The first generation of professional basketball players called the custom "tin canning," and it was a way of life in the early years of the game, shortly after World War I. Tin canning meant multiplying your schedule—and your seven-dollar or twenty-dollar game checks—by joining three or four teams at once, in as many different leagues. A Nat Holman or a Joe Lapchick—or any other well-known New York player—might well play in Scranton, Pennsylvania, one night, in Elizabeth, New Jersey, the next, and then finish up a weekend playing in a dance hall in Harlem or Queens. A top athlete might work five or six games a week, traveling by bus and train between the sites, while holding down a regular job back home. The routine was grueling even by the modern standards that require the top pros to compete in one hundred games a season, but it offered kids money for playing a game that they would have played for nothing; so the players endured it. In fact, tin canning of a sort lasted into the 1940s, when more than a few New York college athletes sneaked off on weekends to play semipro ball under assumed names.

Dave DeBusschere played in 98 of the Knicks' 101 games last season, and he certainly needed no extra paynights in Scranton. Yet if you had to pick a modern ballplayer who would have excelled in the tin-canning era, it would be DeBusschere. At one stage of his career, he was faced with a choice between pro baseball and pro basketball. One season called for 160-odd games, the other for up to 100; each was a full-time job. DeBusschere elected to do both at once. At another point, he was challenged to try both coaching and playing; he accepted eagerly. In his rare hours of spare time, he also became a low-70s golfer. He was a natural athlete, and people insisted that he could have settled down to any one of his roles and become a star; but he was determined to do it all.

DeBusschere was a pitcher and a basketball forward at Austin High School in Detroit and then at Detroit University. By the time he left college, he was hailed as the best athlete that Detroit had ever produced. The Chicago White Sox offered him a bonus to sign with them; the Detroit Pistons lured him with a basketball contract. He signed with both teams, and for four years he worked for both, giving his characteristic all-out effort. But the odds were heavily against him. Only one other athlete, Gene Conley, had managed the dual role, playing for several years as a Milwaukee Braves pitcher and a Boston Celtics forward. But Conley, a fine pitcher, had been a reserve for the Celtics, and had never given them the intense game-long exertion that DeBusschere demanded of himself. The White Sox predicted that DeBusschere could be a starter on their excellent staff, but the basketball schedule robbed him of spring training and he never quite fulfilled their hopes. Soon both teams were pressuring him to quit his "other" sport; in 1964, the Pistons helped make up his mind by offering him still another job—as head coach.

At twenty-four, DeBusschere was the youngest man ever to last more than a few weeks at the head of a pro team. He worked no miracles with the lowly Pistons, but he did improve their record somewhat, and as a local hero, he attracted thousands of extra fans —no mean feat for the Pistons. Being a player-coach in the NBA presents enormous problems. On the most basic level, a man must concentrate on his own play while somehow keeping track of substitutions, time-outs, and the overall flow of the game. Even with aid from an assistant on the bench, the player-coach risks seeing one job or the other suffer. And then there are more subtle difficulties: Does the player-coach go out for beers like a regular player or remain as aloof as most coaches? How does he discipline a man and still get him to play unselfishly alongside him? How does he instruct an older veteran in some schoolboy fundamental? Bill Russell overcame all the obstacles and won two championships as player-coach of the Celtics; but Russell was in his mid-thirties and he was the most dominant personality ever to play the game. Other coaches have not fared as well, but the youthful DeBusschere performed respectably. And when he finally decided to step down and concentrate only on playing, in 1967, he had acquired an invaluable education.

"Coaching changed my approach to the game in a very positive way," he said. "I gained a keener insight into the intricacies of the game, and I learned what's really important to a team. It's not only a matter of scoring, but what goes on at the other end of the floor. It's the defense, the assists, the rebounds." Freed from coaching and with baseball far behind him, DeBusschere found himself focusing on one job for the first time as a professional. He kept improving, but the Pistons didn't. And he began to hear the rumors that he would be traded. Finally, on the eve of a game against the Knicks in December of 1968, general manager Ed Coil called him to tell him the news. Coil was grateful for the years of effort DeBusschere had given Detroit, and he was understandably afraid that Dave would be aggrieved. But DeBusschere could hardly have been more delighted. He was going to a city that loved basketball, a city near his wife, Geri's, home town on Long Island. And he was leaving a losing, unhappy club to join one that seemed to be young and improving. As it turned out, he provided all the improvement the Knicks needed.

In the off-season, DeBusschere is a stockbroker. He is also an author, having kept a tape-recorded diary of last season for publication. But if those occupations have changed his social status, the boys in his neighborhood bar back home in Detroit haven't noticed. A prodigious beer drinker who easily guzzles two six-packs after every game, DeBusschere still visits the same taverns, drinks with the same working-class friends, and plays softball in the same Thursday-night league. He met Geri, a petite, attractive brunette, in a bowling alley; when they go out to dinner, it is for steak and beer. In every phase of his life, his pleasures remain simple. "Relationships don't change," he said simply. "When you're through playing, you go back to your friends. You do the things you've always enjoyed."

Tentatively, leaving his options open, DeBusschere says that he probably won't return to coaching when he stops playing. He undoubtedly means it. But even if he never coaches again, he won't stop thinking like a coach. DeBusschere primes himself for games as if he were getting an entire team ready, working himself up to a high pitch, telling himself how tough his opponent will be. And if DeBusschere felt any frustrations during the Knicks' quest for the title, they stemmed from that habit: the more Dave would kindle himself into a psychological fever, the more upset he would get when Knick coach Red Holzman came in and lowered the temperature.

DeBusschere has always had an old-fashioned conception of leadership. As a coach, he wanted his players to like him, to follow his tireless example, and to be inspired by his words. And last year he found himself playing for a determinedly colorless little man who couldn't have cared less about emotions or inspiration. Occasionally the contrast became painful. DeBusschere would be sitting in front of his locker, visions of Hawkins or Johnson or some other rival dancing in his mind, adrenaline pumping through his body; Holzman would enter and give his monotone pregame talk, and Dave would feel himself slipping from his peak. Frowning, he might sneak a glance at Bradley, who shared many of his feelings about self-psychology. Then he would stare ahead until it ended, with a typical flash of Holzman oratory such as "These guys are tough. Go get 'em." And then DeBusschere would re-ignite his entire mental process and work himself back to his private emotional pitch.

In the long run, however, such annoyances seemed minor, because even the more emotionally attuned Knicks such as DeBusschere, Bradley, and Russell couldn't fail to notice one strange fact about Holzman's low-key method: it worked. If it caused problems for some players, it may have smoothed things out for others; and its overall result was the world championship.

Listening to Holzman's bored, noncommittal analyses of even the most implausible Knick feats, some people understandably concluded that the team was winning in spite of him. Studying his remarkable record in two and a half years as coach, Holzman admirers have cited him as the key to their success. The truth lies somewhere in between. But nobody will ever learn it from Holzman.

"I'm no genius," goes his favorite statement. Then there are his lucid follow-ups: "I've never done anything spectacular or really smart. Just the best I could." When a visiting reporter tries to get more specific, asking why the Knicks played so well on a given night, the reply is: "How the hell should I know?" No one offered a rebuttal when Red's wife, Selma, commented: "I guess you could say we're uninteresting people."

At least a few of Holzman's contributions are tangible. First, he was chief scout for New York during the years when the present club was being built; along with general manager Eddie Donovan, he deserves considerable credit for the Knicks' draft selections and trades. Second, he was the architect of the Knicks' devastating team defense.

Holzman's name has been linked to defense in New York since

his earliest days around high school gyms and union halls. While still at Franklin Lane High School, Red built a wider reputation by playing for Local 102 of the International Ladies Garment Workers Union—the most powerful team in the strong union league. Then he joined the master, Nat Holman, at City College, and brought Holman's theories of defense to fruition. Whenever a team with a heralded individual scorer challenged City, Holzman was assigned to stop him. He seldom failed. Many New Yorkers still remember his confrontation with Bob Davis of Seton Hall, who later became his pro teammate at Rochester. In the early 1940s, Davis became famous as the first great behind-the-back dribbler; then Holzman gained his own fame by being the first to destroy a behind-the-back dribble. For an entire game Davis tried the maneuver, only to have Holzman snatch the ball away from him. Seton Hall, a superior team, won the game, but Holzman's performance became a New York basketball landmark.

Holzman, now fifty, was among the first basketball experts to realize that the old-fashioned "I got my man" approach to defense was being superseded by concepts like double-teaming the man with the ball and directing the flow of the opponent to a special area; and he drilled those principles into his players until they developed possibly the best balanced defense in pro history. Third, Holzman put the Knicks through an unusually rugged training camp last year—getting them off to their fast start.

The effect of Holzman's personality, however, remains all but impossible to gauge. From the moment that people began calling the Knicks a great team, people kept looking for that traditional element of such a team, the "great coach." But except for his keen technical mind, Holzman refused to live up to the phrase. Coaches who win titles are somehow expected to look like Red Auerbach, who led the Celtics through most of their dynasty—gruff, witty, deeply involved with his men, capable of both rare inspiration and harsh discipline; or they are expected to make grand gestures, like Alex Hannum of the Philadelphia 76ers, challenging towering Wilt Chamberlain to fight him if he didn't like the way he was coaching. Holzman, of course, falls far short of such expectations. On the bench and at practices, he yells and growls a lot; but before and after games he resumes his flat monotone. The only hint of "great" coaching stature is in the Knicks' record.

Yet some have theorized that there is an advantage inherent in Holzman's blandness. He is in charge of a group of remarkable individualists. Each of the Knicks has his own life style, his own mental approach, his own swirl of publicity around him. By remaining so completely in the background, Holzman leaves more room for those personalities to flourish. DeBusschere or Bradley can psyche themselves any way they choose before games, while Barnett gets ready in his own low-key way. Reed can drive himself with that fierce pride, while Frazier waits for the crowd and the feel of the ball to awaken his mood. And each man can project his own image, in his clothes or phrases or outside activities, enjoying as much attention as he might want from New York's basketball-crazy fans—with absolutely no competition from the coach. A stronger personality would leave a far greater imprint on the team and the city, but maybe the Knicks are better off making their own imprints without interference.

Perhaps that theory explains Holzman's success. Or perhaps there is no need for a theory to explain it. As the championship coach, Red requires no apologists. Yet many times during the season, one had to fight the urge to barge into his small office, knock his feet off his desk, pull the big cigar out of his mouth, grab him by the shoulders, and loudly remind him that he was presiding over the most emotional basketball season New York has ever enjoyed.

If it ever had happened, of course, Holzman would have propped his feet back up, puffed on the cigar, and muttered, "Yes. Things are going all right." As usual, the coach would sound flat, unsatisfying—and correct.

The cast is complete. These were the men—nine athletes and their coach—who did the most to bring the championship of the city game to the city that wanted it so badly. But there were many others who helped. At the top, Ned Irish finally learned to leave things in the hands of professionals; and general manager Eddie Donovan took full advantage of his newfound free hand to supervise the building of the club. Then there was Dick McGuire, remembered best as the coach Holzman replaced, but still sought after for his opinions in his position as chief scout. There were Bill Hosket, Don May, and John Warren, two second-year men and a rookie, who seldom played but led lusty cheers from the bench—and who have now departed for new teams in the NBA expansion program, taking with them a winning experience they may never duplicate. And there were the New York fans, the chanting, shouting crowds who understood the subtleties of defense as well as the scoring statistics, and who sometimes added so materially to Knick triumphs that Bill Bradley described victories as "collective achievements by everyone in the building."

But there are still others in the cast of the city game: Athletes who may never even see Madison Square Garden, young men who flash briefly across asphalt courts, momentarily suspended in time and memory, finding and sharing something very special with others in the ghetto. Some are unknown to the general public, others have almost been forgotten even in the parks; they may be recalled only by a nickname, or by a remembered "move" with the ball. Their stories are vague and they build to no theatrical climaxes. But before going on to the playoffs that climaxed the Knicks' season, it is worth pausing, to scan other heroes in the panorama of New York city ball.

BOOK III

Playground Profiles

10

"People Wonder Why": The Stars Who Never Made It

In March of 1964, Boys High of Brooklyn faced Benjamin Franklin High of Harlem in the old Madison Square Garden, on Eighth Avenue and Fiftieth Street, for the public high school championship of New York. Boys won the title; but the result was quickly overshadowed by a seat-slashing, bottle-throwing melee that resulted in the end of high school ball in the Garden and established a negative landmark in city basketball. The riot occurred against the tense backdrop of the city's first black school boycott; and it happened on St. Patrick's Day, when many patrolmen who might have handled the crowd were out parading. But administrators were not much interested in the details or causes of the disturbance. It was much easier to run from the problem than to solve it. So the Public School Athletic League swiftly moved its tournaments into small neutral gyms, and the black stars who dominate high school ball in the city were swept quietly out of sight.

Since that time, the Garden has promoted a series of fights featuring Latin American boxers with volatile, bottle-throwing followers. It has hosted rallies for such public figures as George Wallace. But the young black ballplayers have not reappeared. While the Knicks turn on the city, its most talented young stars play in virtual secrecy in musty gyms and youth centers and playgrounds, before only their peers and a handful of college scouts. While the media fall in love with the Knicks, a top high school star searches in vain for a paragraph or two in the *Times* on his team's victories. A year ago, the Boys High team journeyed to New Haven, Connecticut, to face Hillhouse High for the informal championship of the East. Boys won by a point. It was the team's forty-sixth consecutive victory. And it drew more attention in New Haven in one day than Boys had gathered in New York with the forty-five wins that preceded it. The irony was not lost on the athletes. The struggle to establish an identity is basic to city basketball, but many black kids in New York have learned that their identity is a well-kept secret to the general public.

"There are a lot of contradictions in ghetto ball," said Sonny Johnson. "Kids see good players who make it. But then they see players just as good who never get any recognition and never get out of their own neighborhoods. It makes the kids question the value of pushing themselves to get out. It drains the motivation." Howie Jones, former coach at Boys High, stated it more bluntly: "By ignoring these kids, you strangle them at the most basic level. And then people wonder why they get bitter."

The bitterness was not readily apparent at the playground on 135th Street near Lenox Avenue. The June afternoon was warm and the basketball was very good. The games were just pickup affairs, with five-man teams being assembled on the spot to challenge the winners of whatever game was in progress; but a few pro players dropped by, as well as several Globetrotters and the established stars of the neighborhood, and somebody said that it was the best ball you would find in Harlem short of the Rucker Tournament itself. The cars were double-parked all the way down the block, and the crowd was three deep alongside the high fences. The action was fast and noisy and there seemed to be a joy in the scene.

Then one athlete, who didn't want to give his name, began talking about it all, and there was an edge in his voice. "Sure there are good players here, and good ones who have made it in college and the pros. But don't try to write this up as a beautiful breeding ground for future stars, because for every star you hear about, there are many more who never escaped. I mean, I can look back on the group that I grew up with down on 111th Street, and I can tell you all about the one or two who are playing college ball, and it will make a great story. But there were twenty of us. And now maybe fifteen are on drugs and three are dead or just gone, who knows where? So how much do the lucky ones count?" The kid sounded very old. He said he was twenty-one.

Other voices were equally bleak. All spoke of their love of basketball and praised it as a path out of the ghetto. But on every level of the sport, from the pros down to high school, they saw racism. Recently Bill Russell wrote a piece in *Sports Illustrated* in which he mentioned the quota system that some pro teams allegedly utilize to limit the number of blacks. There were anguished reactions, and people said that Russell was fostering bitterness among youths by making such accusations. But he fostered no new bitterness on 135th Street; no player there needed Russell to tell him that the quota system existed. They had seen too many fine players try out for the pros and come back to star in the parks, and they insisted that those players were good enough to be solid reserves in pro ball. "But," they concluded, "the pros aren't looking for blacks who are going to fill their bench. If you can start, fine. Otherwise, go home."

Somebody mentioned the "no dunk" rule, which was instituted in college ball during Lew Alcindor's career at UCLA. Many assumed that the rule was designed largely to keep Alcindor from ruining the game by methodically stuffing one shot after another into the hoop. In the parks, people assume differently. "Look, if a guy is seven feet tall, he is going to score from in close whether he stuffs or just lays the ball in," explained Robert Bownes. "That rule wasn't put in to stop seven-footers. It was put in to stop the six-foot-two brothers who could dazzle the crowd and embarrass much bigger white kids by dunking. The white establishment has an uncomfortable feeling that blacks are dominating too many areas of sports. So they're setting up all kinds of restrictions and barriers. Everyone knows that dunking is a trademark of great playground black athletes. And so they took it away. It's as simple as that."

Bownes, twenty-six, is now an assistant basketball coach at Hunter College in New York. He is respected by the playground kids as a man who made it; but he made it only through tremendous perseverance. A tough product of the streets, he managed to get thrown out of two small colleges for fighting before he finally finished school at Norfolk State University. "I come from a family of five kids," he said proudly. "And four of us are college graduates. My mother and father never got an education, they're just common people, you might say, but they pushed us through. They deserve great credit. But I don't kid myself. If I hadn't possessed basketball talent, I don't know if I would have made it all the way. If you get out of one of the high schools here and you don't play ball, nobody rushes to get you to their college. Let's face it, high school graduates in the ghetto are very poorly educated people."

In fact, many athletes who graduate from ghetto high schools are steered toward "prep schools" such as Laurinburg Institute in North Carolina or Newark Prep in New Jersey—schools that specialize in quality basketball teams, but also offer the ballplayers courses that give them a shot at college. Chuckie Murray, a youth whom Bownes was trying to recruit for Hunter, described his Newark Prep experience: "I was at De Witt Clinton High School in The Bronx, but I had no incentive to study or to play ball. I knew that the teachers didn't care, and I didn't care either. And I was just taking general classes [as opposed to academic ones], and what do general courses do for you? They shove you through school and send you back out onto the street. At Newark, I could aim higher than the streets. I realized that I had a chance at college, so I started to apply myself."

The athletes who do get to college have to "apply themselves" all over again, and many of them fail. Some blame coaches or the schools, but others tend to blame the wider system—the system that begins with the gulf between the Garden and the black playgrounds, the system that keeps black and white worlds so far apart. Keith Edwards was six feet five, a talented player with a sharp mind. But he couldn't make the transition between the two worlds, and he flunked out of Marquette in 1968 after a year and a half. "When I went to college," he said, "I was nineteen and I had known the life of the streets. In other words, I was a man. If I had been sixteen, maybe I could have been changed or molded.

But by the time I got to Marquette, I was too old, too sure of myself, too independent. I couldn't fit into any patterns or accept any discipline. In college ball, a coach owns your body and your mind for three hours a day. A kid may be able to accept that. But a man can't."

Edwards now teaches elementary mathematics at an Urban League Street Academy. He harbors little bitterness. "I went through what so many Harlem cats go through in college," he said. "But the experience taught me a lot about people and about life. When I came back home, I was able to get myself together. In that way, I was more fortunate than a lot of guys." Edwards is twenty-three now. "I still play a little ball," he added. "If somebody challenges me I'll go out and see if I can still do the job. But I don't do it often. I'm an old man now."

The less fortunate grow old even faster, leaving the bright moments behind them on the courts as the real world of the ghetto drags them down to earth. There is a sustaining power to basketball in the playgrounds: a young athlete walks into a bar or luncheonette and hears people say, "That's the dude that dunked on Lew up at Rucker"; the admirers want to talk to him, to ask advice, to be near the star, and maybe that sense of importance and identity will keep a kid going for weeks. But if he is a dropout and he is broke, and the hustlers and pushers are around him with their cars and fancy clothes, the magic of his game can begin to wear off. Sooner or later, stuffing a basketball through a hoop is not quite enough to transcend the reality of his life.

"At one point in most guys' lives," said Keith Edwards, "basketball is the top priority, because it is the one escape valve from the ghetto. But once the paths toward college or pro ball are closed to an athlete, merely playing the game is not as much of an escape. Then the kids get offered a much easier escape—an escape to within themselves—in drugs. A few years ago, I would have said that the athletes I knew looked 90 percent to ball, 10 percent to drugs. Now the ratio is reversed. The kids are looking to drugs 90 percent of the time. And they are destroying themselves."

Everyone in Harlem has watched the process of destruction, but no one feels it more acutely than the ballplayers. "You see somebody who can do everything on the court," said Pat Smith. "You know that his ballplaying can open up a whole new world to him. It gives you a feeling of excitement. It makes you build high hopes. And when you watch him start to deteriorate, it tears you apart." Smith paused, shying momentarily from the subject. Two of Smith's nine brothers have died on the Harlem streets; another was a dope pusher at the age of fourteen. Six years away at school in Milwaukee have not erased the streets from Smith's life. "There's such great waste of humanity," he said slowly. "Such tragic waste." And then the memories came pouring out, a remarkable testament to the darkest side of basketball in the city:

"I remember when I was just developing as a ballplayer, early in high school. I played a lot with a guy named Artie. I never knew his last name, just Artie. He played often at Millbank Center, and his team was known for winning a lot of local tournaments. Artie was capable of scoring every way: jump shots, hooks, lay-ups, set shots. His scoring totals were 40 to 50 points every game. When I knew him, Artie was about twenty-eight, and he was trying to make a comeback. From alcohol. He was a wine drinker. That shows you how far back it was—people still ruined themselves the slow way with wine, instead of drugs.

"Anyway, Artie had been in a hospital, trying to dry out and recuperate. When he started playing again, he was probably a step slower than he once was, but he still had those fantastic shots. He took an interest in me for some reason, and he picked me to play with him in pickup games whenever he could. When we played together, he would teach me, and he would also get so many good passes to me that I was sure of getting 25 or 30 points—while he still got his 50.

"But after a few months he began showing up less at the playgrounds. Then he didn't come at all. And one day I was on the street and somebody asked if I'd heard about Artie. Then the guy told me. They'd found Artie dead in a hallway. He drank himself to death."

"There was another guy we knew only by his first name, Frank," Smith continued. "He came from uptown, around 155th Street, but he would come down to our neighborhood around 128th Street to play. He was a strong guy, very good-looking, with a great build. I didn't know him well, I didn't know what high school he was from, but I always assumed that he had the potential to go on and start for some college team.

"Then we heard the news. Frank had tried to rob a drugstore. The storekeeper had a gun, and Frank got shot in the back. He was paralyzed from the waist down. He was maybe nineteen years old, and it was all over for him.

"People still see him, in his wheelchair. When anyone goes up in that neighborhood they look for him. He's about twenty-four now, and he tries to take the thing very well. Talking to him, you can hardly realize that he knows he'll never walk again. But the way he hides his pain only makes it hurt more to look at him and think of what he could have been."

"Dexter Westbrook was one of the few big men that ever came from the uptown playgrounds," said Smith. "For some reason, most of the taller guys happened to play downtown around 135th Street or 128th Street, while the players up at 155th were known more for quickness and ball handling. But Dexter was about six feet eight, and he was a super big man. Playing with so many fast little guys, he developed the quickness and moves of a guard. He had a beautiful left-handed jump shot, and he could do everything with the ball.

"Dexter went to Providence College for a while. Then he failed out and came home and worked in a few jobs in the poverty program. But with his size and talent, everybody insisted that he could still make the pros, and two or three years ago he tried out. I forget which team it was, but word got back to Harlem that Dexter was doing great. He was the high scorer and the best rebounder in rookie camp; nobody could touch him. Then it came time for the routine physical examination, and he couldn't pass it. There were needle tracks on his arms.

"Now this was a man who could have made it big. But he just couldn't seem to adjust his mind to bigger things than what's here in Harlem. The last time I heard of Dexter was in the summer of 1969. There was a robbery on Riverside Drive, and he was arrested for taking somebody's wallet. His drug habit had gotten beyond his means. Like it always does."

If it hurt Smith to talk of his contemporaries, it seemed to wrench him more to turn to younger kids. "I saw guys I played with get ruined, and it was bad, but it wasn't always unexpected," he said. "You go to school or play a lot of ball with a guy and you get an idea whether he can make it. But watching kids come up, you lose that perspective. You somehow hope they'll all make it. And you forget that the drug thing is much worse now than it was when you were in school yourself. You forget that escaping the streets is harder than ever. And then you see what happens to a kid like Kenny Bellinger.

"Kenny earned a citywide basketball reputation when he was still in junior high school. I was a senior in high school when I played against him, and he was in ninth grade. But he couldn't go on playing against kids his own age, because he was too good. He was always looking for older guys to challenge, and he always held his own. A lot of high school players waited to see where he would decide to go, and we were glad when he chose Franklin. He was a cinch to make all-city, and he had a great future ahead of him.

"Then one day, I was walking on 111th Street between Seventh and Eighth avenues, and I saw four or five squad cars. I asked somebody what was going on, and people said that a lady's purse had been snatched, and someone had run into one of the buildings with it. The next thing we knew, there was a helicopter over the buildings. The purse snatcher was on the roofs, and they were trying to spot him. Nobody had ever seen the police use a helicopter before, but somebody said that the purse belonged to a white lady with some influence. Anyway, it looked like they were fighting the whole Vietcong instead of looking for a purse.

"Suddenly all the cops rushed into an alley, and in a few minutes the word spread: the thief had tried to hurdle a six-foot gap between the buildings, and he hadn't made it. I went home, and I didn't find out until the next day that the kid who had plunged into the alley had been Kenny Bellinger.

"I couldn't believe it. I thought there must have been a mistake. Kenny couldn't have risked so much—and anyway, he could have leaped a six-foot gap with no problem at all. So I went up onto the building and checked out the gap, and it was more like fifteen feet. Then it began to sink in. All that potential was gone. Whether it was drugs or despair or what, Kenny hadn't been able to stay straight. One more victim. Kenny was sixteen years old when he died."

"Boobie Tucker was also in junior high when he first came around to play with us older guys," said Smith. "He was about six feet nine, but he wasn't as advanced as Kenny Bellinger. He was still clumsy and uncoordinated. He didn't know how to take advantage of his size. But while I was at Franklin and he was in junior high, he would come to our gym and try to learn, and we watched him develop into a really good ballplayer. He learned to get position under the boards for rebounds, and he practiced a short jump shot until he could make it regularly. Here was a kid only about sixteen, and he was six feet nine and still growing. He might have had the world in front of him. The year I went away to college, he started playing for Franklin.

"Every so often I'd ask somebody about Boobie. First I heard that he was coming along fine, scoring nicely. But gradually the other rumors reached me: 'Yeah, Tucker's on stuff. . . . Yeah, he's snorting pretty heavy. . . . Yeah, Tucker's strung out.' Boobie stopped playing altogether and went out onto the streets. And finally I learned that he had died of an overdose. It was a shock, because he hadn't been strung out for that long. He probably hadn't even developed an expensive habit yet. But of course, when times get hard, pushers will put anything into that white bag and sell it. Some guys have shot up rat poison and died instantly.

"It was a terrible, frustrating thing to imagine Boobie dead. I felt very close to his career, because I'd watched him develop from a clumsy kid into a ballplayer. Day to day, I'd seen the improvements. I'd watched him work at the game, and I couldn't help thinking that he would be repaid for all that work.

"But the one thing I wasn't thinking about, the one thing you never think about, I guess, until it's too late, was that the pusher was watching him develop, too."

11

The Fallen Idol: The Harlem
Tragedy of Earl Manigault

IN THE LITANY of quiet misfortunes that have claimed so many
young athletes in the ghetto, it may seem almost impossible to
select one man and give him special importance. Yet in the stories
and traditions that are recounted in the Harlem parks, one figure
does emerge above the rest. Asked about the finest athletes they
have seen, scores of ballplayers in a dozen parks mention Connie
Hawkins and Lew Alcindor and similar celebrities. But almost
without exception, they speak first of one star who didn't go on:
Earl Manigault.

No official scorers tabulate the results of pickup games; there
are no composite box scores to prove that Manigault ranked highest
among playground athletes. But in its own way, a reputation in the
parks is as definable as a scoring average in the NBA. Cut off from
more formal channels of media and exposure, street ballplayers
develop their own elaborate word-of-mouth system. One spectacular
performance or one backward, twisting stuff shot may be the seed
of an athlete's reputation. If he can repeat it a few times in a
park where the competition is tough, the word goes out that he
may be something special. Then there will be challenges from
more established players, and a man who can withstand them may
earn a "neighborhood rep." The process continues in an expanding
series of confrontations, until the best athletes have emerged.

Perhaps a dozen men at a given time may enjoy "citywide reps," guaranteeing them attention and respect in any playground they may visit. And of those, one or two will stand alone.

A few years ago, Earl Manigault stood among the loftiest. But his reign was brief, and in order to capture some feeling of what his stature meant in the playground world, one must turn to two athletes who enjoy similar positions today. Herman "Helicopter" Knowings, now in his late twenties, is among the most remarkable playground phenomena; he was a demigod before Manigault, and he remains one after Earl's departure. Uneducated and unable to break into pro ball, the Helicopter has managed to retain the spring in his legs and the will power to remain at the summit after many of his contemporaries have faded from the basketball scene. Joe Hammond, not yet twenty, is generally recognized as the best of the young crop. Neither finished school and vaulted into the public spotlight, but both pick up money playing in a minor league, the Eastern League—and both return home between games to continue their domination of the parks.

The Helicopter got his name for obvious reasons: when he goes up to block a shot, he seems to hover endlessly in midair above his prey, daring him to shoot—and then blocking whatever shot his hapless foe attempts. Like most memorable playground moves, it is not only effective but magnetic. As Knowings goes up, the crowd shouts, "Fly, 'copter, fly," and seems to share his heady trip. When he shoves a ball down the throat of a visiting NBA star—as he often does in the Rucker Tournament—the Helicopter inflates the pride of a whole neighborhood.

Like Connie Hawkins, Knowings can send waves of electricity through a park with his mere presence. Standing by a court, watching a game in progress with intent eyes, the Helicopter doesn't have to ask to play. People quickly spot his dark, chiseled, ageless face and six-foot-four-inch frame, and they make room for him. Joe Hammond is less imposing. A shade over six feet, he is a skinny, sleepy-eyed kid who looks slow and tired, the way back-court star Clinton Robinson appeared during his reign. But like Robinson, Hammond has proved himself, and now he stands as the descendant of Pablo Robertson and James Barlow and the other backcourt heroes of the streets.

The kings of playground ball are not expected to defend their titles every weekend, proving themselves again and again the way less exalted players must. But when a new athlete begins winning a large following, when the rumors spread that he is truly someone special, the call goes out: If he is a forward, get the Helicopter; if he's a guard, let's try him against Joe Hammond. A crowd will gather before the star arrives. It is time for a supreme test.

Jay Vaughn has been in such confrontations several times. He saw the Helicopter defend his reign, and he watched Joe Hammond win his own way to the top. He described the rituals:

"When I first met the Helicopter, I was only about seventeen, and I was playing with a lot of kids my age at Wagner Center. I was better than the guys I was playing with and I knew it, so I didn't feel I had anything to prove. I was playing lazy, lackadaisical. And one of the youth workers saw how cocky I was and decided to show me just how good I really was. He sent for the Helicopter.

"One day I was just shooting baskets, trying all kinds of wild shots, not thinking about fundamentals, and I saw this older dude come in. He had sneakers and shorts on and he was ready to play. I said, 'Who's this guy? He's too old for our games. Is he supposed to be good?'

" 'The coach sent for him,' somebody told me, 'He's gonna play you.'

"I said to myself, 'Well, fine, I'll try him,' and I went out there one-on-one with Herman Knowings. Well, it was a disastrous thing. I tried lay-ups, jump shots, hooks. And everything I threw up, he blocked. The word had gone out that Herman was there, and a crowd was gathering, and I said to myself, 'You got to do something. You're getting humiliated.' But the harder I tried, the more he shoved the ball down into my face. I went home and thought about that game for a long time. Like a lot of other young athletes, I had been put in my place.

"I worked out like crazy after that. I was determined to get back. After about a month, I challenged him again. I found myself jumping higher, feeling stronger, and playing better than ever before. I wasn't humiliated again. But I was beaten. Since that time, I've played against Herman many times. He took an interest in me and gave me a lot of good advice. And now, when I see he's going to block a shot, I may be able to fake and go around him and score, and people will yell, 'The pupil showed the master.'

"Then, of course, he'll usually come back and stuff one on me. . . ."

"Joe Hammond was playing in the junior division games in the youth centers when I was in the senior games," Vaughn continued. "He was three years younger than me, and sometimes after I'd played, I'd stay and watch his game. He wasn't that exceptional. Just another young boy who was gonna play ball. In fact, at that time, I didn't even know his last name.

"Then I came home from school in the summer of 1969, and one name was on everyone's lips: Joe Hammond. I thought it must have been somebody new from out of town, but people said, no, he'd been around Harlem all the time. They described him and it sounded like the young kid I'd watched around the centers, but I couldn't believe it was the same guy. Then I saw him, and it was the same Joe, and he was killing a bunch of guys his own age. He was much improved, but I still said to myself, 'He's young. He won't do much against the older brothers. They've been in business too long.'

"But then I heard, 'Joe's up at 135th Street beating the pros. . . . Joe's doing everything to those guys.' I still didn't take it too seriously. In fact, when Joe came out to Mount Morris Park for a game against a good team I was on, I said, 'Now we'll see how you do. You won't do anything today.'

"Now I believe in him. Joe Hammond left that game with seven minutes to go. He had 40 points. Like everybody had said, Joe was the one."

Many reputations have risen and fallen in the decade between the arrival of the Helicopter and of Joe Hammond. Most have now been forgotten, but a few "reps" outlive the men who earn them. Two years ago Connie Hawkins did not show up for a single

game during the Rucker Tournament. When it was time to vote
for the Rucker all-star team, the coaches voted for Hawkins. "If
you're going to have an all-star game in Harlem," said Bob
McCullough, the tournament director, "you vote for Connie or
you don't vote." (Having been elected, The Hawk did appear for
the all-star game—and won the Most Valuable Player award.)
One other reputation has endured on a similar scale. Countless
kids in Harlem repeat the statement: "You want to talk about
basketball in this city, you've got to talk about Earl Manigault."

Manigault played at Benjamin Franklin High School in 1962 and
1963, then spent a season at Laurinburg Institute. Earl never
reached college, but when he returned to Harlem he continued to
dominate the playgrounds. He was the king of his own generation
of ballplayers, the idol for the generation that followed. He was
a six-foot-two-inch forward who could outleap men eight inches
taller, and his moves had a boldness and fluidity that transfixed
opponents and spectators alike. Freewheeling, unbelievably high-
jumping, and innovative, he was the image of the classic playground athlete.

But he was also a very human ghetto youth, with weaknesses
and doubts that left him vulnerable. Lacking education and motivation, looking toward an empty future, he found that basketball
could take him only so far. Then he veered into the escape route
of the streets, and became the image of the hellish side of ghetto
existence. Earl is now in his mid-twenties, a dope addict, in prison.

Earl's is more than a personal story. On the playgrounds, he was
a powerful magnetic figure who carried the dreams and ideals of
every kid around him as he spun and twisted and sailed over all
obstacles. When he fell, he carried those aspirations down with
him. Call him a wasted talent, a pathetic victim, even a tragic
hero: he had symbolized all that was sublime and terrible about
this city game.

"You think of him on the court and you think of so many incredible things that it's hard to sort them out," said Bob Spivey,
who played briefly with Earl at Franklin. "But I particularly recall
one all-star game in the gym at PS 113, in about 1964. Most of
the best high school players in the city were there: Charlie Scott,

who went on to North Carolina; Vaughn Harper, who went to Syracuse, and a lot more. But the people who were there will hardly remember the others. Earl was the whole show.

"For a few mintues, Earl seemed to move slowly, feeling his way, getting himself ready. Then he got the ball on a fast break. Harper, who was six feet six, and Val Reed, who was six feet eight, got back quickly to defend. You wouldn't have given Earl a chance to score. Then he accelerated, changing his step suddenly. And at the foul line he went into the air. Harper and Reed went up, too, and between them, the two big men completely surrounded the rim. But Earl just kept going higher, and finally he two-hand-dunked the ball over both of them. For a split second there was complete silence, and then the crowd exploded. They were cheering so loud that they stopped the game for five minutes. Five minutes. That was Earl Manigault."

Faces light up as Harlem veterans reminisce about Manigault. Many street players won reputations with elaborate innovations and tricks. Jackie Jackson was among the first to warm up for games by picking quarters off the top of the backboard. Willie Hall, the former St. John's leader, apparently originated the custom of jumping to the top of the board and, instead of merely blocking a shot, slamming a hand with tremendous force against the board; the fixture would vibrate for several seconds after the blow, causing an easy lay-up to bounce crazily off the rim. Other noted leapers were famous for "pinning"—blocking a lay-up, then simply holding it momentarily against the backboard in a gesture of triumph. Some players seemed to hold it for seconds, suspended in air, multiplying the humiliation of the man who had tried the futile shot. Then they could slam the ball back down at the shooter or, for special emphasis, flip it into the crowd.

Earl Manigault did all of those things and more, borrowing, innovating, and forming one of the most exciting styles Harlem crowds ever watched. Occasionally, he would drive past a few defenders, dunk the ball with one hand, catch it with the other—and raise it and stuff it through the hoop a second time before returning to earth.

"I was in the eighth grade when Earl was in the eleventh," said

Charley Yelverton, now a star at Fordham. "I was just another young kid at the time. Like everybody else on the streets, I played some ball. But I just did it for something to do. I wasn't that excited about it. Then there happened to be a game around my block, down at 112th Street, and a lot of the top players were in it—and Earl came down to play. Well, I had never believed things like that could go on. I had never known what basketball could be like. Everybody in the game was doing something, stuffing or blocking shots or making great passes. There's only one game I've ever seen in my life to compare to it—the Knicks' last game against the Lakers.

"But among all the stars, there was no doubt who was the greatest. Passing, shooting, going up in the air, Earl just left everybody behind. No one could turn it on like he could."

Keith Edwards, who lived with Earl during the great days of the Young Life team, agreed. "I guess he had about the most natural ability that I've ever seen. Talent for talent, inch for inch, you'd have to put him on a par with Alcindor and the other superstars. To watch him was like poetry. To play with him or against him— just to be on the same court with him—was a deep experience.

"You can't really project him against an Alcindor, though, because you could never picture Earl going to UCLA or anyplace like that. He was never the type to really face his responsibilities and his future. He didn't want to think ahead. There was very little discipline about the man. . . ."

And so the decline began. "I lived with the man for about two or three years," said Edwards, "from his predrug period into the beginning of his drug period. There were six of us there, and maybe some of us would have liked to help him out. But we were all just young guys finding themselves, and when Earl and another cat named Onion started to get into the drug thing, nobody really had a right, or was in a position, to say much about it. And even as he got into the drugs, he remained a beautiful person. He just had nowhere to go. . . ."

"The athlete in Harlem," said Pat Smith, "naturally becomes a big man in the neighborhood. And if he goes on to college and makes his way out of the ghetto, he can keep being a big man, a respected figure. But if he doesn't make it, if he begins to realize that he isn't going to get out, then he looks around, and maybe he isn't so big anymore. The pusher and the pimp have more clothes than they can ever get around to wearing; when they walk down the street they get respect. But the ballplayer is broke, and he knows that in a certain number of years he won't even have his reputation left. And unless he is an unusually strong person, he may be tempted to go another way. . . ."

"You like to think of the black athlete as a leader of the community," said Jay Vaughn, "but sometimes the idea of leadership can get twisted. A lot of the young dudes on the streets will encourage a big-time ballplayer to be big-time in other ways. They expect you to know all the big pushers, where to buy drugs, how to handle street life. And if they're fooling with small-time drugs, maybe they'll expect you to mess with big-time drugs. It may sound ridiculous at first, but when you're confronted with these attitudes a lot, and you're not strong enough, well, you find yourself hooked."

It didn't happen suddenly. On the weekends, people would still find Earl Manigault at the parks, and flashes of the magnetic ability were there. Young athletes would ask his advice, and he would still be helpful; even among the ones who knew he was sinking deeper into his drug habit, he remained respected and popular. But by early 1968, he seldom came to the parks, and his old friends would find him on street corners along Eighth Avenue, nodding. "He was such a fine person," said Jay Vaughn, "you saw him and you wished you could see some hope, some bright spot in his existence. But there was no good part of his life, of course. Because drugs do ruin you."

In the summer of 1968, Bob Hunter was working on a drug rehabilitation program. He looked up Earl. They became close, building a friendship that went deeper than their mutual respect on a basketball court. "Earl was an unusual type of addict," said Hunter. "He understood that he was a hard addict, and he faced it very honestly. He wanted to help me in the drug program, and he gave me a lot of hints on how to handle younger addicts. He knew different tricks that would appeal to them and win their trust. And he also knew all the tricks they would use, to deceive me into thinking they were getting cured. Earl had used the tricks himself, and he helped me see through them, and maybe we managed to save a few young kids who might have got hooked much worse.

"But it's the most frustrating thing in the world, working with addicts. It's hard to accept the fact that a man who has been burned will go back and touch fire. But they do it. I have countless friends on drugs, and I had many more who have died from drugs. And somehow it's hard to just give up on them and forget that they ever existed. Maybe you would think that only the less talented types would let themselves get hooked—but then you'd see a guy like Earl and you couldn't understand. . . ."

Some people hoped that Earl would be cured that summer. He did so much to help Hunter work with others that people felt he could help himself. Hunter was not as optimistic. "The truth is that nobody is ever going to cure Earl," he said. "The only way he'll be cured is by himself. A lot of people come off drugs only after they've been faced with an extreme crisis. For example, if they come very close to dying and somehow escape, then they might be able to stay away from the fire. But it takes something like that, most of the time."

Earl was not cured, and as the months went on the habit grew more expensive. And then he had to steal. "Earl is such a warm person," said Vaughn, "you know that he'd never go around and mug people or anything. But let's face it: most addicts, sooner or later, have to rob in order to survive." Earl broke into a store. He is now in prison. "Maybe that will be the crisis he needs," said Hunter. "Maybe, just possibly . . . But when you're talking about addicts, it's very hard to get your hopes too high."

Harold "Funny" Kitt went to Franklin three years behind Earl Manigault. When Funny finished in 1967, he was rated the best high school player in the city—largely because he had modeled himself so closely after Earl. "We all idolized Earl in those days," Kitt said. "And when you idolize somebody, you think of the good things, not the bad. As we watched Earl play ball, we had visions of him going on to different places, visiting the whole world, becoming a great star and then maybe coming back here to see us and talk to us about it all.

"But he didn't do any of those things. He just went into his own strange world, a world I hope I'll never see. I guess there were reasons. I guess there were frustrations that only Earl knew about, and I feel sorry for what happened. But when Earl went into that world, it had an effect on all of us, all the young ballplayers. I idolized the man. And he hurt me."

Beyond the hurt, though, Earl left something more. If his career was a small dramatization of the world of Harlem basketball, then he was a fitting protagonist, in his magnitude and his frailty, a hero for his time. "Earl was quiet, he was honest," said Jay Vaughn, "and he handled the pressures of being the star very well. When you're on top, everybody is out to challenge you, to make their own reps by doing something against you. One guy after another wants to take a shot, and some stars react to all that by bragging, or by being aloof from the crowd.

"Earl was different. The game I'll never forget was in the G-Dub [George Washington High] tournament one summer, when the team that Earl's group was scheduled to play didn't show. The game was forfeited, and some guys were just looking for some kind of pickup game, when one fellow on the team that forfeited came in and said, 'Where's Manigault? I want to play Manigault.'

"Well, this guy was an unknown and he really had no right to talk like that. If he really wanted to challenge a guy like Earl, he should have been out in the parks, building up a rep of his own. But he kept yelling and bragging, and Earl quietly agreed to play him one-on-one. The word went out within minutes, and immediately there was a big crowd gathered for the drama.

"Then they started playing. Earl went over the guy and dunked. Then he blocked the guy's first shot. It was obvious that the man had nothing to offer against Earl. But he was really determined to win himself a rep. So he started pushing and shoving and fouling. Earl didn't say a word. He just kept making his moves and beating the guy, and the guy kept grabbing and jostling him to try to stop him. It got to the point where it wasn't really basketball. And suddenly Earl put down the ball and said, 'I don't need this. You're the best.' Then he just walked away.

"Well, if Earl had gone on and whipped the guy 30 to 0, he couldn't have proved any more than he did. The other cat just stood there, not knowing what to say. The crowd surrounded Earl, and some of us said things about the fouling and the shoving. But he didn't say anything about it. He didn't feel any need to argue or complain. He had everyone's respect and he knew it. The role he played that day never left anyone who saw it. This was a beautiful man."

12

"You Grow Up Quick": The Comeback of Duane Smith

THE GLASS in the outside door was broken and the smell of urine in the hallways; the housing-project elevator creaked as it lurched its way up to the eighth floor. Yet inside the apartment it was cool and quiet, and as clean as the freshly polished glass on the trophy case full of basketball awards. The trophies belonged to Billy and Edward Smith, former local stars, and to Gene and Pat, who both played at Marquette. Only a few belonged to the youngest brother, Duane, but there was an open space in expectation of more. Duane will fill that space soon. He is a six-foot-five-inch sophomore at Long Island Lutheran High School; he is a very good ballplayer now and he is getting better. More important, the streets will never claim him. Duane has been there, and he has come back.

The grim ghetto pattern began for Duane Smith when he was fourteen years old and already capable of playing basketball with his talented older brothers and other high school and college stars. For a year he gave it all up, dropping out of high school and hustling in the streets. He did very well for himself and soon he had to find extra clothes racks, because his closet did not hold all his dazzling threads. But the wardrobe never impressed his mother or his brother Pat, and somehow Duane, a very wise man of sixteen, got the message. He gave up his big-time image on the streets and his bravado with his family, and decided to go back to school. Now instead of the specter of drugs and jail, his future holds a college career. He has a long way to go and the work will be hard. But you listen to Duane Smith tell his story, first haltingly and then in more detail, and you know that he will make it all the way. At sixteen, his is already a story that deserves to be told in the ghetto: a ballplayer and a man who, like Melville's Ishmael, has "looked in the face of fire" and survived to tell of it.

"My school is in Upper Brookville, Long Island, and I'm living with one of my teachers in Westbury, which is nearby. The Association of Black Athletes, which helps a lot of brothers, is paying for half of the thousand-dollar tuition. I'm working, vacuuming and cleaning up around the school, to pay the other half. That doesn't give me time to come back to Harlem, and that's the way it should be. I waited too long to get away. I don't want to come back too often."

"Why did you want to get away?" he was asked.

"Because I was getting in trouble. My mother was worried about me, and my brothers. I had put them through some terrible things and I decided it was time to do something good for them. And for myself, in the long run. Because I wasn't going nowhere in the street. I had tried everything else, so I figured it was time to give school an honest try."

"You were out of school?"

"Yeah, for about seven months—a full year, actually. I should be in my junior year now, but I'm still a sophomore because I lost that year. I left Brandeis High School, downtown. The reason I left? I was too involved in other things, things I considered more important at the time."

"Like what?"

"Like the streets. That was what I wanted. I started out going to school half a day and then splitting. Then I just wouldn't go at all. But gradually, through my brothers and whatnot, I found out that there was more to life than the streets. So I went back. I'm doing good now, too. Good in my grades and good in basketball. I've gained a lot of weight and I'm playing well. My brother Pat is a great leaper, but I got two inches on him, and I can jump even higher. The people I'm living with, they understand me, give me a place to come home to. You know, it seems to me that everything is working out all right. This is what I needed, in every way. Looking back now, I see that there's nothing out on the streets for me.

"I always did love to play ball. But I had something in the way. It took me a while to find out what was most important. Finally I said, 'If I can't do it for myself, let me do it for my mother.' It was hard, man. It was very hard. But at least I found out, finally, that the streets are nothing. Some people still aren't finding that out. Some people out there are thirty-five and forty years old and they still think that's the place to be. I'm sixteen and I'm lucky to have found out so young."

"What did you do on the streets?"

"I was involved in—you know—let's say . . . illegal doings. To be frank, that's what it was, illegal stuff. Like, I wasn't working and I wanted nice clothes and the other things the older guys had. So illegal doings was the thing to do. That's what I did."

"You didn't get caught?"

"No. I was lucky. A lot of young fellows are in the same bag, and they get caught. They're less fortunate than I was, and their lives are ruined. But I was very lucky—a year out there, twenty-four hours a day, doing the things I did and not getting caught."

"What kind of things were you doing?"

"Selling drugs. It could have got me in very big trouble. But like I said, I came through it."

"Were you on drugs yourself?"

"No. Never. My mind was always above that. Most of the sellers are like that, the ones that have got any sense. Unless they're strung out beyond help, they stay off it. They see what drugs can do. So they decide to get what they can out of the drug, without letting it destroy them. I was in that bag."

"Were there a lot of guys your age on the street with you?"

"Oh, yeah. A whole lot of them, who never will come back. Too many. They were my age, they grew up on the same block, did the same things. And like me, they figured, 'I can't do this and go to school, too,' so they dropped out. And a lot of them wound up getting hooked on the drug themselves. At this time right now,

I can go out and see them, strung out, walking around like old, old men. They're only sixteen, seventeen and they're strung out, with nothing else to do with their lives. It's really bad.

"I was fortunate to have my family behind me, to help me. Not really to help me, but to tell me, 'Oh, man, look into what you're doing. Is it worth it? Just don't do it and say it's the right thing. Have some feelings about it.' So that's when I started examining it. And I said, 'Wow, can't I do something better than this with my life? Or am I gonna do this for the rest of my life?' So I told my brother I was ready to go back to school.

"Pat got in touch with Ron Torrance, the head of the Black Athletes Association, and Ron said he could help me get back. But even then, it was hard. I hesitated. I said, 'I need this, I owe that'—giving myself reasons to stay on the street. But finally I said, 'I got to go.' And that's what I did.

"I could have stalled for one more day and lost my whole chance. Because after a while, your life is on the line. People on the streets can get jealous of a person who's doing better than they are. And if they're addicts, they can also get desperate. So pretty soon you've got to be afraid of your own people out there, as well as the police. When you know your life is on the line, you've got to make decisions. You grow up quick."

"You were fifteen when you started on the streets?"

"Fourteen and a half. I was out there for my whole fifteenth year, before I realized there had to be something better than that. I went through a lot. I'm sixteen now, and it feels like I've lived a whole life already. Not just a life. A long life."

13

"Searching for Myself": An Athlete Called Funny

THERE ARE countless city athletes on the spectrum between Earl Manigault and Duane Smith. Most of their struggles cannot be described as dramatically; their lives are shaped in subtler ways. Far-reaching choices can be made on the basis of whether a youth happens to spend an afternoon with an articulate, straight-talking college graduate like Pat Smith—or with a pusher with a smooth and enticing "rap." A life can turn on whether an impressionable teen-ager looks up to a Bob McCullough, barely making it on a schoolteacher's salary and pleading with wealthy people for the money needed to keep the Rucker Tournament alive—or to one of the charismatic personalities in the silk suits and Cadillacs along the Eighth Avenue drug pickups at dusk.

Invariably, basketball is a first step toward the right decision: the athlete has a much better chance to escape than the non-athlete. This is not meant to overemphasize the sport. A game played with a bouncing ball doesn't cure drug problems or build housing or prevent crime. But it does offer what Robert Bownes called "an elevator to better things." The elevator isn't always used and it doesn't always work properly. But Harlem athletes are glad that it is there.

Bernard McLean was a talented backcourt man but a small one, and even when he starred in uptown parks and then at Aviation

149

High School in Queens, he had no illusions about his basketball future. "People used to say to me, 'Why are you killing yourself playing ball, when you know you won't make major college ball or pro ball?' " he said. "Well, I knew I wouldn't go that far, but I also knew that basketball could finance my education. When I chose a college, I didn't choose it to become a big star. I chose it to get into something else. I got a four-year basketball scholarship to the New York Institute of Technology, and that was the start I needed. The people there got me a fellowship to graduate school at Adelphi University on Long Island. Now I have my master's in electrical engineering and a stipend to work for my PhD at City College. Without basketball, I might never have been able to afford any education. I'm sure a lot of guys who will never be big stars got the same benefit out of the game."

Few have performed as brilliantly in school as McLean, but thousands of athletes have gained enough exposure to education to get solid jobs. "Basketball scholarships have opened many doors to black athletes," said Robert Bownes. "But the game has also been very instrumental in developing young blacks psychologically. Basketball is the great criterion in the ghetto, and the man who excels at it gains a better sense of his own worth, even if he doesn't benefit in schools and jobs."

"It's a moral thing," interjected an observer named Ernest Bino. "It's much more important than money to know that you are good at something. If you know that you can go out and play fairly and win, because of your own determination and abilities, you make people appreciate and respect you, and you appreciate and respect yourself."

That self-respect is a head start, but many times it is not quite enough to keep an athlete going. Yet when men falter, Harlem athletes are reluctant to accept the standard sociological explanations. Robert Bownes echoed the sentiments of almost every athlete I spoke to: "I disagree with a lot of people who blame failures and problems on the environment. Sure, the ghetto presents many barriers. But if an individual is psychologically strong, he can overcome the barriers. If he gets some kind of incentive from his family or friends, or if he can somehow motivate himself, he can make it. It's not hopeless."

"People are made up differently," said another athlete. "Some can stand up to certain stresses and some can't. It has something to do with community surroundings, but the most important factor is the self. You've got to have self-inspiration. Take me; when I went to school and didn't do well, I could have given up. But I refused to give up. I went to prep school and corrected my problems and kept going. It happens to many athletes. You reach a crossroads, and you have to decide whether you're going to quit or keep going. It's as simple as that."

Funny Kitt is at a crossroads. Three years ago, at Benjamin Franklin High, he was generally hailed as the best high school player in the city. Athletes as good as Dean Meminger and Charley Yelverton were ranked just below him. But while Meminger and Yelverton have gone on to star at Marquette and Fordham, respectively, Funny has spent two confused years around Harlem and one unhappy year at an obscure junior college in Wyoming. Funny has never done well in school. Scores of colleges have sent out feelers toward him, only to back away when they examined his grades. So staying in school has been a struggle for him—and continuing will be just as hard. Sometimes his voice betrays a severe discouragement, almost a hopelessness; but then it fills with deep determination, a feeling that, somehow, he has to make it. It is a feverish voice, full of sudden rises and plunges; it is the voice of countless young ballplayers in his city.

Funny sat deep in a big easy chair, his legs stretched out in front of him. His wife, Linda, sat on the ledge by the open window of their small Harlem apartment. On the floor, their year-old son, Harold, Jr., scrambled between them, vying for attention. Funny had seen little of his family. He had been forced to leave them home while he played ball at Sheridan Junior College in Wyoming. Now his eyes seemed to drink them in as he talked. He had been back in Harlem for only a few days.

"In high school, people said I was the next Earl Manigault," he said. "But I knew I was never as great a player as Earl. I just shot the ball, dunked the ball, grabbed the rebounds like anybody else. I didn't want to try to match Earl. I just wanted to be myself, Funny Kitt."

"Why do people call you Funny?" he was asked.

"The way I act, the way I play, I guess. I joke around a lot, and on the court I had some moves that some people thought were pretty wild. But I don't really know what they were. I didn't think about them, you know. I just went out and did them."

Others described Funny as a superb six-foot-two-inch forward, with moves that merited comparison—if not equality—with Manigault. "But Funny has a lot to learn," said Sonny Johnson. "He'll get a five-minute spurt in which he'll kill everybody and score about 15 points, but then he'll be so tired that he'll have to sit down. He tries to do everything by himself instead of fitting in with a team. If he makes a bad pass or misses a rebound, he'll go crazy trying to make up for it. His adrenaline will drive him for five or ten minutes and he'll be sensational. But then he'll fade. Funny is definitely one of his generation's playground superstars. But he still needs to work, to develop, and to get his priorities straight."

At twenty-one, Funny is just sorting out the priorities. "In high school," he said, "I was partying, drinking wine, playing ball— doing everything but studying. In senior year it really hit me: 'When you gonna graduate?' So I worked a little more and got my high school diploma. But I still hadn't taken the courses that would get me to college, and my marks were low. I went to Newark Prep for two years to get some academic courses, and it was all right. But I was still listening to too many people and getting into too many different things. Finally I decided to accept a scholarship to Sheridan. And that was a big mistake.

"I grew up in The Bronx and lived in Harlem. I'm used to talking and socializing and playing ball with black people. And suddenly, there I was, in a town with six blacks in the whole community, all of us in the college. It was the usual story—five blacks on athletic scholarships, one African student, and that was it. I went through changes I had never dreamed of. I mean, I had never even known people like that existed. Sometimes it had me actually crying. . . ."

"You just weren't prepared for what you ran into?" asked Linda.

"Nobody from Harlem could be prepared for that. You sit all day in class listening to white teachers and then you play ball for a white coach, and you need some outlet, some social activity—and they tell you there isn't any. You're there to play ball. Period. They don't want you for anything else.

"Kids on the campus would tell me to go home. They'd say they don't need any blackies. Girls' fathers would call up the school if they even suspected that their daughters were talking to us. One night we were driving around—me, another brother from Pennsylvania, a white ballplayer from California, and a white girl who hung around with us quite a bit. Suddenly we got pulled over to the side of the road, and a guy stuck a gun in the car. It was the girl's father. He was a detective in the town, and he said he'd shoot any nigger who ever tried to ride around with his daughter again. The coach heard about it, and he warned us that we'd better stay away from that girl. Like I said, it could make you cry."

"What about basketball?"

"I know I disappointed a lot of people, because I just couldn't be another Earl. I couldn't even get my own thing together. And halfway through the season I went to a party and broke curfew, and they kicked me off the team. I thought about coming right home, but then I forced myself to stay there and finish the year. I couldn't give up a year of education. I had to get what I could out of that place. If I'd come back here, maybe I would have gotten into things and lost interest in getting ahead. I couldn't let that happen.

"Anyway, as bad as it was, Sheridan taught me a lot. I traveled to a lot of places—Colorado, Nebraska, North Dakota—and I met a lot of ballplayers, and I saw a whole new world that exists outside of Harlem. Around here, you see people who can't think or understand anything because they're on drugs. Out in Wyoming, they're not on drugs, but they might as well be, because their minds are so bigoted and twisted that they can't see you or understand you. I don't want to go back to that world. But I guess it's worth something to know it's there, to go through it.

"And the Indians—that scene was really deep. I mean, you

think that things are tough in the ghetto and you're blocked off from a lot of things, but then you see the Indians and it's just unbelievable. I had an Indian friend in school and he took me out to the reservation, a Crow reservation in Montana. My friend, Calvin—I can't pronounce his last name, a long Indian name— had been telling his people about basketball and all, and he took me out there for a couple of days. I couldn't believe what was happening to those people.

"They have programs for them, like the Urban League or other groups here, but the idea is: 'Here, Indian, take some money and get back in your cage.' In Harlem, people can at least speak up. The Indians, they're just supposed to keep quiet and drink their problems away.

"The leaders of the reservation, they're proud people and they have some political action. They police the town and they don't allow hard liquor. But many of the Indians will drink cases and cases of beer, as if they want to stay in a stupor and not face what's happening to them. Calvin showed me some new housing they were building and some improvements they were making, but I kept looking at the people and it was worse than seeing the winos or addicts here. They had some monuments and historical stuff to show me, and there was a lot of stuff about Custer— here it is 1970 and, boy, they're still talking about Custer. And that's the way the white people want them—living in the past.

"On the reservation, you can do anything you like. You don't need a license to fish, you don't need a driver's license. They more or less tell the Indian: 'Do anything you want, we'll give you a little money—just as long as you stay here.'

"I told Calvin's older brother, 'Instead of letting the government tell you what you want, why don't you tell them what you want?' He said that they were trying to get political action and all. But they got a long way to go. They really opened my eyes. They can't even live like real people out there."

As he talked, Funny had jumped up from his chair, gesturing to emphasize his feelings. For a moment he stood in the center of the room, still shaking his head over the Indians. "For a black athlete from Harlem," he concluded, "an experience like Wyoming is wild. I've talked to other blacks in other white schools, and it was the same for them. It makes you confused, it makes you cry. It can make you say, 'What am I doing? I'm going home.' But you can't give up. I won't go back to Wyoming, but I will go to some school. I'm trying to find a black school, where I can have Linda and my son with me. And somehow I will find one, because all I've gone through has just made me more determined."

After a few quiet days at home, Funny returned to the playgrounds. The moves and the ten-minute spurts of brilliance were still there, and when people watched him they couldn't refrain from the familiar comparison to Earl Manigault. Funny said that he hoped to get into Winston-Salem College, the black school that produced Earl Monroe, and his admirers felt sure that if he did get there, he would finally fulfill his potential. The presence of Linda, proud and forceful and beautiful, would undoubtedly help him. But Funny knew he would have to do most of it on his own, and he was preoccupied with finding himself.

"Sometimes I want to just play ball and say good-bye to everybody," he said. "Everybody's been around me ever since I came home, saying, 'How you doing? What happened to you?' and all that. I know they're just being friendly, but I've got to fight the urge to tell them to leave me alone. I mean, they want to hear all about me. But I don't know all about myself yet.

"Today, I was coming home and there was a guy on the stoop, and he wanted to talk. I'd seen him before, but I didn't really know him. But he wanted to know all about where I'd been and what it had been like. You'd think I went out and made a million dollars someplace, he was so interested in it."

"You've been outside Harlem," said Linda. "To a lot of people, that's very special. So they want to rap with you."

"I know. So I talked to the guy. He was kind of drunk, and I thought of cutting out on him. But he was so interested, I sat down and told him a lot of things. And before I knew it, I'd been talking to him for an hour and a half. I don't know why. Maybe after being away so long, I just like to get close to the people back here again. Or maybe I was really talking to myself, studying myself. I don't know. But it was beautiful. It was me."

Funny will probably keep searching for himself for years, and the quest may not be smooth. But he won't run away from it, any more than he ever ran from the endless challenges of starring in the parks. "I see what happened to Earl Manigault and Boobie Tucker and so many others I played with," he said. "And then I see myself. And I know that I have to keep going." He was up out of the chair again, as if physically confronting the challenge before him, the crisis that had beaten back so many young athletes. His voice rose and the words tumbled over one another. "Oh, yes, I have to make it. I look at my son here, and my wife—and I look at myself—and I know that if the opportunity's out there, I don't care where, I'm going to find it. That's one thing I know about myself now: I won't quit."

BOOK IV

The Giant Killers

14

Approaching the Playoffs

"I WON'T QUIT." Funny Kitt's phrase echoes through all levels of city basketball, a part of the game as real as the moves to the basket or the jostling for position under the boards. In describing sports, a word like "determination" is so overused that it becomes a cliché. But when you see the differences between the Earl Manigaults and Duane Smiths and Funny Kitts, the word takes on a genuine significance. Determination is an integral part of the game on every level. It decides who makes it out of the ghetto and it often decides which of two almost equally skilled teams wins an important pro game. But it remains an elusive quality, far easier to demonstrate than to define. And the Knicks last year provided a remarkable demonstration in the championship playoffs.

The Knicks' rise to the top of basketball in the first part of the season could be recounted in terms of artistry and superior performances; but the playoffs brought out the inner elements of the club's personality. If the regular-season story was one of physical excellence, the playoffs probed deeper. In three short series against three dangerous—and very different—rivals, the Knicks could not win on talent alone. Playing with the haunting knowledge that a playoff defeat would dull a lot of the glitter of their lavishly praised season, they encountered superb opponents, some shocking setbacks, and finally the crushing injury to Willis Reed. Yet they

rose to the challenges, and every frantic fan in Madison Square
Garden was wrapped up in their victory. The intense communal
experience of the season was only multiplied by the playoff pressures, and on the May night when it reached its climax, one man's
voice boomed out of the balcony and seemed to sum up the
Knicks and their fans and an entire city of basketball players.
Pounding his heart, the man yelled over and over: "They got it
in here."

Not surprisingly, the final months of the regular season seemed
somewhat anticlimactic, a lull before the explosive climax of the
playoffs. The Milwaukee Bucks injected some vague suspense into
the Eastern Division race by playing extremely well over the last
part of the season; in fact, the Bucks, with Alcindor improving constantly, outplayed the Knicks from the end of the New York
winning streak until the finish of the season. The Bucks were
43–16 over that span and the Knicks 37–21. The Knicks' early
lead was insurmountable, however, and they always played just
well enough to keep the Bucks at bay; so Milwaukee's efforts contributed little real tension to the race—but, like almost everything
else that happened late in the season, they added considerably
to the feeling that the Knicks might be beaten in the playoffs.

Bradley's ankle injury slowed the New York attack during the
closing stretch, and Frazier also missed a few games, including one
ignominious rout by the Bucks at the Garden. But again, the
injuries were less damaging physically then psychologically. They
only served as a reminder that the Knicks had been incredibly
lucky all year in escaping serious ailments—and that the percent-
ages could even out in the playoffs.

As the players themselves had often cautioned, no team can
stay mentally on edge for eighty-two games, many of them virtually meaningless. So the Knicks seemed to level off, giving their
fans an occasional Saturday night of excellence in the Garden,
recalling just how sensational they could be—but also playing
enough uninspired games to shut off the torrent of "greatest of
all time" quotes that had poured out through the early part of
the season. The weaker performances were explainable in terms of

injuries or a letdown, but they also contributed to an uneasy suspicion that disaster could strike in the playoffs. "Sure it's been a great year," said Mike Riordan, speaking for many of the Knicks, "but if we can't do it all over again in the playoffs, what will it mean?"

The Knicks clinched the division title on March 14 in San Diego, but the feat provoked no outbursts of glee. In fact, they had been expected to do it the night before in Portland, against the weak Seattle Supersonics; champagne had been stocked for a party, but the Knicks had lost the game. So when the victory did come, there was no champagne and minimal exuberance. "The real celebration," said Reed, "will have to wait for the playoffs." The following night the Knicks lost again, in Los Angeles, and even more New Yorkers, understandably cynical after twenty-four years without a title, harbored doubts about their heroes.

In a final ironic twist, the media that had helped create the Knicks seemed to work against them as the playoffs approached. The television specials and magazine cover stories had ceased shortly after midseason; then the American Broadcasting Company began its series of Sunday NBA telecasts, hoping to give viewers the super team they had heard about, live and in color. In fact, the network crowded as many Knick appearances as possible into its schedule—only to have the Knicks respond with a strange Sunday-afternoon slump. In a half dozen television appearances, the Knicks managed to look anything but super; they pulled off only one victory, and presumably left Middle America convinced that they had been a vicious figment of the New York–Washington media axis' imagination.

In addition, players around the league had ample time to contemplate the Knicks' love affair with the media. Like stars on the playgrounds, the Knicks had been elevated so high that all their rivals knew that they could gain instant recognition by beating them. "There's no doubt that all the publicity we've gotten antagonized other teams," said Dave DeBusschere. "An athlete has his vanity, and a lot of guys will want to kick the hell out of us. We've done a great deal for the sport, we've given it new national awareness. But the other teams will be out to get us."

"I'm very happy for the Knicks," said Earl Monroe of Baltimore, referring wryly to a widely used Knick television commercial. "If they want to use Vitalis, let them use Vitalis. I hope they get everything that's coming to them."

Monroe and the rest of the Bullets had particular cause for sarcasm. A year earlier, they had won the Eastern Division race themselves, inspiring hardly a ripple of national media attention or endorsement money. Then the Knicks had trounced them in four straight playoff games and they had dropped quietly from sight. Even while they played very well to finish third in the division last year, the Bullets were known best for their principal negative distinction: they had an uncanny talent for losing to the Knicks. They had followed their playoff debacle by losing five of six regular-season games to New York, salvaging only one—on Sunday-afternoon television, of course—in the final weeks against a tired and ailing group of Knicks.

In New York, writers and fans liked to joke about Baltimore's propensity for bowing to New York teams. The Baltimore Colts had succumbed to the New York Jets in the most shocking of Super Bowls, the Orioles had been the foil for the incredible Mets in the World Series, and the Bullets seemed capable of defeat by the Knicks in any setting. The quips were repeated endlessly, and Knick fans came to think of the Bullets as helpless, star-crossed victims. But Monroe, Wes Unseld, Gus Johnson, and the other Bullets were proud and talented athletes in their own right, and every clever New York sally cut deeply into them. "We just can't let it keep happening," said Baltimore guard Kevin Loughery. "They're a good team but so are we. We've lived with this thing long enough. Now we've got to do something about it." The first 1970 playoff series gave the Bullets their long-awaited chance.

15

The Baltimore Scare

JACK PRICE stood next to one of the high round tables that surround the bar at Harry M's, the restaurant under Madison Square Garden, sipping beer from a goblet. Alternately he looked at the wall clock and then peered over the heads of the crowd toward the door. His hand went into his inside jacket pocket and he fingered a sheaf of courtside tickets. Price was the Garden executive in charge of the Knicks' television and radio networks, among other things. A dour man, he seemed even more annoyed than usual; several of the chosen friends to whom he had offered the precious tickets were late, and Price was not about to miss the tip-off he and the other Knick regulars had been awaiting for months.

This was the night of March 26, 1970, when the team would take on the Bullets and begin its drive to its first championship. Diehard Knick devotees clustered in Gallagher's 33 and Spats and the other bars around the Garden. And as the opening game neared, they were unusually edgy, irked by the elbows and noise of the twice-a-year dilettantes who thronged around them, frustrated by the fact that so many cherished $12.50 tickets had slipped away from other deserving regulars to the expense-account set. The nervousness of the evening was summed up in every frown and shrug that greeted headwaiter Tony Triola in Harry M's as he confronted friends with the familiar query, "Got any extras?" In the agonizing hour before the seven-thirty starting time, it was impossible to escape the haunting suspicion that had built up over the months of waiting—the fear that everything the Knicks had accomplished could be lost so quickly in the playoffs.

The crowd inside the Garden wasn't the astute New York gathering that senses the nuances and patterns. It yowled wildly when the Knicks were introduced and booed the Bullet starters, and then it commenced to cheer every pass and every play, no matter how sloppy or simple. It was too similar to the groups that assemble annually for the opening game of baseball's World Series, full of men who know that the game is the place to be and have the influence to make sure they get there. Many of the long-suffering, knowledgeable Knick followers were also on hand, from the kids in the balcony down to the season-ticket holders in the courtside and loge sections. But in the early minutes they were drowned out by the novices, who failed to sense the sluggishness of the Knick attack and kept screaming madly for two full minutes while the Bullets burst to a 12–2 lead. Was this the way it would end, with Earl Monroe stealing the ball and Jack Marin scoring from outside and half the crowd unaware of what was happening? The seconds raced by and the Knicks kept missing shots, and the noise was ironic, discomfiting.

Then the old pro, Barnett, restored order. Slipping gracefully away from Monroe, Dick found himself open in the corner, took a pass from Frazier and scored. Seconds later he faked toward the corner and drove up the middle to score again. The Knicks regained their composure and the crowd seemed to find its sense of perspective, mixing lulls with shouts of appreciation as the home team began to click. Quickly the Knicks ran off a 12–1 burst of their own, to take the lead, 14–13.

For a moment one suspected that the Bullets had spent their fury in the first two minutes, managing only one headlong dash from the starting gate before recalling that they were supposed to be helpless against New York. But this was a new Baltimore team, one that New Yorkers had not seen all year. Instead of their usual concentration on individual feats, they were playing a team defense as tight and aggressive as that of the Knicks. Their offense was as awesome as ever. And they refused to become panicky or discouraged in the face of Knick rallies, retaliating with spurts of their own.

"All year we watched the Knicks generate their offense with bold defense," explained Marin. "We finally realized that to beat them, we'd have to do the same thing."

"We sat down in a team meeting and figured out that we'd all get our own points," said Monroe, "and our big job was to cut down the Knicks' scoring."

"If there was a special team meeting," said Gus Johnson, "I wasn't at it. But we didn't need any meeting. Our coach, Gene Shue, taught the right defensive theories long ago—overplaying your man, helping out, double-teaming the ball—and they helped take us to the Eastern Division title last year. Lately we just stopped doing those things. And if we were going to win the playoffs, we knew we'd have to start doing them again."

With the Bullets playing so astonishingly well, the first game became a microcosm of the entire series: two evenly matched teams performing superbly and then poorly—with the result in constant doubt. New York fans were left in a state of tortured apprehension. It soon became clear that the Knicks could not rout the Bullets simply by outplaying them, as they had done all season; the Knicks would need all the toughness and togetherness that had driven through their early-season successes.

Near the end of the first half, with Reed taking a brief rest, the Bullets gained the upper hand. At half time they led, 52–46, and one hardened New York fan had visions of past Knick failures as well as last spring's monumental collapse by the city's hockey team, the Rangers. Undoubtedly speaking for many others, the cynic leaned over the entrance to the dressing-room corridor as the Knicks filed off the court, bellowing the phrase that Bill Bradley would later recall with a smile: "I knew it. When it counts, you guys turn out just like the Rangers."

Most fans were less discouraged. All season long, half time had been a reassuring interlude for them; they all knew that the third period would belong to the Knicks. Vintage New York performances had often fit into a pattern: a fast start, a slight letdown near the end of the first half, and then a third-period explosion that broke the game apart. The pattern could be explained in part by Holzman's employment of substitutes. Late in the first half he almost invariably rested Reed; all the other starters enjoyed even longer second-period breathers. So after half time, the starting five would be refreshed and ready, while their rivals, without benefit of such talented replacements, might be exhausted. But whatever the logic behind the Knicks' third-period superiority, many fans came to think of it as an occult phenomenon.

Against the Bullets that phenomenon was far more physical than mystical; the Knicks dominated the third period with sheer hard work. Typically, DeBusschere was the leader of the drive, shoving his way around Johnson for important rebounds, then flashing away from Gus to block several shots by Marin. Picking up the beat, all the Knicks began hustling, moving, forcing Baltimore into mistakes. After trailing by 6 at the half, they led by 3 going into the final quarter.

But they still had to reckon with Monroe. Bobbing, jerking, gyrating, Earl the Pearl captured the Garden as if it were one more South Philadelphia playground. Some of his moves were too subtle for the uninitiated in the crowd to comprehend, and only the aficionados responded with applause or groans of fear. Other shots were so miraculous that the entire audience was left gasping. With the outcome riding on every shot, Monroe scored the Bullets' last 8 points in the fourth quarter—but Frazier distracted him into missing the final try that could have won the game. Monroe had staged the ultimate individual show, but the teams were still tied at the finish.

After four minutes of the first five-minute overtime, the Bullets led by 3 points. Reed, wide open, missed a short-range jumper. The Bullets brought the ball up, and Kevin Loughery shook free for a twenty-footer that could have virtually clinched it. It was the kind of shot around which the steady, competitive Loughery had built an eight-year career. But this time, Kevin was playing with a heavy brace protecting the four cracked ribs and collapsed lung he had suffered a month earlier in a collision with Lew Alcindor. The brace had enabled him to get back into action far sooner than anyone had dared expect; but it also hampered his delicate shooting touch. His shot missed, and the victory slipped away, as had so many Baltimore games against New York.

The Knicks tied the score again with twenty-three seconds left, and Monroe brought the ball up against Frazier. Clyde slapped it away and Barnett drove for the winning lay-up—only to have it blocked with a prodigious leap by Fred Carter. To almost everyone in the Garden, it appeared that Carter had slapped the ball on its way down toward the hoop—an act of illegal goal tending that, if called by the official, would have given the Knicks the basket and the victory. But officials Ed Rush and Mendy Rudolph didn't call the infraction. The game was sent into a second overtime. And the Knicks and their fans were driven into a frenzy.

The controversial call welded the disparate crowd into a unified one, with the casual observers joining the Garden veterans in the clamorous outpouring of venom—"Mendy is a bum"—and the pleas for swift retribution—"Let's go, Knicks." The entire second overtime was played in a sustained din. In the stands, several of Bradley's friends from Italy looked at one another with expressions of wonder. Having watched Bill capture many Italian crowds when he played weekend games for Simmenthal of Milan during his Oxford days, they had assumed that those Italian crowds had scaled a peak of noisy devotion. "But those last five minutes tonight," they told Bradley afterward, "were beyond anything we ever imagined."

"A disputed call like that," said Bradley, "whatever its merits, can have a tremendous effect on the way a game is being played. It turned on the crowd, and it forced us to reach back and find something more to give." Responding immediately, the Knicks reeled off 5 straight points. Again the Bullets fought back, getting within 2. But Monroe and Wes Unseld missed desperate shots in the final seconds, and after fifty-eight frantic minutes of play, the Knicks escaped with a 120–117 triumph.

"Yes," said Red Holzman, answering a question laconically, "I thought it was an exciting game."

The opener had indeed been a preview. The Knicks and Bullets were two exceptional basketball clubs, quite similar in age and talent, different in offensive styles but, at their best, equally devoted to aggressive team defense. Their confrontation was both pyrotechnic and unpredictable, with games hinging on spectacular shots as well as crafty maneuvers under the boards. With the clubs so even, the officials sometimes played a disproportionate role: the lack of a goal-tending call on Carter was one example, and the adjudication of fouls was critical in the nightly wars between DeBusschere and Johnson. But the most crucial single factor, it developed, was the advantage the Knicks had earned by winning the division title—the home-court edge in the seventh and final game.

Early in the series, however, there was hardly any reason to expect it to last seven games. After the opener, Gus Johnson spoke bravely about the end of the Knick mastery over Baltimore: "I thought the Knicks played a little scared out there. They know we can beat them now." But another question lingered over the subdued Bullet locker room. Did the Bullets themselves believe they could beat the Knicks? After all, they had played as well as they could have hoped. Monroe had been incomparable, Unseld had outrebounded Reed, and the entire club had executed what DeBusschere called "the best team defense I've ever seen Baltimore play." Yet after two overtimes, they still had lost. "You do begin to wonder," Loughery said quietly, "what we have to do to beat these guys."

Two nights later Baltimore had more cause for despair. Playing at home, the Bullets led by 6 points entering the final period. Then it all caved in around them once more. Mike Riordan, in the game mainly to defend against Monroe, erupted with 11 points in the fourth quarter, and New York drew out to a 99–93 lead. Then the Knicks wrapped it up on a bizarre series of plays that left the Bullets shell-shocked.

The Knicks had the ball, with their allotted twenty-four-second time limit running out; if they didn't hit the backboard or rim with a shot within seconds, the ball would be turned over to Baltimore. Deep in the corner near the baseline, Bradley took a desperate shot; it hit the side of the board. The Bullets didn't seem to think that hitting the side of the board constituted a legitimate shot. They looked toward the refs, expecting to be awarded the ball; the reserves jumped up along their bench. But the rule specified that the ball needed only to touch any part of the boards. So the officials signaled for play to continue, the twenty-four-second clock was reset—and in the confusion Bradley grabbed his own rebound.

Bill killed more valuable time, then hurled another wild shot that missed the rim completely. Unseld had secured position under the basket. He went up to snare the ball and ignite a fast break that might bring the Bullets back to within four. But somehow DeBusschere leaped from behind Unseld and slapped the ball to Reed—who stuffed it triumphantly to extend the lead to eight points and clinch the 106–99 victory.

Again the Bullets had played well, and lost. Johnson found it more difficult to sound confident. "For three quarters we kick the hell out of them," he muttered, "and then . . ."

"I'm tired," snapped Marin, "of this 'Mission Impossible' script."

The fans may have believed in such a script, but the Knicks themselves were wary. At the height of the celebration after the opener, Bradley had injected a cautious note—and one that took on increased meaning with every game of the series. "The playoffs are an incredible psychological exercise," he said. "The important thing is not to let any one game seem too big, too climactic— because we've got to come back to the same pitch twelve times if we're going to win the championship."

In the third game, on a snowy Easter Sunday in New York, the Knicks lost their pitch. They stayed even with the Bullets for a half, then crumbled. Their shooting was cold, their ball handling slovenly; and they all seemed glued to the Garden floor, watching Unseld, high above them, take complete control of the boards and the game.

Unseld, a hulking man with a broad, almost gloomy countenance and a subdued manner, was an ideal counterpoint to the Bullets' flashier stars, Monroe and Johnson. At six feet seven, he was the shortest center in the league, but he was also one of the strongest. Like DeBusschere, he was "tall" for his height; an awesome power

was coiled in his redwood legs, and he always seemed to be in
perfect position under the boards. Arriving as a rookie from Louis-
ville in 1968–69, he had been an even more dramatic catalyst for
Baltimore than DeBusschere had been for New York. With
Unseld securing rebounds and releasing accurate outlet passes to
acknowledged scoring threats like Monroe, the Bullets had raced
from last place to first—and Wes had become the second man ever
to win both Rookie of the Year and Most Valuable Player honors
in the same season. (Wilt Chamberlain had been the first, in 1960.)

Last year Reed had overshadowed him, but Unseld had remained solid, scoring modestly but finishing a close second to
San Diego's Elvin Hayes in NBA rebounding. In that third game,
he reminded Knick fans just how good he could be: his thirty-
four rebounds surpassed the total of thirty managed by the entire
New York team. That imbalance made the result inevitable. The
Bullets led by as many 21 in the fourth period and breezed to
a 127–113 victory—as sound a thrashing as the Knicks had
suffered all season in the Garden.

The game seemed to have a profound effect on Baltimore. The
Bullets had shown both fans and opponents that they could
handle New York; and they had convinced themselves. Returning
jauntily to Baltimore, they promptly dismantled the Knicks again,
102–92. "I was so elated," said Johnson, "that I wanted to jump
on somebody's shoulders. I'm a grown man, thirty-one years old,
and basketball stopped being fun for me a long time ago. But
tonight it was more fun than ever."

The fans of that dreary city were equally manic. Baltimore's
Civic Center is an informal arena, an all-purpose theaterlike
auditorium that offers cotton candy and pizza at small concession
counters and Dixieland music between periods—as if to compensate the patrons for their abysmally poor view of the game. A
low-slung, sprawling structure far longer than the court itself,
the Civic Center has many seats at angles distant from the action.
Because of those angles, the noise seldom batters the court as it
does in most arenas. Instead it seems to filter down in disjointed
cries and cheers; and in that fourth game, the cries reflected all
the pent-up frustration of a year and a half of snide jokes by

New Yorkers about Baltimore teams. "Who the hell are the Knicks?" they shouted. "Earl the Pearl is king of the world."

At first there seemed to be a desperation in the cries. Even as the Bullets pulled away, drubbing the Knicks completely, the crowd seemed unready to believe it. In fact, when the Knicks staged two futile spurts near the finish, wiping out big deficits and getting within six points, the fans howled with fear. But each time the lead narrowed, Monroe would go into the most effective time-killing ritual in basketball, simply dribbling the ball in his high, jaunty style for twenty-two or twenty-three seconds, while defender Riordan slapped at him, climbed on him—and still couldn't stop him. Then, with the twenty-four-second clock running out, the Pearl would rise suddenly, nonchalantly, not even bothering to look at his target. And he would score, frustrating Riordan and keeping the Knicks at arm's length.

Finally it began to sink in among the fans. This was a Baltimore team that was actually humiliating a New York team. The individual shouts merged into chants: first, "Whirl, whirl, you Pearl," then, inevitably, "We're Number One." At the finish, the Civic Center was drowned in full-throated ovation for the local heroes. "These fans have never shown the enthusiasm they did tonight," said Loughery, a New Yorker who played at St. John's and knew how cheering was supposed to sound. "That 'We're Number One' sounded great."

In New York, the Knicks no longer looked like strong favorites. And the bars and newspapers of the city were echoing with the nagging question: "What's wrong with the Knicks?"

The real question should have been: "What's right with the Bullets?" Why had they stopped playing the tentative, almost respectful basketball that had made them such easy marks during the season? How were they outhustling and outrunning the vaunted Knicks, breaking up the New York patterns and dictating the pace of the game? "We're working harder than ever before," answered Unseld simply. "We're playing desperation basketball."

Holzman accepted the turnabout matter-of-factly: "They're a very good ball club. This shouldn't surprise anyone." But the

Bullets were unquestionably a surprise. Nobody could have been shocked at the genius of Monroe, the rebounding of Unseld, the multiple skills of Johnson, or the uncanny shooting of Marin. But those ingredients had been there all along; the unforeseen elements were the performances of rookie Fred Carter and the taped-up Loughery—as well as the Bullets' newfound willingness to sacrifice themselves to their team.

Carter, twenty-four, was the major revelation of the series. During the regular season he hadn't seen much action until two higher ranked guards, Loughery and Mike Davis, had been injured; he had averaged only 5 points a game. In the playoffs, he averaged 14, defended admirably against Frazier—and infused energy and exuberance into the entire team. Like Monroe, Carter was a product of the Philadelphia parks, and he treated the playoffs as if they were a high-class series of pickup games. Postseason pressure games are supposed to humble mere rookies; they brought out the best in Carter, who had played college ball at tiny Mount St. Mary's, in Emmitsburg, Maryland. "I love it," he said. "I love to go into the Garden before all those people, and hear the silence come over the crowd when we've got the Knicks whipped."

Carter easily led both teams in diving to the floor after loose balls. Observing his reckless defensive play in training camp, his teammates had named him Mad Dog—and he was justifying the epithet with every frenetic performance. Cocky and outspoken, he bragged openly about how he was exhausting the older Barnett with his offensive running, while cutting down Frazier's assists with his defense. And he was making good on his boasts.

Loughery was even more remarkable. Fighting for a rebound on February 25 in Milwaukee, he had been smashed by the knee of the high-flying Alcindor. When his friends heard that his lung had collapsed, they understandably feared for his career; but Kevin worried only about recovering for the playoffs. Then, when his heavy brace hindered him, he removed it early in the third game. "It was strictly my own decision," he admitted. "If I had asked my wife or my mother, they might have disagreed. But I was sick and tired of what the Knicks were doing to us. I had to try something."

It was a high-stakes gamble. A month before there had been a plastic tube in his right lung and his ribs had been slowly knitting back into place; now he was exposing them to the prospect of another collision. Loughery tried to play down the danger. "A collapsed lung isn't as serious as it sounds. The only way it could be really serious is if it kept recurring. . . ."

"Aren't you worried about it recurring if you get hit while you're not wearing the brace?" he was asked.

"Well . . ." Loughery hesitated, then spoke softly. "I guess if I took one direct shot, it could be all over."

Like rookie Carter, the veteran Loughery was supplying much more than solid play to the Bullets. With their enthusiasm and courage, the two men were important additions to a team bent on "desperation basketball."

After the fourth game a reporter offered Holzman the truism: "Well, it all comes down to a two-out-of-three series now."

"I guess so," deadpanned the coach. "I thought it was three out of five, but somebody straightened me out."

"What will you do with the team now?" another writer persisted.

"I guess our first worry," said Holzman, "is to make sure we catch the plane in the morning."

Behind the bland façade, however, the coach was planning some tactical changes. He would have been the first to emphasize that two losses don't force you to shake up a combination that has succeeded all season. On the other hand, the Knicks were being outplayed in the series; they had barely escaped with their two victories and been severely battered in their two defeats. Their 92 points in the fourth game represented a nadir for the entire season; something had to be done to break loose from the tenacious Baltimore defenders.

Problems abounded almost everywhere. Reed, plagued by nagging knee problems, was not shooting well, and he was failing to challenge Unseld enough to keep Wes off balance and detract from his superb rebounding at both ends of the court. Bradley and Barnett were not contributing their requisite bursts of outside shooting. Bradley, in particular, had been all but eliminated from the action in the two losses as Jack Marin tracked his every step and nullified Bill's efforts to twist free for open shots. The rugged Johnson had also slowed down DeBusschere's offense at times; in the fourth game, all the Knick forwards, including reserves, had combined for only 33 points on a pitiful shooting average of 30 percent.

But the key was Frazier, who was supposed to hit the open man and set up the plays. Clyde was scoring well in the series, but the Knicks weren't. Holzman decided to reverse that formula. He told Frazier to forget about scoring in the fifth game, and devote himself exclusively to stopping Monroe and feeding the other Knicks. "I felt that I had been moving and shooting well," said Frazier. "But we weren't winning. So if the man wanted to switch things around, it was okay with me." At a team meeting, Holzman made another suggestion: "Let's get the ball into the forecourt faster and give ourselves more time to move around and get free."

"That was an important adjustment," said DeBusschere. "When we run, Bill and I can get open. When we don't have to play one-on-one against Gus and Marin all the time, it makes things a lot simpler."

Finally Reed, ignoring the pain in his legs and quietly gathering himself and his teammates for a massive effort, said, "If the unity and closeness of this club is ever going to pay off, it's now. This is our moment of truth."

It turned out to be Willis' finest hour. Offensively he overwhelmed Unseld, scoring 36 points; he also set a Knick record with 36 rebounds and anchored an impregnable defense. The other Knicks followed the captain's example. DeBusschere held Johnson to only one basket in fourteen tries. Bradley, at last managing to elude Marin with consistency, scored with his first five shots. Barnett smashed any illusions Carter had about wearing him down, smothering the rookie completely and eventually driving him to the bench. And Frazier, following his orders to forget about scoring, limited Monroe to 18 points, sparked the offense with his perfect passes—and even crashed to the boards for sixteen rebounds. The Knicks were erratic in their shooting, but their defense won for them, 101–80. To the chanting, stomping fans, the Knicks were back in early-season form. "What do you know?" said Barnett after the game. "We finally stopped all that standing around."

The time seemed propitious for a quiet Baltimore collapse, a recognition that, for all their efforts, they couldn't handle New York. The Bullets, however, refused to concede. "I have just played the worst game of my life, including high school," said Johnson. "Now I've got to do something about it."

"It's impossible," said Monroe, "for any team to play that kind of defense against us twice in a row. The sixth game will be different."

It began very similarly. The Bullets had been held to 11 points in the final period of the fifth game; they added only 15 in the opening quarter of the sixth. But the Knicks were unable to take advantage of the Baltimore mistakes. Although Monroe and Johnson were ice cold, New York led by only 43–41 at the half. The half had been sloppy on both sides; the crowd was tense and restless. There was a sense of an impending explosion: "Gus and the Pearl," shouted one Baltimore fan, "never stay this cold for a whole game."

The shout was prophetic. Johnson made the first three shots of the half, boldly challenging DeBusschere, who had already drawn four personal fouls. Then Monroe scored 5 quick points, and the Bullets had a lead they never surrendered. DeBusschere, in danger of fouling out with six personals, was replaced by Stallworth for long stretches; Bradley, thoroughly contained by Marin, was also benched in favor of Cazzie Russell. Stallworth amassed 16 points with some fine one-on-one moves, but he was no match for Johnson's offense, and Gus hit on nine of eleven shots in the half. Cazzie and Mike Riordan also were first-rate, but they couldn't compensate for the strangely lethargic performance of the starters. Once more the Knicks had misplaced their rhythm and teamwork, forcing themselves to play one-on-one against Johnson and Monroe—a hopeless task. The Bullets won, 96–87, as the Knick offense sank to another new depth in point production.

There was a thick silence in the New York locker room. On the threshold of a major victory, the Knicks had played one of their most inept games, and they were puzzled and annoyed. DeBusschere, who had been in action only twenty-four minutes and scored all of 4 points, seemed most distressed. Someone approached him and asked what Johnson had done in the second half.

"He made his shots," snapped Dave. "Anyway, I was on the bench watching most of the time."

"Would you have liked to play more?"

"Yes. I thought I could have helped if I'd been in there more."

Frazier also had criticism for Holzman. "If we'd send Monroe down the middle more," he said, "we could surround him better and stop him. But Red wants us to send him to the outside. And Earl's killing us from there." With things going poorly, the formulas that had worked all season were open to question. But there was little time to search for answers. It was late Sunday afternoon. On Monday night in New York, the seventh game would begin. And the season might end.

The players dressed very slowly, avoiding conversation. Then they walked out through a corridor full of kids, signing a few autographs, brushing others aside. The bus to the airport was parked at the wrong side of the building. Waiting for someone to bring it around, the Knicks stood in a cluster on the deserted sidewalk. "Well, this is it," Barnett said to Reed. "Tomorrow night it all hits the fan."

Hours before the seventh game, Holzman was asked if he was worried. "I'm always worried," he said.

"More than usual tonight?"

"I try to keep my worrying on an even keel."

Frazier admitted to being more keyed up. "I tried to eat and dropped the fork, the salt, everything. I had bad hands with the food. And during warmups I couldn't come near the hoop. But I told myself that it didn't matter. I wasn't going to be shooting much anyway. My job was defense."

On a blackboard in the locker room, somebody had scrawled: "How bad do you want it?" Dick McGuire, the chief scout, erased it. "They're high enough," he said. And, indeed, the players needed no chalked slogans for this game. "There were reminders everywhere of what was at stake," said DeBusschere. "But if you're a professional, you don't need reminders."

Then the Knicks demonstrated how thoroughly professional they could be; in their most important game, they came up with their finest all-around effort. In their defeats, they had allowed the Bullets to set the pace by running and going one-on-one on them. This time the Knicks seized the initiative. Barnett and De-Busschere consistently challenged their defenders with daring drives to the hoop; each scored 28 points. Russell, who had suffered through a mediocre series due to leg troubles, came off the bench to add offensive power. And Frazier did it all, scoring on seven of ten shots and picking up ten rebounds and eight assists. The Knicks led by 15 at the half and rolled to a 127–114 triumph. The crowd seemed to breathe a vast sigh of relief.

"We're not normally a one-on-one team," explained DeBusschere, "but tonight we caught them by surprise. We'd been playing too casually, waiting for things to happen. Tonight we wanted to dominate the action from the start. And we proved that we could do it."

Frazier sat on his stool, studying the statistic sheet with a smile. "It was the first time we really exploded," he said. "I was thinking about it today. We had this team down 2–0 and let them off the hook. If great champions like the old Celtics had a team down 2–0, they put them away. But we didn't have that championship toughness, and we let the Bullets come back. Then it came down to one game, and we reacted—and I think that shows that we're developing a toughness. The next time we get a team down, we'll finish them off."

Bill Bradley, surrounded by well-wishers, put the victory in another perspective. "Last year, when we were eliminated from the playoffs, I said to myself, 'I wish there could be some more basketball this year. It's sad to see it end.' I thought of that tonight. I wanted some more basketball, and so did all those fans. Now we'll all get some more. That's a good feeling."

16

The Bucks: Holding Off the Future

LEW ALCINDOR was fourteen years old and six feet eight inches tall when he first leaped toward a ten-foot-high hoop, moving with only a hint of the grace he would later acquire, and exultantly dunked a basketball. The gangling, awkward teen-ager, his body fully extended against the dim background of his small grade-school gymnasium in Manhattan, cast a shadow over the entire future of basketball.

As Alcindor developed and grew remarkably agile, his shadow enveloped seventy-one consecutive opponents of New York's Power Memorial High School, where Lew grew to seven feet and towered over all high school competition. Later, as he added depth and finesse to his skills, the shadow would frustrate all pretenders to the college championship; Alcindor and UCLA won three straight NCAA titles. And inevitably, the shadow would loom over the pro game, threatening to alter drastically the balance of power in the NBA for years to come.

As rookie Alcindor led the Milwaukee Bucks from last place into second in the Eastern Division last year, the only question about his future seemed to concern timing: Would he win the championship immediately, or allow the Knicks or another club one more season at the top? Actually, it was grossly unfair to expect Alcindor to transform the young, erratic Bucks into instant champions. But as the season progressed and both Alcindor and the Bucks improved, the big man brought the questions on himself. Offensively, he was comparable to Wilt Chamberlain in his early, record-shattering years with Philadelphia; defensively, he still lacked the cunning tactics of Bill Russell, but at seven feet two or more, he was so much bigger than the six-foot-ten-inch Russell that he was able to show flashes of the intimidating defense of the Celtic center. And though Lew was only a rookie, he had an enormous dignity that made him a magnetic, dominant figure on and off the court—a man who, much like Russell, projected the sense that he could accomplish the impossible.

While the Knicks had been clawing their way past Baltimore, the Bucks had made short shrift of the diehard Philadelphia 76ers. The young Bucks stifled their more experienced opponents in five games, and set an NBA playoff record by pouring in 156 points on one of their triumphs. Responding to his first playoff pressures, Alcindor had shot even more accurately than during the regular season. So the fears that had been generated in New York by the narrow squeak against the Bullets only magnified when the Bucks arrived for the opening game of the next series —and the Knicks' own giant, Reed, walked out to stand in Alcindor's shadow and peer up at a rival who appeared at least a head taller.

The Knicks, however, seemed more relaxed than they had been against the Bullets. They had a game plan ready for the Bucks. It was no secret that Reed alone could not harness Alcindor, and that if he tried, he might get into foul trouble and place the entire team in peril. But his teammates had no intention of leaving him alone in the middle. In fact, they were prepared to slack off their own men even more than usual to aid Willis. They were willing to gamble that Alcindor's supporting cast would be unable to capitalize on the situation, because, as Frazier put it, "They're a rookie team. And in the playoffs, rookie teams make mistakes."

The gamble paid off, and the scheme for the series was established early in the first game. Bradley was defending against Greg Smith, a fleet second-year man who lacked a strong shot; Frazier was assigned to Flynn Robinson, a streak-shooting guard who found himself mired in one of his most frustrating phases of ineffectiveness. So both Knicks felt free to leave their positions and collapse around Alcindor, slapping and grabbing at any pass in his direction or any dribble he dared to make. DeBusschere, meanwhile, emphasized rebounding, leaving Reed free to concentrate almost totally on defending against Lew.

Reed showed up for the opener with a day's growth of beard, looking like a prizefighter entering the ring. He explained that he had simply slept late, allowing no time to shave; but somehow his truculent appearance seemed apropos. Willis knew that he could not expect to leap or score on a par with Lew, but he could certainly force Alcindor to struggle for every point and rebound, while the rest of the Knicks took care of the other Bucks. "You don't stop a man like Lew," Willis said. "You just keep him busy. And we have the ideal kind of defense to accomplish that."

The Knicks maintained constant pressure on Alcindor. They stole countless passes intended for him, and they batted the ball from his hands several times. Reed always seemed to have a massive leg planted in Alcindor's path to the hoop, and he shoved and elbowed the bigger man as much as the rules would allow. Alcindor remained superb, spinning off Willis or leaping over him to hit with fourteen of twenty-four tries for a total of 35 points. But as the game wore on he appeared increasingly isolated, a stag circled by snapping dogs, forced to fight the entire battle alone.

"Lew did one thing wrong," said Frazier. "He put the ball on the floor and gave us a chance to take it away. If he keeps the ball above his head, we can triple-team him all day and we'll never touch it. He should have held it high and waited for an open man to clear so he could pass to him."

"He hit the open man very well," corrected Reed. "But what good did it do him?"

None at all. One hot outside shooter might have disrupted the New York defensive plan and opened up the middle for Alcindor. But the Bucks offered no one. Flynn Robinson hurled sixteen shots at the basket and made only four. Freddie Crawford was three for thirteen, Jon McGlocklin four for nine. So Alcindor's passes produced only scattered baskets by his teammates, and inexorably the Knicks pulled away. With Cazzie Russell coming off the bench to spark the rally that broke it open, they led by as much as 14 points and coasted to a 110–102 decision.

After the game, the specter of Alcindor seemed less forbidding. The Knicks had provided a solid team effort; six men had scored in double figures while Frazier had troubled to notch only 6 while he concentrated on decimating the Milwaukee offense. And after facing Baltimore's balanced team, the Knicks had appeared far more at home subduing what amounted to a one-man challenge. "You can never underestimate Lew," cautioned Reed. "On a given night he can kill anyone. But our team is one of the best suited to play against him. Our team defense can bother him, and on offense we don't drive much, so we aren't too intimidated by his shot-blocking ability."

"You're becoming one of the foremost authorities on him," Reed was told.

"I may be an authority, but that doesn't mean I can stop him."

In the second game, also in New York, Alcindor put Reed to the supreme test. For the greater part of his career in organized ball, Lew was so superior to most rivals that occasionally he appeared almost bored on the court, and a few critics wondered if he was fierce enough to excel against the pros. But Alcindor, who grew up in a predominantly white housing project in the Inwood section of Manhattan, played much of his basketball on Harlem playgrounds. He was well aware of the principles of head-to-head competition—principles that dictated that if a man threw a dunk shot or a matchless game at you, you consumed yourself with the idea of "getting back."

He applied the principle only once in college, with awesome results. Midway through his junior year at UCLA, Alcindor suffered a scratched eyeball; he missed eight days of practice but, still hampered by blurred vision, he returned for a key game in the Astrodome against the University of Houston and Elvin Hayes, the cocky high-scorer who now leads the San Diego Rockets. Alcindor had the most dismal night of his career while Hayes played excellently, and Houston ended a forty-seven-game UCLA winning streak, 71–69. Immediately Houston catapulted above UCLA in the national rankings; Hayes was lionized as practically a peer of Alcindor. Characteristically, Lew offered no excuses. He refused to mention the eye injury again. But as his team kept winning, he brooded constantly on the most challenging mission of his college career—to "get back" at Houston.

UCLA met Houston again in the semifinal match of the NCAA tournament. Hayes was brash and flamboyant as the game approached, vehemently predicting another Houston victory. Alcindor and his teammates were silent. Then they rose to the occasion. Hayes, hounded by UCLA's Lynn Shackleford outside and smothered by Alcindor near the boards, managed 10 points in the game. UCLA won, 101–69.

The pros had offered more competition, but Alcindor's detractors—a durable legion—pointed out that he was a fortunate rookie, entering the league in a year unusually barren of big men. Russell had just retired, Chamberlain missed almost the entire season after knee surgery, and San Francisco's Nate Thurmond sat out half the schedule with his own knee injury. With the ranks so depleted, Alcindor faced only occasional confrontations with near equals—and was thus better able to prepare for them.

Against Reed, however, Alcindor saw a direct need to "get back." True, Reed had been assisted by his teammates, and Lew still had played well. But in the forty-eight hours between the first and second games, Lew steeled himself for an even better performance, one that hopefully would knock Reed off balance and carry the floundering Bucks to a victory.

Reed, of course, had the same thought. Despite all his praise of the team defense, he knew that if the threat of Alcindor was to be overcome, he would have to lead the Knicks. "I look like his little brother," said Willis. "It must be great to be that tall. But I can't stand back and admire him. I've got to take it to him."

The result was a titanic ballet, an exhibition of strength and grace worthy of the most memorable playoff duels of the past between centers such as Russell and Chamberlain. Alcindor furnished graphic evidence of the talent and competitive fire that appears destined to dominate the sport. But Reed countered with a matching display of the skill and courage that made him the leader of the champions. Alcindor finished the game with 38 points, twenty-three rebounds, and eleven assists; Reed had 36 points and nineteen rebounds. But statistics couldn't capture the essence of either man's achievements.

Lew stuffed the ball over Reed, drove around him and watched vigilantly for teammates who were clear, hitting them with perfect passes. Reed countered with sharp outside shooting, often scoring with Alcindor's hand apparently in his face; and once he brought the crowd to its feet with a whirling drive around the bigger man for a 3-point play. Milwaukee coach Larry Costello, who played twelve years in the league with Russell and Chamberlain, summed it up: "I never saw two centers play so well in the same game."

The game was as even as the personal battle, with the lead constantly changing hands. And finally the noise abated and all the bold moves and physical strains were put aside; it came down to Alcindor, alone at the foul line in the waning seconds, with two shots that could win the game. For a big man he is a good foul shooter; under pressure he generally becomes more accurate. But this time the tension and wear of the game had apparently sapped him. He grimaced with anguish as he watched both his shots hit the rim and bounce out.

That left the score at 110–109, in favor of the Knicks. Seconds later Cazzie Russell converted two chances at the foul line. Though Alcindor stormed back for a final basket, the game was decided, 112–111. Lew had carried a team that was giving him scant assistance, and his overall performance ranked with any individual feat in the playoffs. But one flaw had negated everything. He strode from the court with his head high and his face an impassive mask once more, ignoring the jubilant New York kids who had scrambled out of their seats. He was a towering figure and yet a defeated one, and as he improves still further and rules his sport, perhaps images like the one forged that night will be most vividly recalled: a portrait of Olympian grandeur, with just a split second of frailty to reveal the human being within.

Alcindor dressed quickly, answering a few questions monosyllabically. Then he snapped his traveling bag shut and stalked out. Some athletes annoy their teammates with similar reactions, gaining reputations as prima donnas. But as the remaining Bucks watched Lew depart, there was only awe in their expressions. "He thinks he lost the game," said Jon McGlocklin, who, along with Robinson and Crawford, had suffered another abysmal shooting night. "He lifts us with as great a game as anyone could play, and we let him down—and just because of those two lousy foul shots, he thinks *he* lost it. He's an incredible competitor."

In the other locker room, Reed admitted that the game was one of the most satisfying of his career. He was asked if he and Lew had exchanged any conversation. "You kidding?" he replied. "We're too busy working out there."

Nearby, Frazier was looking ahead: "We can't let them off the hook like we did with Baltimore. We've got to win one of the two games in Milwaukee."

In the Milwaukee Arena, a carnival atmosphere prevailed. During the Bucks' first playoff round against Philadelphia, the arena had been occupied by a commercial home show, and the Bucks had been exiled to Madison, Wisconsin, for their "home" games. Most of their fans had followed them eagerly, but now they seemed raucously elated by the fact that their club had survived the opening series to bring the playoffs back to the true parental city. The Bucks were a joyous phenomenon, a two-year-old NBA entry that had left fans no time to wax cynical or ill-tempered about minor matters like the ghastly shooting of the backcourt men.

The coming of Alcindor had made the Bucks the most successful expansion team ever, on the court and at the gate; a town that had been deserted by one NBA team—the Hawks, who went to St. Louis and then Atlanta—and one major league baseball team, the Braves, was now embracing its Bucks avidly. So was the owner, young, imaginative Wes Pavalon, an engaging hustler from Chicago who made his fortune with a correspondence school and seemed anxious to lavish it as quickly as possible on his team. He outbid the American Basketball Association for Alcindor in order to transform the Bucks into winners; then he rewarded their success with gestures such as Christmas bonuses, thousand-dollar-a-man bonuses for beating Philadelphia, and shares of stock in the franchise. "It took the Knicks twenty-four years to get to this point," Pavalon quipped. "It took the Bucks two. I've got to show my appreciation."

In the third game, the Bucks—with a generous assist from the Knicks—repaid Pavalon and the rest of their fanatical adherents. After his two stellar performances in New York, Reed seemed depleted, and his teammates followed him downhill. In many ways, the game was reminiscent of the losses to the Bullets: DeBusschere and Bradley suffered ineffectual nights, Reed was glaringly outrebounded, and the Knicks were uncharacteristically static at both ends of the court.

Bob Dandridge, the skinny rookie forward from Norfolk State, finally broke the hold DeBusschere had clamped on him in the earlier games and hit with ten of fifteen shots for 22 points; with Dandridge's output added to Alcindor's 33, the two men had 55—as many, unbelievably, as the entire New York starting five. New Yorker Crawford, replacing the slumping Robinson at guard, combined with Alcindor on adroit give-and-go maneuvers they had often executed together on the Harlem playgrounds. And with his teammates sharing the scoring load, Lew played his most aggressive, venturesome defense of the series, blocking several Knick shots that might have altered the game.

Yet when the debacle was over, Milwaukee had won by only 5 points; and coach Costello had been forced to call old Guy Rodgers off the bench in the closing minutes when the other Bucks seemed panicky in the face of a Knick press. Rodgers had saved the game with his ball-handling legerdemain but the narrow margin consoled the Knicks. Their locker room held none of the despair that had descended after the Baltimore defeats.

DeBusschere looked surprised when he saw the scorers' sheet. "I didn't know it was that close. How could they outplay us so badly and win 101–96?"

"If we'd played well and lost," said Reed, "we'd have reason to worry. But we played our worst, so we can just forget about it and concentrate on playing better."

"It means nothing special," added Frazier. "We played lousy. I'm glad we got it out of our system."

Nearby, Dick Barnett needled Cazzie Russell, who for the second game in a row had approached some kind of dubious record by driving in for a lay-up, trying to dunk, and missing. "Show us how you make that dunk, Russ," Barnett said. "How do you manage to do it so consistently?"

Cazzie laughed, buoyed by the fact that after his bad Baltimore series, he was scoring well. "I promise," he said solemnly, "that the next time I drive in alone, that ball is going to be placed gently up on that backboard."

The first time Cazzie drove for a lay-up in the fourth game, he executed it as promised, banking it cautiously off the board and into the hoop. The Knick bench erupted in cheers and laughter. All suspense was gone from the game. The lay-up, near the end of the half, put the Knicks ahead by 18 points. Seconds later, Dave Stallworth scored on a forty-foot heave at the buzzer, and New York completed the half with a 65–45 lead. They were playing like the accomplished pros they were, and the Bucks were once again vulnerable rookies. Unlike the Bullets, the Bucks were being gifted with no chances to even the series.

Then, in one of those puzzling sequences to which the Knicks had become agonizingly susceptible, the game turned around. The Bucks had the stamina for one more all-out rally. And the Knicks were caught off balance. Grasping desperately for the points that had eluded him all series, Flynn Robinson finally hit a few shots; so did Freddie Crawford. The Knicks missed their shots and their margin was slashed to 13 before Holzman called time-out to regroup.

It didn't help. After five minutes the lead was down to 7, and then Reed drew his fourth personal foul; Willis would have to play cautiously, and there were still twenty minutes left. Seeking any change that might shift the momentum, Holzman even shuttled John Warren in for a minute, when Barnett got into foul trouble and Riordan was ineffective. But the Bucks kept surging, and with five minutes remaining in the third period, the score was 69–67. The Bucks had scored 16 in a row. The crowd was in a frenzy and the Knicks were reeling, and for the first time in the series, Knick followers had reason to suffer the same profound doubts that had engulfed them in the battles with Baltimore; it was frightening to contemplate what blowing a 20-point lead might do to their playoff future.

The next few moments illustrated why the Bucks, for all their potential, were still a year or so away from the championship—and why the Knicks were en route to a title. Milwaukee had three quick chances to tie the score, and everybody in the Arena should have sensed what they had to do: Alcindor was wheeling in and out of the foul lane under the basket, pleading silently for the ball and the opportunity to drive up over Reed. Willis, in foul trouble, would have been obliged to slack off and allow Lew a big advantage—or else commit his fifth personal and put the Knicks in desperate straits.

But the Bucks couldn't or wouldn't get the ball in to him. Bradley and DeBusschere managed to close some lanes toward Lew; the overeager Bucks didn't look for alternates. Crawford took two shots, Robinson one. All three missed, and by then the Knicks were able to take advantage of their brief reprieve. "The guys were tight," said Russell. "And I had to loosen them up. I can't afford to be tight. I only get so many chances to come off the bench and score, so I have to be ready to hit right away."

The same Knicks who had razzed Cazzie about his abortive stuff shots now looked to him for help. "Give him the ball and a second in the clear," Reed said later, "and I'll bet on him to score every time." Frazier had experienced moments, especially late in the season, when he was leery of giving Russell the ball; Cazzie was too anxious to shoot, too prone to dribble in one spot and slow down the attack. Russell, in turn, had expressed his impatience with the lack of passes from Frazier. But now a game was on the line and there was no hesitation. Frazier moved into the front court, surveyed the scene, whipped a pass to Cazzie. Reed took a giant stride toward Russell, setting a pick that blocked off Cazzie's defender, Greg Smith. Twenty feet from the hoop, Cazzie jumped and shot. 71–67.

Alcindor came back with a vengeful stuff shot over Reed, but it wasn't enough to restore the Bucks' spell. "When a team scores 16 points in a row," commented Barnett, "you just know that sooner or later you're going to get a few of them back." Russell managed 2 of them; Barnett hit a long floater; Frazier made a 3-point play, and the scare had evaporated. The Knicks led by 9.

Milwaukee scrambled back to within 3 as the turbulent period ended. In twelve minutes, the Bucks had outscored the Knicks, 34–17—a feat worthy of the Knicks' own third-period outbursts earlier in the season. But their fury was spent. Russell made 3 more quick jumpers early in the final quarter, and New York reassumed control. The final score was 117–105. The Knicks led the series, three games to one, and few of the fans filing out of the Arena expected the teams to return to Milwaukee for a sixth game.

"I couldn't give you guys any more to joke about," Russell chortled in the cramped dressing room. "I've seen enough of your imitations of my dunk shots." Barnett and DeBusschere, seated near him, went right on mimicking him, and the room filled with relaxed laughter. Only Reed took Cazzie's crucial 18-point performance with suitable sobriety. Leaning into the group around him, the captain jabbed Russell's arm to get his attention, then raised his fist in warm appreciation.

The fifth game was no more than a formality. The Bucks had hurled all their weapons at the Knicks in that one third-period streak. Repulsed, they resembled playground kids who have suf fered their first humiliation at the hands of Herman "Helicopter" Knowings or Joe Hammond; it would take months for some to recover. Their first several passes sailed wide of the targets. The Knicks reaped the errant throws and fed them to their hot shooter of the moment, Barnett. Dick, again playing better with only one day's rest than he had with two- or three-day breathers, connected with his first five attempts.

The Knicks led by 16 at the quarter and 24 at the half, and this time there would be no retaliation. Frazier, who scored only 2 points and couldn't have cared less, had the offense in high gear all the way. There was no idle dribbling, no wasted motion. The fans might have been watching a film roundup of the Knick highlights of the year.

Frustrated, Alcindor tried to salvage the game singlehandedly. He tried long jump shots, razzle-dazzle hooks, audacious defensive gambles—even an incredible stuff over Reed. But he couldn't faze Willis and he couldn't breathe life into his teammates. Lew would have to wait at least a year for his first championship. With the score 95–66 late in the third period, Costello conceded defeat and brought his big man to the bench, sparing him further humiliation.

Then the chant began, high in the balcony. Quickly it spread into the lower seats, until perhaps five thousand voices were raised in derisive song. "Good-bye, Lewie. We hate to see you go."

It was the most tasteless moment of the season in the Garden, a shameful ending to a Knicks spectacular. Frazier tried to be charitable, terming it "a sigh of relief." Crawford also made light of the behavior of his home-town citizens: "Lew's a legend, right before their eyes. . . . They were singing an ode to him." But it wasn't an ode; it was a nasty, rancorous taunt that embarrassed several Knicks as it persisted.

"Lew's a great athlete and he played a great series," said De-Busschere. "New York fans are supposed to appreciate greatness. They should never have chanted like that."

"It was only a minority," said Reed. "The real fans here wouldn't have done it."

Alcindor endured it without expression, slouched on the bench with a towel across his legs. He understood the motives behind it, and he knew he would suffer similar injustices throughout his career. It wouldn't matter. From his grade school days he had been a head taller and a great deal more intelligent than many of those around him; being different, he had sometimes felt condemned to hear and see and feel more than the others. Classmates and even a coach had seared the word "nigger" into his brain; cruel or patronizing whites had driven him very quickly to seek peace in black power and pride.

By so doing, he had only spurred on his critics. At UCLA he had bewildered some whites by becoming a Muslim. In 1968 he had incensed many more by joining professor Harry Edwards and trackmen like Tommie Smith and John Carlos in a movement to boycott the Olympics. His picture appeared on posters with Smith and Carlos above the legend: "Rather than run and jump for medals, we are standing up for humanity." While the trackmen went to Mexico City and raised black-gloved fists in protest on the victory stand, Lew remained home and worked with young blacks in New York's ghettos. The effect was the same: many whites would never quite accept the militant Alcindor—unless he happened to be leading their particular team to a championship.

The Los Angeles press had long since inured Lew to vicious or condescending commentary; on the morning before the fifth game, New York *Daily News* columnist Dick Young allied himself with that rich journalistic tradition by branding Alcindor a racist. So a small part of the crowd undoubtedly took a special racial pride in watching him defeated.

Not all the Garden singers were racists, of course. As a massive threat to the Knicks, Alcindor was a natural sports villain, and everyone who pays for a ticket claims the right to bait his villains. In any case, he accepted it all stoically, then flashed a peace sign at the crowd as he left the court. "I don't feel anything at all about it," he said later. "If they want to act that way, that's their problem."

There was no champagne in the locker room of the Knicks, the new Eastern Division playoff champs. The only celebration was staged for photographers, when Frazier poured a ceremonial beer over his own head. A breathless radio reporter thrust a microphone at Barnett and shouted, "You scored 27 points. Did you ever have a more satisfying game?"

"Yeah," said Dick, concluding the interview.

The Bucks filed in to congratulate their conquerors. Then the Knick conversation turned to the Los Angeles Lakers, who had destroyed Atlanta in four straight games to win the Western series.

The Milwaukee series was already past history. The shadow of Alcindor had disappeared, at least for another year.

Lew was the first man dressed and out of the Garden. The kids who hang around the players' entrance mobbed him. He refused to sign autographs and clambered into the team bus, taking a seat by the window. The kids gathered around the window, shouting and jeering. Alcindor could have moved across to a seat that didn't face the sidewalk. But he didn't bother. His eyes were fixed straight ahead, his face serene. The kids' voices seemed to bounce back to them off the closed window. Lew was far away, perhaps achieving once more the state he always seeks—"harmony with my universe." There would be other playoffs with different endings, and there would be hundreds of black youngsters awaiting his summer appearances in the streets. The Knick victory wouldn't haunt him. "I didn't come in with exaggerated expectations," he had said earlier. "I'm proud that I gave my best."

17

Champions

TIME WAS running out on the Los Angeles Lakers. Their years were cluttered with last-minute shots that just missed and injuries that crippled them at the most inopportune moments; and above all, there had been the recurring nightmare of Bill Russell. Six times in the nine seasons since they had moved west from Minneapolis, the Lakers had reached the final championship series. And six times they had bowed to Russell and the Boston Celtics. If not for Russell, the Lakers might have been acclaimed as the team of the 1960s in the NBA. Instead, they were left with an awesome collection of scoring records—and a painful reputation as also-rans. The Celtics had won a total of eleven championships, and their legend would endure long after the Knicks or Bucks ascended to rule the 1970s. The Lakers held only consolation prizes.

But as the 1970s began, there was yet another chance. The Lakers' three superstars—Elgin Baylor, Jerry West, and Wilt Chamberlain—were all reasonably healthy, their battered bodies ready for one more playoff grind. Perhaps it would be their last genuine shot at the title. Baylor, thirty-five, was playing on courage and memory, but injuries and age were catching up to the gallant team captain. Chamberlain was thirty-three and recovering from serious knee surgery that raised questions about his future. And even West, better than ever at thirty-one, had reason to wonder if he would ever wear a championship ring.

Maimed by injuries, beginning with the bad step that tore Chamberlain's knee apart, the Lakers had finished second in the Western Division race, two games behind the Atlanta Hawks. But for a change, instead of fading in the playoffs, they picked up momentum. Down three to one against Phoenix, they won the last three games to save the series; then they steamrollered the rugged Hawks in four straight. The seven consecutive triumphs represented an NBA record and propelled the Lakers into the Knick series at full speed. And their confidence wouldn't be diminished by the fact that at last their opponents in the finals were not the Celtics.

There was irony in the frequently expressed criticisms of the Laker stars. Every sport has its chronic runner-ups, teams or athletes cursed with an unerring capacity for losing the big games. The National Football League's Dallas Cowboys, a crushing machine during every regular season, sputter to a halt annually in postseason playoff games; baseball's San Francisco Giants have a genius for finishing second. But the Lakers had not faltered and submitted to weaker teams in crucial games; they had been defeated by the most powerful dynasty pro basketball had ever seen. To call them losers because they couldn't beat Russell and the Celtics was to classify the entire NBA as a league of losers.

West, for example, had become under pressure the most prolific scorer in playoff history; Baylor ranked right behind him. And Chamberlain—who did manage to overcome Russell and win one title while playing in Philadelphia—moved into third place on that all-time list during the Knick series. If the Bucks had confronted the Knicks with the specter of the future, the Lakers brought a rich past—a past that was very much alive last spring.

Chamberlain was the center of speculation as the final series began. In ten years, he had won the NBA's Most Valuable Player award four times. He was the highest scorer ever to play the game and, as if to underline his versatility and unselfishness, he had also been the only center ever to lead the league in assists for a season. Yet Wilt was always an enigma. Unlike Russell and Alcindor, he never quite seemed to adjust to the demands of being a seven-foot superman. In between his magnificent performances he would sulk and complain and skip practices; sometimes, in frustrating moments on the court, he appeared to give up. Teammates called him a prima donna, outsiders questioned his courage. And some people wondered whether his towering presence might be more of a hindrance than an asset to a team. The rare superstars of sports are almost never traded; Chamberlain has been traded twice, at the height of his career—an indication of the doubts he has always provoked.

When flamboyant Laker owner Jack Kent Cooke acquired Chamberlain from Philadelphia in 1968—largely because the 76ers were unwilling to meet Wilt's huge salary demands—the reactions had been varied. Some insisted that a team with Chamberlain, West, and Baylor would hardly ever lose. Others thought they would have to play with three basketballs at once to maintain harmony. Both forecasts proved partially correct. The Lakers won the Western Division handily, but 1968-69 was a rancorous season. Chamberlain battled heatedly with coach Bill van Breda Kolff over strategy and performed fitfully on the court. Then, in the final game against the Celtics, Wilt reached the depths of his confusing career by removing himself from action with a minor injury and, from a seat on the bench, watching the title slip away. It was too much for his old rival Russell, and the Boston player-coach commented, "With the championship at stake, one of our guys would have to break his back before he'd take himself out of a game."

To many, this seemed a suitable epitaph for the puzzling giant's career. But, contrary as always, Wilt revealed a whole new aspect of himself last year. In his ninth game of the season under new coach Joe Mullaney, Chamberlain crumpled to the floor, the tendons of his knee severely torn. He was declared finished for the year; at his age, it was uncertain whether he would ever regain his mobility. But he insisted that he would make the playoffs, and he exercised and worked ceaselessly to get his leg back into shape. Amazing his doctors, Wilt rejoined the Lakers in the final weeks of the regular season—and renewed their championship hopes.

"I still don't have it all back," he said before the opener. "I'm testing, finding out just how much I can still do."

"Those people who knock Wilt ought to watch how hard he's pushing himself now," said Baylor. "After the operation he had, it's amazing that he's even playing. I don't know how anyone could ever question his courage after this. He deserves all the credit in the world."

The Knicks had no time to pause and heap credit on Chamberlain; there was no compassion in their game plan. "We've got to check him out early," said Frazier. "If he can't move too well on that knee, maybe we can drive on him."

"Our basic weapon is outside shooting anyway," added De-Busschere. "It won't matter too much if we can drive to the hoop. But if Wilt can't move, we'll have to run him into the ground. If he can't keep up with the action, then we'll always have an open man."

The main task, of course, fell to Reed, whose own knees were aching after weeks of hand-to-hand combat against Unseld and Alcindor. "I'm earning my pay in these games," Willis said with a smile. "But it's no time to stop now. I'm anxious to see how far Wilt has come."

Throughout the first two games in Madison Square Garden, the Knicks put the question to Wilt. Driving, rotating, moving constantly around the large figure of Chamberlain, they dared him to block their shots and prove that he could still leap and run. And as with so many aspects of his personality and career, Chamberlain provided contradictory answers.

The opening moments of the Reed-Chamberlain match were reminiscent of a Muhammad Ali–Sonny Liston heavyweight fight: While Chamberlain seemed as rooted to the floor as "Big Bear" Liston, Reed floated like a butterfly and—with a series of deadly jump shots from out of Wilt's range—stung like a bee. Against Alcindor, Willis had been forced to use strength to keep his taller, faster rival in check. Against the almost immobile Chamberlain, Reed turned the opening game into a virtuoso demonstration of finesse and delicate shooting. He began by hitting from the corners and from out near the foul line. When it became clear that Wilt was not going to venture out to stop him, Reed moved even closer to the hoop, still Wilt ignored him—and he kept on scoring.

On the bench, Joe Mullaney suffered with each Reed basket and clapped his hands to encourage Wilt. "I know that Wilt can't be expected to play nose-to-nose with a smaller, quicker man like Reed," Mullaney said later. "But he will have to go out far enough to stop those eight-to-fifteen-footers. You can't leave a shooter like Reed completely open."

But Chamberlain did. Enveloped in one of the private worlds that sometimes seem to carry his mind miles away from the competition, Wilt played into the Knicks' hands. Laying back near the hoop, he might have helped to deflate another team that kept driving inside. But the Knicks were content to leave him alone in there and work their patterns outside—playing five-on-four basketball. By the time Reed went to the bench for a breather before half time, the Knicks led by 17 and Willis had scored 25.

In the second half, the Lakers resorted to their basic weapon. On play after play, four of them drifted to one side of the court, and left West to operate on the other side. West's jump shots have little of the showmanlike, electric quality of Monroe's; he doesn't seem to uncoil suddenly into the air and shoot without looking at the hoop. His form has a simpler, more economical beauty. There is no wasted motion, no lost time; he dribbles, jumps, then releases the ball even more quickly than Monroe— and his accuracy is uncanny.

Barnett and Frazier had covered West successfully in the first half. But time always runs out on defenders who stop Jerry. In the third period Barnett played him as if he were manipulating a pinball machine, his hands on West's sides, jiggling him, shoving him, slapping occasionally at the ball. Five times the officials called "tilt" and pasted fouls on Barnett; the rest of the time, West scored. Jerry totaled 16 points in the period and Los Angeles took a 3-point lead. With their early margin gone and both Frazier and Barnett in foul trouble, the Knicks' situation looked bleak.

But the game's furious pace was to New York's advantage. Russell and Riordan took to the floor to keep the club running at top speed; the older Lakers grew weary. West lost the ball several times while bringing it upcourt; when he turned that chore over to rookie Dick Garrett, the Knicks made more steals. Baylor, spent from a fine 21-point effort, slowed noticeably. And Wilt grew even more sedentary. Riordan and Russell challenged him with bold drives to the basket, and he failed to block them. Literally running away from the Lakers, the Knicks won it, 124–112.

"They played just the way we hoped," exulted Frazier, who ignited the final New York rally with his ball-hawking defense. "If Wilt doesn't come out on defense, my job becomes the easiest thing in the world. Everybody is open."

At the other end of the Garden corridor, Chamberlain answered the inevitable questions.

"How long can you go, letting Reed shoot like that, Wilt?"

"Judging by the score, I guess I went too long."

"Did you learn something from it?"

"I'm not sure. I'll have to think about it."

"Does your knee hamper your style of play?"

"My man," Wilt said slowly, "I don't have a style." As the reporters dispersed, Chamberlain finished dressing, inserting large gold cuff links into wide cuffs decorated with the insignia "Dipper." Beginning in his college days at Kansas, he had been called The Big Dipper. Few referred to him by the nickname anymore. In fact, following Alcindor into the Garden, Wilt appeared far less intimidating than he once was. Even a few people who had detested him when he was a force to conjure with on the court saw him as a strangely sympathetic figure.

On his way out, Chamberlain talked quietly to a few friends from Harlem. "We'll read a lot of crap tomorrow about whether I'm going to stay inside or come out," he said. "But you know it's not that simple. It's a matter of degree, a question of positioning. Maybe I can adjust by a few feet and it will make all the difference. I'm not sure. I've got to figure out just what I can still do."

On the afternoon before the second game, the Lakers were supposed to view the film of the opener. But the movies didn't arrive until an hour and a half before game time, and most of the players didn't see them. Chamberlain did. He sat in a darkened room under the Garden and squinted at the first three periods. Then he got up and told Mullaney, "That's enough. I know how it ends." On the way into the locker room he gave the coach a silent look that was somehow reassuring. "I knew he didn't think he had been as bad as people said," said Mullaney. "But I also knew he was going to make some changes."

The changes were startling. The first time Reed took aim from near the foul line, Chamberlain came out to shove a hand in Willis' face. From that moment on, Wilt was a positive force on defense, the key man in a strong team effort. He was still far from agile, and occasionally he was as stationary as he had been in the opener; but the subtle adjustments in his positioning and a fierce determination made a difference. Reed, bothered by a shoulder he had wrenched while stuffing a shot in the opener, hit on only twelve of twenty-nine shots. Now the fans found nothing sympathetic or vulnerable about Wilt.

West played his normal game—sensational. But Bradley and Barnett matched him with outside shooting of their own. With the big men battling to a draw inside, no one could break open the deadlock. Once, briefly, a Barnett shot put New York in front by 5. But seconds later Frazier drew his fifth foul trying to stop West; then Barnett drew his fifth—also on West. The game was quickly tied again, and it stayed that way until the final minute, when Chamberlain reached back into the years when his jumping and maneuverability were never a question, and made the plays that won it.

Dick Garrett scored to give Los Angeles a 103–101 lead. Riordan charged back, recalling the previous game and his success in driving. But this time Wilt was waiting. Mike looked for Reed to hit him with a pass, but Wilt's body blocked his vision. Desperately, he tossed a high floater over Chamberlain—and far over the basket. Reed closed in for the rebound, but Wilt whirled and slapped the ball downward. It slipped off Willis' hands and out of bounds, giving the ball back to Los Angeles.

Following another steal, Frazier did tie the score; but West drew

a foul and made two shots. The Lakers led, 105–103, with time
running out. The Knicks went back to Reed. He took a pass
from Barnett and backed toward the hoop, looking over his
shoulder at Wilt. His body leaned first one way and then another
as he feinted a drive. For a moment they could have been up
at Rucker in Harlem, where they had faced one another during
several summers; and as Wilt recalled, Reed had beaten him on
many similar plays in the park. Finally Willis wheeled and went
up. Chamberlain countered with his most prodigious leap of the
series and slammed the ball down. The Lakers held on to win,
105–103.

They cited several reasons for the victory. "We didn't allow them
to organize their offense as much," said West. "We didn't give
them a chance to whip that ball around us the way they like to."

"We switched men better," said Baylor, "and played good team
defense."

But both statements came down to the man who anchored the
defense and came out to break up the Knicks' five-on-four picnic.
"You have good games and bad games," Chamberlain philoso-
phized. "And maybe the guy you're playing has different kinds of
games. Maybe Reed was a little slower and made me look quicker.
I don't know. . . ."

But he did know. "Even before I got hurt, I never had much
lateral movement. I never had the moves of an Alcindor. I have
to rely on height and jumping ability, and to do that, I have to get
good position. Tonight, I worked a little harder for that position."

An intrepid reporter tried to sum up the moment in a cliché:
"Would you say, Wilt, that you came to play?"

Chamberlain glared at him. "Man, I always come to play. Do
you think I worked four months on my knee so I could come
here and jive?"

The Knicks flew to Los Angeles in one of the huge new 747s.
With its high ceilings and broad aisles and endless supply of
food and drink, the plane seemed specially designed for basketball
players. Tourist class is like a vast cattle car, but the first-class
section gave the Knicks ample room to move around, stretching

legs and pacing off restless moods. In addition, the upstairs lounge provided a luxury long coveted by several members of the club's entourage—a spacious accommodation for their floating poker game. The game was a feature on all Knick trips, flourishing in hotel rooms and on buses and planes. Its principal members were Barnett; Phil Jackson, the forward who missed the season with a back injury but covered the team as a photographer; publicity man Jimmy Wergeles; and whatever sportswriters happened to join. The most popular game was something called Spit in the Ocean; but anyone who could dream up enough wild cards and crazy stipulations could suggest variations in the routine. It was a lively game, with a lot of kibitzing and conversation. Only Barnett was always quiet; only Barnett, from all reports, was a steady winner. As the plane approached Los Angeles, Wergeles said, "Barnett just won so much, he shouldn't bother to draw his pay this month."

"The day Barnett doesn't pick up his paycheck," replied the traveling secretary, Frankie Blauschild, "the whole franchise will collapse."

Blauschild and Wergeles were promoters in the traditional mold, and at times last year they seemed uncomfortable amid the mass of television and magazine people who wanted to publicize the Knicks. They grew impatient with those who demanded to talk endlessly to the players or pose them for pictures; their idea of keeping the press happy meant stocking the team hotel suite with liquor and feeding reporters sumptuous free meals. Blauschild and Wergeles remembered vividly when the Knicks were considered minor sports attractions and they had to beg for "ink," and they remained loyal to the men who had been there—Lennie Lewin of the *Post* and Murray Janoff of the Long Island *Press*, and a handful of other veterans. They also remained loyal to the idea that, no matter how many high-powered media types crowded around, the whole thing was faintly humorous. Once Blauschild gazed with wonder on the painting of *The Last Supper*. "Hey," he finally cried, "the third guy from the end looks like Janoff—and he's signing my name to the check."

In the airport, a friend told Blauschild, "I want to get back to New York in the worst way."

"The worst way?" said Frankie. "Then take the bus."

The Knicks were not quite as frivolous as their companions as they arrived on the Coast, but their mood was relaxed. At a glance, this seemed surprising. They appeared to be in their most dangerous position of the playoffs. When Baltimore had been tied with them, the Knicks had always been consoled by the fact that more home games remained; but now the Lakers were even with them—and three of the final five games would be in Los Angeles.

Yet there was no sense of foreboding, because Los Angeles is the best place in the league for a visiting team. Cooke's Forum is the most spectacular and well-planned arena in basketball, but it also offers the least advantage to the home team. The plush seats are set far back from the court, and the fans in them are equally removed from the tension of the game. Los Angeles sports enthusiasts come to be entertained rather than to root desperately for their team. They may marvel at the scoring of West or the occasional flashes of Baylor's incomparable form driving to the hoop, and then cheer appreciatively. But they do not give way to hysteria when the Lakers break a game open, nor do they gnash their teeth when the Lakers lose. It is not unusual to see the crowd begin to file out with three minutes left and the Lakers ahead or behind by only 10 points—a gesture that would be sacrilegious in the Garden. If the Knicks failed, they were confident that it would not be because of the surroundings.

The Knicks had already played ninety-six regular-season and playoff games, the Lakers ninety-five. Reed was gobbling cortisone pills to ease the ache in his knees. Laker forward Keith Erickson was having fluid drained from a painful ankle after each game. Almost every other player was nursing lesser ailments and annoyances, and battling simple weariness. The Forum fans were entitled to wonder what new forms of entertainment they could expect from the exhausted warriors. Then they found out: The Knicks and Lakers split two overtime games that were as implausibly theatrical as anything that had happened all year.

If Chamberlain had been the focal point of the action in New York, center stage in Los Angeles belonged to West. In the two games he scored 71 points and added twenty-seven assists; but the statistics were minor compared to the drama he contrived at the end of the third game of the series.

Erickson, a five-year veteran from UCLA who generally concentrates on defense while the Lakers' big-name players gather points, sparked Los Angeles to a 14-point half-time lead. Keith scored well himself, and as Marin had done for Baltimore, he cut off Bradley from the Knicks' offensive flow. That left the rest of the Knicks to stand around watching Reed keep them in the game with another big night. But in the second half the Lakers seemed to lose their own movement, and DeBusschere and Barnett brought the Knicks back. With time running out, the game was tied at 100–100; but the entire forty-seven minutes and fifty-seven seconds of hard-fought defensive ball turned out to be a mere prelude to the night's action.

With three seconds showing on the clock, DeBusschere scored to make it 102–100. The Knicks prepared to leave the court with their victory; Mullaney had used all his alloted time-outs, so there was nothing for the Lakers to do but heave a long desperation shot. Chamberlain fed the ball to West. Jerry took a few loping strides and chucked, from a distance later estimated at anywhere from fifty-five to seventy feet. It was the kind of futile gesture that ends many NBA games; it figured to draw halfhearted cheers if it even hit the backboard.

But it went in. From far beyond midcourt, with a game and possibly a championship riding on it, the ball sailed in a gentle arc and dropped into the net as the buzzer sounded. West has scored about 23,000 points in NBA competition, but no two will be remembered longer.

DeBusschere watched its flight from near the basket. "No," he said to himself, "it can't be. Not in my wildest dreams . . ." As the ball went through the hoop, Dave fell backward and sat on the floor.

Chamberlain, at the other end of the court, blinked in disbelief and headed for the locker room to go home. He was so stunned that he thought the shot had won the game instead of tying it.

The other Knicks walked slowly back to their huddle to prepare for the overtime. Holzman had to call Frazier twice; Clyde was mesmerized, standing under the basket, trying to absorb what he had seen. "It drained me," he said. "After seeing that, I had to pull myself together just to walk back out for the overtime."

West himself took it almost casually. "Honestly, it felt good leaving my hand," he said. "I wouldn't call it a desperation heave. I aimed it and got my body behind it. I've made them from that far before. But never, of course, with so much at stake."

Knick fans should not have been too shocked. They had seen 5 points made in the final sixteen seconds that beat Cincinnati and kept the winning streak alive. They remembered Christmas night in the Garden, when Detroit led by a point with one second on the clock and the Knicks were taking the ball in from out of bounds; the clock would not start until a Knick touched the ball in play, so Frazier tossed a long pass toward the basket—and Reed jumped up to tap it in. Such things, in other words, could happen— but New Yorkers had assumed they could only happen for the Knicks.

It was a demoralizing moment. The Knicks had struggled from far behind and won a game, only to have it snatched away. Now they faced five more minutes of play against a team that had been reanimated. "It's incredible," said Reed in the huddle, "but we got an overtime to win now. Let's forget it and do the job." The Knicks snapped out of their shock and, defying every rule of sports momentum, won the game all over again, 111–108.

West had two more chances to save his team late in the overtime. Both shots were from reasonable range; both missed. Like Alcindor in his finest playoff game against the Knicks, West had done everything imaginable for his club—only to lose it at the end. He was disconsolate after the game; Mullaney appeared on the verge of tears. Emotions had been yanked in more directions than seemed possible in a basketball game, and when it ended the Knicks were riding the crest.

"It was some shot," said Barnett. "But to come back and beat them anyway, we've got to be some team."

West had scored 100 points in three games and gained only one victory. His left thumb, jammed during the third game, had swollen badly. Baylor was limping visibly on a bruised heel. The

Lakers appeared beatable once more, old men who had fought themselves out, left with one fruitless fifty-five-foot basket to serve as a last hurrah. The Knicks, healthy and confident as the fourth game began, moved in for the kill.

And then West and Baylor, veterans of all those losing years and hints that they couldn't win the big ones, called on hidden reserves of strength. West took control of the game, scoring steadily and drawing the Knicks around him, then feeding open men for more baskets. Baylor, even more remarkably, challenged DeBusschere with those tantalizing, suspended-animation drives of which his legs were no longer supposed to be capable; forgetting the pain and the years, he mixed it up under the boards like a strapping rookie. West scored 37 points and added eighteen assists; Baylor scored 30 and grabbed thirteen rebounds. With the two other stars scoring, Chamberlain devoted all his efforts to the war under the boards and got twenty-five rebounds. Barnett and DeBusschere led a commendable Knick effort, but when it ended in another tie, West took full advantage. With Jerry hitting from all over, the Lakers scored 20 points in the five-minute overtime, to win, 121–115.

The situation didn't seem unpromising as the Knicks returned to New York for the fifth game. They had weathered any psychological storm that West's shot might have generated; and with each passing day their physical edge over the Lakers increased. While the Knicks exuded confidence, the Lakers issued medical bulletins. West was still pressing ice packs against his thumb. Erickson's ankle was still being injected and drained. And Baylor, in throwing himself so courageously into the fourth battle, had reinjured a stomach muscle that had sidelined him for twenty-five regular-season games.

Conceivably, the Knicks could have gone on to defeat the Lakers with a few solid games. After the two tumultuous dramas in the Forum, a pair of straightforward victories might have been slightly anticlimactic, but the New York fans wouldn't have minded a bit. Yet somehow the Knicks were not meant to win the championship simply by wearing down their foes. From the start, the playoffs had tested their spirit and resiliency as well as their shooting and rebounding. Striving for their first title, they were undergoing a rite of manhood. Like kids ascending to playground supremacy, they had to overcome a range of confrontations and obstacles. After Monroe and Alcindor, and West's performances on the Coast, it was difficult to envision a more profound test. But after eight minutes of the fifth game, the new challenge arose: the Knicks were forced to play without Reed.

Reed was driving to the basket when he tripped over Chamberlain's leg, landing heavily on his right hip. At first there was a collective groan from the crowd, followed by silence as Willis struggled to his feet and hobbled to the dressing room. Then strange vibrations affected everyone in the Garden. The Lakers, already 10 points ahead and faced with an undermanned opponent, became sloppy and inaccurate. The Knicks, with Nate Bowman and then Bill Hosket at center, were equally inept. And the fans grew anxious and preoccupied, watching and cheering with part of themselves, but devoutly hoping that in the locker room deep beneath them, Reed would be miraculously cured.

With four minutes left in the half, Holzman gambled on putting DeBusschere in the pivot against Chamberlain. Dave shoved and scrambled mightily, but the Knicks remained tight. At the half the Lakers led by 13. When the teams reappeared for the second half, Reed was not among them. Again there were moans of dismay, feeble words of hope. Then, late in the third period, announcer John Condon told the crowd: "Willis Reed suffered a contusion and strain of the right tensor muscle and will not see any further action this evening."

Willis put it more graphically: "I would have done anything to come back. But I couldn't lift my leg."

When the announcement was made, the Knicks trailed only by 10. Every rational observer knew that the Lakers should have opened up a 30-point lead under the circumstances; but somehow they hadn't, and both teams seemed to sense the improbability of it all. The Knicks suddenly realized that they could do more than wage a gallant fight; the Lakers felt control of the game slipping away from them.

"At half time Willis was lying on that table," said Russell, "and we just knew we had to get this one for him. He's done so much for us. This was our chance to repay him."

"When Willis got hurt," said DeBusschere, "I was awfully depressed. I envisioned all we had worked for going down the drain. But we were playing great team defense and they were making incredible mistakes, and after a while it dawned on me. We could win the thing."

The Laker mistakes defied belief. Consumed with the desire to take advantage of the mismatch at center, they forced passes desperately toward Wilt, ignoring the Knicks who swarmed around him. Few of the passes reached Chamberlain; he got off only three shots in the second half. Worse yet, the Lakers entirely forgot about their one stabilizing influence. Unable to get the ball to Wilt, they were unwilling to give it to West. Mullaney called time-outs, begged his men to return to their normal patterns, inserted substitutes who only worsened the situation. The Lakers were engulfed in a wave of insanity—a wave that was sweeping the entire building.

There was no division of effort by the Knicks. Each man was aiding in every phase of play. Bradley and Russell, both of whom had been slumping during the series, caught fire simultaneously— and both crashed recklessly to the boards in uncharacteristic displays of rebounding. "All year I've been getting my hands on rebounds and forgetting to hold on so other guys could grab them," said Cazzie. "Tonight I snatched one out of Baylor's hands and said, 'Hey, that should've been the other way around.' It was unreal."

Frazier staged another premier ball-swiping show, but also broke a scoring drought; Barnett, who had been scoring nicely, played his finest defense. And DeBusschere and Stallworth never ceased tormenting Chamberlain. After three periods the Knicks trailed by only 7. Four minutes later they were tied, and the crowd was beside itself. Then Bradley, Russell, and Stallworth went on a streak that crushed the Lakers. The final score was 107–100. In another five minutes the margin would have been wider; the Knicks were racing away from their rivals at the finish. As they leaped in the air in incredulous triumph, the message board on the scoreboard flashed: "THE GIANT KILLERS . . ."

"Let me through," bellowed Cazzie in the corridor. "God dog. What a thrill."

"Caz and Bill started the momentum," said Stallworth. "I just joined in. How could I help but join in?"

"I had been rushing my shots too much," said Bradley. "But when I got caught up in this whole thing, I seemed to get my feeling back. But the big thing was the defense. We applied all Red's principles tonight. We changed our plans constantly, switching and adjusting. We had great communication, both through talking and through intuition. There was an intuitive aspect to the entire game. We were thinking as a group. Even the crowd was in on the collective experience. The crowd has never participated as directly as it did tonight."

Somebody brought statistic sheets. They were astounding. The pressing defense had forced the Lakers into thirty turnovers. Los Angeles had taken only twenty-nine shots in the second half, sinking to an unprecedented level of futility. Chamberlain, who had 18 points early, scored only 4 more after DeBusschere and Stallworth began guarding him. West, with 20 at the half, didn't score again.

"Did you see that West only got two shots in the half?" Stallworth was asked.

"That's his business," said Dave, letting out another whoop.

Even Holzman betrayed genuine emotion. "These guys can do anything," he kept repeating. "There's nothing they can't do."

Unfortunately, they couldn't sustain a miracle for two days and three thousand miles; or, more accurately, the Lakers wouldn't let them. Back in Los Angeles, the Lakers reviewed the game films and cringed; then they resolved to forget all about mismatches and revert to their normal game. It was more than enough. Reed made the trip, but was never close to playing—or even walking without an agonized limp. Bowman started, followed by Hosket and then DeBusschere and Stallworth; but the magic was missing. Chamberlain scored on twenty of twenty-seven shots, many of them breathtaking stuffs over his defenders. And when the Knicks left men open in order to surround Wilt, Garrett and West kept their poise and hit from outside. The score was 135–113, and all who witnessed the slaughter had to suspect that the glamorous Knick season had ended in the fifth game.

The victorious Lakers, on the threshold where they had been turned back so often, had mixed emotions. "You don't like to see a team lose when they're not at their best," said West. "It's like stealing something. We can look back and remember the games we've lost the same way. But it still takes something out of it, seeing Willis on the bench."

"We Americans emphasize winning too much," added Chamberlain. "Both teams in this series have played well under adversity. Even the loser will deserve a lot of credit."

Frazier winked and put up the bravest front in the Knicks' locker room. "All we were doing," he quipped, "was getting them overconfident." But the words that hung over the room were DeBusschere's: "Without Willis, we are an ordinary team."

Reed hobbled out of the Forum quickly to catch a night flight home for further treatment. He made no promises or predictions, and judging from the pain that twisted his face as he moved, he couldn't possibly return to action within forty-eight hours. The Knicks knew better.

Back in New York, Reed was treated for two days. On the afternoon of the game, he tested the leg gingerly. It hadn't improved. "I was still sure I could play," he said. "It was just a matter of getting enough Novocain in my leg."

An hour and a half before game time, he flexed the leg again. The pain stung sharply. "By that time," he said, "it didn't matter. I knew I'd play." He went back into the locker room and prepared for the first of the three injections that would fill the leg with 300 cc. of Carbocaine, a more powerful derivative of Novocain. It was enough pain killer to disqualify a racehorse if found in its system.

The real question, of course, was never whether Reed would play, but what effect he could exert on the game. It was answered before the opening tap, as Reed appeared and the roars thundered down on him; the adrenaline surged through his teammates. "I knew I couldn't go at all on offense," said the captain. "And I wasn't even sure I could contain Wilt on defense. But I felt I could give the guys a big psychological lift by just walking out there."

He had expressed his motives more succinctly in a parting word to trainer Danny Whelan in the dressing room: "Well, this is it. There's nothing to save up for now." The entire team got the message.

Reed didn't even try to jump as Chamberlain won the opening tap. He didn't have to. Bradley stole the first Laker pass and steered it to Frazier. Clyde fed Willis and he scored. Seconds later Reed scored again, as the crowd sensed what was happening and increased its ovation. Soon it was 9–2, then 38–24. Reed couldn't jump or run, but somehow during his twenty-seven minutes of play he blocked Chamberlain's route to the hoop—and that was all the Knicks needed from him. "When he made the first shot," said Frazier, "I thought, 'He ain't hurt.' Of course I knew he was, but after the first few minutes it didn't matter. Just having him out there with us, I got so turned on I couldn't stop."

Throughout the playoffs Clyde had been forced to select priorities, sacrificing offense for defense or shooting for passing. But in the final game, all the elusive, explosive forces within him erupted. He did everything well: 36 points, nineteen assists, a half dozen clean steals. "Clyde devastated them," said Riordan. "It had to be the best game of his life." Frazier couldn't help agreeing: "I was dynamite."

By half time it was 69–42. Bradley and Barnett were scoring from outside; DeBusschere was muscling inside to assume Reed's share of the rebounding (Willis himself scored 4 points and had three rebounds). The game was never close. Only a forlorn Laker rally late in the final quarter narrowed the final margin to 113–99. "We should save the films of this game for training camp," said Bradley, "to show the rookies the kind of ball we aim for."

In the dressing room, champagne was sprayed around ceremonially but the players merely drank beer and talked happily. Perhaps after 101 games, they were emotionally drained; or perhaps their somewhat subdued expressions of joy seemed more suitable tributes to the massive, quiet man who had made it possible.

Reed sat on the bench in front of his locker for a long time, looking around at his teammates, explaining what he had done to Wilt. "It's tough enough to play him on two legs. On one leg, I had to conserve myself and get good position at all times. I had to play a thinking man's game." A wince of pain momentarily contorted his broad smile. Reed glanced down at his right leg. "I can't even lift it now without using my arm," he said. "But it will have a long time to heal."

Across the room, Bradley analyzed Reed's psychological coup. "In warm-ups, you start high and then tone down," he explained. "We were just toning down when Willis appeared. So there we were, two minutes before game time, sky high all over again. And when he made that first basket, I thought, 'Maybe the man's got something inside him that we've never even seen.'

"Reed's presence demonstrated what he thought of us as men, and of the team," Bradley continued. His voice picked up as he recalled the plays and baskets and steals that had broken it open.

"Hey," somebody needled him, "remember that this is only a game."

"It's a game," said Bradley, "but we're at the top of it. You can't minimize the significance of the achievement."

The Knicks will be hard pressed to maintain their place at the top. Through clever behind-the-scenes dealing, they managed to avoid losing any of their important men in the expansion draft and they will continue to be a fine team, a spectacular form of entertainment. But Oscar Robertson, obtained in a trade, is joining Alcindor in Milwaukee; as Lew improves even further, the Bucks may be hard to withstand.

Yet even if the championship should pass on, the significance of the achievement will endure, in everyone who played and watched and felt it. Reed's majestic entrance and Frazier's quick steals and the other Knick heroics will be imitated and recounted on every patch of asphalt where kids aim basketballs toward a hoop. As Reed told a luncheon audience a few days after the final: "All we've gone through has made us all better men. And I'd like to think it's made the city just a little better place."